CLEANING MAGIC!

1,593 Better, Faster, Cheaper, and Smarter Ways to Clean Everything from A to Z

by Jerry Baker
America's Do-It-Yourself Expert™

Published by American Master Products, Inc.

Other Jerry Baker Books:

Jerry Baker's Solve It with Vinegar!
America's Best Practical Problem Solvers
Jerry Baker's Can the Clutter!
Jerry Baker's Homespun Magic
Grandma Putt's Old-Time Vinegar, Garlic, Baking Soda, and
   101 More Problem Solvers
Jerry Baker's Supermarket Super Products!
Jerry Baker's It Pays to be Cheap!

Jerry Baker's The New Impatient Gardener
Jerry Baker's Supermarket Super Gardens
Jerry Baker's Dear God...Please Help It Grow!
Secrets from the Jerry Baker Test Gardens
Jerry Baker's All-American Lawns
Jerry Baker's Bug Off!
Jerry Baker's Terrific Garden Tonics!
Jerry Baker's Backyard Problem Solver
Jerry Baker's Green Grass Magic
Jerry Baker's Great Green Book of Garden Secrets
Jerry Baker's Old-Time Gardening Wisdom

Jerry Baker's Backyard Birdscaping Bonanza
Jerry Baker's Backyard Bird Feeding Bonanza
Jerry Baker's Year-Round Bloomers
Jerry Baker's Flower Garden Problem Solver
Jerry Baker's Perfect Perennials!

Healing Fixers Mixers & Elixirs
Grandma Putt's Home Health Remedies
Nature's Best Miracle Medicines
Jerry Baker's Supermarket Super Remedies
Jerry Baker's The New Healing Foods
Jerry Baker's Amazing Antidotes!
Jerry Baker's Anti-Pain Plan
Jerry Baker's Oddball Ointments, Powerful Potions, and Fabulous Folk Remedies
Jerry Baker's Giant Book of Kitchen Counter Cures

To order any of the above, or for more information on Jerry Baker's
amazing home, health, and garden tips, tricks, and tonics, please write to:

Jerry Baker, P.O. Box 1001, Wixom, MI 48393

Or, visit Jerry Baker online at:
www.jerrybaker.com

Copyright © 2009 by Jerry Baker

Executive Editor: Kim Adam Gasior

Managing Editor: Cheryl Winters-Tetreau

Writer: Sally Roth

Copy Editor: Nanette Bendyna

Production Editor: Debby Duvall

Interior Design and Layout: Trish Field

Cover Design: Kathleen B. Johnston

Indexer: Nan Badgett

Illustrations © 2009 Jupiterimages Corporation, except for the Great Clean-dini and Grandma Putt illustrations

Publisher's Cataloging-in-Publication
(Provided by Quality Books, Inc.)

Baker Jerry.
    Jerry Baker's cleaning magic : 1,593 better, faster, cheaper, and smarter ways to clean everything from A to Z
    p. cm.
    Includes index.
    ISBN-13: 978–0–922433–94–0
    ISBN-10: 0–922433–94–1

    1. House cleaning. 2. Housekeeping. I. Title.
II. Title: Cleaning magic.

TX324.B35 2009   648.5
              QBI09-600058

Printed in the United States of America
4 6 8 10 9 7 5 3 hardcover

Contents

Introduction

Step right up, folks, and get ready to enter the magical world of The Great Clean-dini! I'm gonna pull all kinds of cleaning secrets out of my hat, and that means you'll be turning dust and grime into sparkle and shine. You'll see spots and stains vanish right before your eyes…grease and grit disappear in a flash…and bathrooms go from blech to beautiful in no time flat!

In fact, you'll find tons of terrific tips and tricks for any cleaning challenge you can think of, from Air Filters to Zippers and everything in between. Just flip this book open to your toughest cleaning problem, roll up your sleeves, and unleash the power of my super solutions.

I've been cleaning up ever since I was living with my Grandma Putt way back when. She was a real whiz, whipping up homemade cleaning concoctions from household products. And I'm proud to say that her tried-and-true tonics still work their magic today! Here are a few of my favorite **Grandma Putt's Magical Methods** that you'll find sprinkled throughout this book:

★ Zap can opener rust with wax paper.

★ Polish your precious gold jewelry with ammonia.

★ Shine copper with leftover pickle brine.

★ Write off ink stains with shortening.

To help you put these magical methods to work, I dug deep into my bag of tricks and pulled out plenty of **Powerful Potions.** These remarkable recipes cost only pennies to make, yet they have enough muscle to pack a potent punch. Mix up a few batches of grime-fighting brews like these to stop dirt dead in its tracks:

★ Daily Shower Spray keeps dirt away.

★ A Silver Shine is mighty fine.

★ Anti-Skunk Shampoo sinks the stink.

Of course, you should always use any DIY potion with a dose of common sense. Keep all ingredients out of reach of children and pets, always wear

Powerful Potions

Super Sanitizing Wipe

Use this potion on any hard surface that needs a quick cleaning. One swipe will cut through grime and kill germs at the same time!

1 part rubbing alcohol

4 parts water

Mix the ingredients in a handheld sprayer bottle. Simply spray the solution on the surface to be cleaned, and wipe it away with a soft, clean cloth.

rubber gloves, and crack open a window for good ventilation. And last, but certainly not least, before using a cleaning solution on any surface, test it in an inconspicuous spot first to make sure it doesn't cause any damage.

By now, you're probably rarin' to go and whip everything into shape. But what if you've got a housecleaning horror that's too tough to tackle? No problem! I get letters all the time from folks who are just plain stumped by goop, gunk, grease, and grime. So bring it on! When **The Great Clean-dini Speaks,** you'll learn no-nonsense answers to your most mystifying cleaning questions, including these:

★ Got anything to dazzle dull brass? (Try homemade "bug juice.")

★ Can bread really restore dingy paintings? (Yes—if it's white!)

★ What do I do when the old ivories turn yellow? (Tickle 'em with mayo.)

★ How can I clear out coffeemaker crud? (Plop, plop, fizz, fizz it away.)

But wait, the show's not over yet! I've also thrown in some of my best **Hocus Pocus** tips to take care of things that bug you the most. Got an army of ants on your countertop? No problem. Clothes moths in the hall closet? Lemme at 'em. Hard-water deposits in your showerhead? Not to worry—just say the magic words and—POOF!—the problem's gone in a flash.

So now that you've seen the opening act and had a sneak peek at what's inside, it's time to put my Cleaning Magic to work for you. If you keep this book close at hand, your hearth and home will soon be happier, healthier—and a whole lot cleaner!

Air Filters

Dirt catchers deluxe. You probably have a number of filters lurking in your house. Here's a rundown of the most common ones:

★ *Air cleaners.* Whether you depend on a tabletop model, room-size unit, or whole-house air-cleaning system, the time to rinse the filter off is *before* you start sneezing. Don't wait until you're running for the tissues to suddenly decide to clean the filter.

★ *Central vacuuming systems.* That vac serves your whole house—and that means a lot of dust! So clean the sponge or pleated paper filter every time you empty the dust collector, and your system will keep on sucking it up like it should.

★ *Furnaces.* That monster in your basement means double your filter "fun" because two different filters are connected to most furnaces. You'll find one of them in the intake part of the system. That's the cold-air return, which is often set into the floor like a heating vent; it may be larger than other vents—all the better to draw in air. You'll know you have the right one when you see a filter lurking inside it, instead of the opening of a duct. And, when the furnace is running, you won't feel any hot air coming from it. The second filter is usually located where the ductwork leaves the furnace. Clean or replace both of them each year before the heating season starts, then check them monthly to make sure they're not clogged.

Meet MERV. My house used to be dusty, even though I changed my filters regularly. Why? Because I wasn't paying attention to MERV, which stands for Minimum Efficiency Reporting Value. You'll find this number on any air filter you buy. The higher the MERV, the more efficient the filter will be because it'll trap smaller particles. FYI: Most filters run from 1 to 12 on the MERV scale; hospitals use 14 and up to filter out germs. Stick to MERV 5 or higher to reduce dust in your house.

Go permanent. I like things that are built to last, so permanent air filters get my vote. For one thing, I don't ever have to run to the store to buy a replacement, and that saves me time, not to mention gas! And as a bonus, permanent filters work better, too—some are rated at 90 percent or higher efficiency (MERV 8 and up). Disposables rated MERV 1 to 4, on the other hand, catch less than 20 percent of the dust floating around in the air, while those rated MERV 5 to 7 snag about 35 to 65 percent. On the downside (you knew there was going to be a downside, didn't you?), permanent filters can be a little pricey, with some models running more than $50 apiece. Still, since you won't need to buy any replacement filters, you'll end up saving money in the long run, so they're well worth the heftier price tag. One other drawback: Some heating and cooling pros say the higher-efficiency filters cut down on airflow. So if you have trouble with hot or cold spots in your house, have a pro come in to balance your system, and then get his or her advice about filter ratings.

You get what you pay for. Going to the hardware store to buy an air filter can be a mind-boggling experience. You'll find pleated filters, flat filters,

The Great Clean-dini Speaks

Q. Jerry, help! I can't find the filter in my furnace. Do you have any ideas on where I should look?

A. Sure—try the owner's manual. Then again, if you can't seem to find the manual, either, look for a manufacturer's name and a model number on the device. When you find them, call up a local heating and cooling company and ask the friendly folks who work there just where that doggone filter is. They're usually more than happy to help. Just remember to say thank you—and the next time you need to call in a professional, keep them in mind!

and filters with more than one layer of dust-trapping material, with price tags that vary just as widely as the selection. "Bargain" filters are less efficient than the pleated or multilayer filters that are priced a few bucks higher, and they'll need to be changed more often. So unless you're on a really tight budget, don't grab the cheapest filter on the shelf. And if allergies are a problem in your family, then buy the best filter you can find that's got the highest MERV available. You'll breathe easier because the filter will trap lots of sneezy, wheezy pollen and dander.

Cover your nose. Think about it: Your schnoz is an air filter, too. So why not make its job easier when you're kicking up some dust? All it takes is a disposable paper mask. I keep a pack of lightweight dust-filter masks—less than a dollar apiece!—at the ready in my cleaning cabinet. Whenever it's time to change my furnace filter or do any other dusty job, I just reach for my own personal air filter and breathe a whole lot easier.

Dealing with disposables. By definition, disposable filters can't be cleaned and reused. But since they only cost a few bucks, buying replacements shouldn't put too big a dent in your wallet. Still, if you're of a rather thrifty nature and want to save a little money (and who doesn't?), buy your disposable filters by the case, instead of one at a time.

Aluminum Siding

Pressure-washer power. Often, all it takes to spiff up shabby siding is a blast from a pressure washer. If you don't own one of these handy machines, you can always rent one from your local home-improvement center. Then just spray plain water on the siding, using the lowest pressure setting so you don't wash (or blast) off any of the siding's finish.

Age spots. On the other hand, if it's been a few years since the last time you really scrubbed your aluminum siding, you may need to do some real "house" cleaning to get rid of any lingering mildew and dirt stains. The DIY Ammonia Cleaner below, or ¼ cup of powdered, bleach-free laundry detergent dissolved in 2 gallons of water, should do the job nicely. Scrub either of these mixes onto the siding with a stiff brush, and rinse it clean with a garden hose. And if you need more potent cleaning power, pick up some trisodium phosphate (TSP) at your local hardware store. Just make sure to follow all package directions when using this cleaner.

Powerful Potions

DIY Ammonia Cleaner

This mix gets rid of grime like magic. But remember, folks—ammonia is powerful stuff with powerful fumes, to boot! So always handle it with care.

¼ cup of ammonia
2 gal. of water

Mix these ingredients together in a sturdy, plastic 3-gallon pail, and dip a sponge or a cloth into it to clean windows, mirrors, and appliance surfaces—anywhere that you'd use its commercial counterpart, Windex®. And because this homemade version is way cheaper than the store-bought stuff, you can even use it for big jobs like cleaning dingy aluminum siding. Just remember to wear a pair of rubber gloves whenever you work with this potion. And never, ever, ever mix it with bleach—the resulting fumes can be deadly!

Ready, set... Before you clean your siding, turn off the power to any outside lights that may get wet. Then sweep the cobwebs away from the area; wet spiderwebs can be mighty stubborn to spray off. Remove any hanging baskets, patio furniture, or other objects that may be in the way, and cover the shrubs and flowers below the area so that no cleaning solution drips on them. Finally, send Fido and Kitty inside, and shut all your windows and doors. Then when you do turn on the hose or pressure washer, direct the spray away from any doors, windows, or other openings. And make sure the whole family knows where you'll be working, so they don't get a surprise shower when they come running around a corner.

Work your way up. Whenever you clean your siding with anything other than water, start at the bottom and work your way up. Why? Because liquids always run down. If you start at the top or the middle, you'll end up with stubborn streaks down below where the cleaning solution has run through the still-dirty part. And those telltale drip paths are hard to remove. So remember: Vertical surface + liquid cleaner = bottoms up!

Antique Furniture (See also Furniture)

Preserve that patina. If there's one thing I've learned from watching *Antiques Roadshow*, it's to leave those precious antique finishes alone! A mellow patina or the original paint can mean the difference between a priceless museum piece and a candidate for the neighborhood garage sale. So if you're lucky enough to get your hands on a quality piece of antique furniture, keep it as close to its original condition as you can.

Dusting does it. Put away that spray can of furniture polish—it'll only leave an oily film on the wood's delicate surface. Instead, dust your antique furniture with a soft, dry cloth (an old cotton T-shirt is perfect). To apply a protective glossy shine, give it a nice gentle rubdown with beeswax (see "Mind your own beeswax" below).

Shimmy with a chamois. The thought of damaging the inlay, veneer, or other valuable details on my old furniture makes me nervous. So to keep it clean, I play it safe and simply wipe down detailed areas with a chamois. The lightweight leather (or imitation leather) glides smoothly over the surfaces, so I don't snag (and damage) any loose edges.

Mind your own beeswax. You will, when you try my candle-stub trick to wax your antique wood furniture. I save leftover beeswax candle stubs just for this purpose. First, soften a stub by warming it in your hands for a bit. Next, use a soft piece of flannel (cut from an old shirt), and rub a light coat of the beeswax onto the wood. Then refold the cloth to a clean spot, and buff gently in small circles.

Keep out of crevices. Believe it or not, there is such a thing as "too clean"—at least when it comes to antique furniture. The dust that gets tucked up in the grooves or carvings is part of the charm of an antique piece. So don't be too tempted to wipe it away. (And don't worry—I won't tell anybody that it's actually just plain, old...dirt!)

Paste, not polish. I want you to pledge to leave that bottle of spray-and-wipe furniture polish in the cupboard! When it comes to an old finish, only an old-fashioned paste wax will do. It's just the ticket for protecting wood from getting wet, or from drying out. So rub a good-quality paste, such as Minwax®, into the wood. Then buff it out to a shine with a soft, clean cloth. And don't worry—you don't need massive muscles to get the job done, just a little more time.

Hocus Pocus

A Little TLC

Antique wood furniture is mighty sensitive—it can warp or crack when the temperature or humidity levels inside your home are too high. So help your vintage pieces live a nice long life by following these guidelines:

★ Keep the antiques well away from woodstoves, fireplaces, furnace vents, and any other heat sources that could dry them out.

★ Use a dehumidifier if your home tends to get a little steamy, and don't ever keep an antique vanity in a bathroom that steams up easily.

★ Always use coasters. If you set an ice-cold drink on your antique furniture, it'll sure as shootin' leave an unsightly white ring behind.

Asphalt Driveways

Keep that curb appeal. Nothing boosts curb appeal like a clean, black, asphalt driveway with no cracks, crevices, and/or weeds popping up here and there. So keep yours looking fine and dandy by using a stiff-bristled push broom and plain old water to scrub off any dirt. Rinse it clean with a strong spray from your garden hose and you're done.

Patch those cracks. Driveway cracks are like wrinkles: They're a normal part of aging. Unfortunately, they continue to get bigger, deeper, and more unsightly as time marches on. But there's no need to spend big bucks having the whole surface repaired. If your driveway looks like it needs a facelift, just head to your local hardware store and pick up a bag of sand, a cartridge of "crack filler," and a container of asphalt sealant. Pull any weeds out of the cracks, sweep the area clean, and fill each crevice with sand up to about ¼ inch from the surface. Squeeze in the crack filler, and after it hardens, apply the asphalt sealant (according to package directions) to seal the deal.

Stop those spills. An ounce of prevention is worth a pound of cure. So before you change the oil in your car or fill your lawn mower's gas tank, put a flattened cardboard box, an old plastic tablecloth, or an old shower curtain down on the driveway to prevent any oil or gasoline spills from damaging the asphalt.

After the fact. If your driveway does happen to be the scene of a gas or oil spill, use paper towels or old rags to mop up as much of the spill as you can. Cat litter, sand, or a commercial oil-drying solution will also absorb any liquid in a hurry. Once the excess liquid is gone, squirt the area generously with a grease-cutting dishwashing liquid, and scrub it in with a stiff-bristled broom. Blast it off with a stiff spray from your garden hose, and the spill should be history.

Hocus Pocus

TAR-STAIN REMOVAL 101

As any paving crew knows, if tar, asphalt, or asphalt sealant finds its way onto your shoes, clothes, carpet, or car, it can be next to impossible to remove. Fortunately, I've got some tricks that'll get rid of the sticky black goo:

On shoes or tools. Spray tar marks with WD-40® or Goo Gone® to loosen them, then scrape the gunk off with an old putty knife. Or try cooking oil or nail polish remover; just dab it on the stain, give it a minute to penetrate, and rub the tar off. An orange oil–based cleaner (available at auto-supply and hardware stores) will also do the trick.

On clothes. Spray the black areas with an orange oil–based cleaner, let it soak in for two to three minutes, and then hold the garment under running water to rinse away the tar. Launder the item as usual.

On carpet. Blot up as much tar as you can with an old cloth, but don't rub it because that will drive the goo deeper into the fibers. Then use an old putty knife to gently scrape away as much tar as possible—and be careful not to drop those sticky bits elsewhere! To get the rest of the stain out, try any of these:

★ Mix 1/4 cup of dishwashing liquid into 1/4 cup of warm water, and use the mixture to saturate the stain. Wait about an hour so it can loosen the tar, then blot away the gunk with a clean cloth.

★ Spray a paper towel with WD-40 or Goo Gone, and blot up the black spots. Fold the paper towel as you work so that you're always pressing a clean part against the stain. If a stubborn spot remains, spray a little more of either product onto the stain, wait a few minutes for it to penetrate, and blot it up.

★ Pour rubbing alcohol onto a cotton ball and blot the stain, being careful not to wet the fibers all the way to the backing, which could damage it. Blot dry with a clean cloth, rinse well, and blot it dry again.

On cars and bikes. This one's easy—just buy a commercial tar-removal product from an auto-supply store, and follow the directions on the label.

Easy does it. A freshly sealed asphalt driveway looks so great, you might be tempted to make it an annual event. Well, don't! According to the experts, one coat of sealant every two to three years is plenty. Any more than that will lead to a buildup of excess sealant, which can crack even easier than the asphalt itself. And if you'd rather not mess with applying a commercial sealant yourself, hire a pro to do this very messy, but necessary job.

Athletic Shoes (Sneakers)

A new lease on life. Have your sneakers seen better days? Before you start shopping for a replacement pair, check the care label to see if it's safe to wash them in a machine. If the answer is "yes," then spray the shoes with a fabric-stain remover, and launder them with a couple of neutral-colored towels (it prevents your sneaks from taking a pounding in the machine). Chances are, they'll come out looking as good as new!

Toothy solution. Believe me, nothing beats an old toothbrush for getting the grime out of all the nooks and crannies in your sneakers. Those skinny bristles are just the ticket for cleaning around the eyelets and for loosening up ground-in dirt along the seams. You can also  use the toothbrush on stubborn stains to help your cleaning products penetrate better. And speaking of cleaning products, why not grab a tube of non-gel toothpaste to use with that toothbrush? Just work a dab of paste onto your leather sneakers or rubber trim, so its gentle, abrasive action can remove scuff marks and stains. Remember, though, that whitening toothpaste includes a bleaching agent, so use that kind only on white shoes. When you're done brushing, simply wipe the paste off with a damp cloth, and your sneakers will be smiling again!

Heavy-duty help. If your shoes are really grubby, pick up a commercial cleaner like KIWI Sport Shoe Stuff Scrub-Off Heavy Duty Cleaner®, and use it according to package directions. Presto, pristine! And if the rubber or vinyl trim on your sneakers seems hopelessly soiled, try a product that car buffs use to clean their tires: Wesley's Bleche-White® (yep, that's the real name of the stuff). Just spray it on the rubber trim of your sneakers, scrub with an old toothbrush, and wipe it off with a wet cloth. This stuff is mighty powerful, so keep it away from any nearby chrome or paint, and be sure to wipe it off your sneakers right away. But, if it can make whitewalls gleam, just imagine what it will do for those scuffed "treads" on your feet!

Powerful Potions

Leather Cleaner and Conditioner

This recipe will spiff up the outside of your leather athletic shoes quicker than you can say "Holy cow!" And it works every bit as well as any store-bought shoe cleaner ever would.

½ cup of food-grade linseed oil or neat's-foot oil

¼ cup of white vinegar

Combine these ingredients, and use a soft, clean cloth to rub the mixture into the leather in small circles. Let it soak in overnight, then buff the shoes with a different soft, clean cloth the next morning to bring out the shine.

Erase dirt like magic. If your white sneakers are looking dingy, brighten them up with a Mr. Clean® Magic Eraser®! The regular and duo types are good for touch-ups; for tougher cases, reach for the Extra Power version. Just wet the eraser, squeeze it out, and rub it lightly over every inch of your sneakers to lift the dirt right off. And here's some more great news: You'll be able to wear the sneakers right after cleaning because they won't need time to dry. You can try a Magic Eraser on colored sneakers, too, but it may lift the color as well as the grime. So test it first in an inconspicuous spot, like the part of the tongue that's usually hidden beneath the laces.

Hand wash how-to. Your sneakers don't have a care label? When in doubt, always hand wash. (After all, you've got nothing to lose!) First, take out the laces and throw them in your regular laundry, or replace them if they're just too grungy. Then toss the old insoles—clean sneaks definitely deserve a pair of new liners. Now fill a bowl with warm water and a few squirts of dishwashing liquid. Wet each shoe down in the sink, and use a short-bristled brush dipped in the soapy water to scrub it clean. Rinse 'em and then you're finished.

How dry I am. Want to keep your freshly cleaned tennies in tip-top shape? Then take a word from the wise—keep them out of the dryer and away from the fireplace, heater, or oven. The heat can damage the adhesive that holds the sole in place, or it can shrink your shoes down a size.

The best way to dry freshly washed shoes is to blot out as much water as you can with a clean bath towel. Then stuff the shoes with paper towels, and set them outside to air-dry in the sunshine. Replace the damp paper towels once or twice to help the insides of your shoes dry faster. And don't ever use newspaper to do this job because the ink will run and ruin your shoes!

Stop the stink. Try one of these terrific tricks to keep people from running away when they smell your sneakers coming:

★ Pull out the old insoles, and replace them with a pair of odor-controlling inserts.

★ Tuck a small piece of a scented fabric-softener sheet into the toe of each shoe.

★ Sprinkle a little baking soda in your shoes after you wear 'em. It'll absorb odors in your sneakers, just like it does in your fridge. (But remember to shake it out before you slip the shoes on.)

★ Buy a second pair of athletic shoes, so you can switch shoes between wearings. Letting each pair dry out thoroughly after an outing goes a long way toward stifling the smell.

Awnings

Steady as she goes. Positioning the ladder is half the battle when it comes to cleaning an awning. First, you never want to climb any higher than the second-to-last step on a ladder, so make sure yours is tall enough to do the job. Then enlist the aid of a helper to hold the ladder steady as you climb aboard. Once you're up, the rest is easy—just brush off the loose twigs and other debris, and then follow the rest of the tips in this section to get your awning squeaky clean.

Managing mildew. If you have a canvas awning on your home, especially in a humid climate, then you already know that mildew positively thrives in the corners. To clear it out, prepare the area as you would if you were cleaning aluminum siding (see "Ready, set…" on page 4). Then mix up a solution of 2 cups of color-safe household bleach in 2 gallons of water, and wipe down the awning, paying extra attention to any areas where mildew often crops up. Rinse immediately with the garden hose, and you're done.

Borrow a trick from boaters. Come on, landlubbers, let's try a little marine magic! How? It's simple: Head to a store that stocks boating supplies, and pick up a bottle of spray-on fabric protector. You'll find a whole slew of products that boaters depend on to keep their cabins and canvas looking like new. These handy helpers are easy to recognize because they have names like Armada AquaBlock Fabric Waterproofer and Stain Repellent® and Heller Glänz Fabric Waterproofer and Stain Repellent Spray®. Choose the product that's right for your awning material, whether it's cotton, polyester, vinyl, or what have you. Once your awnings are nice and clean, periodically give them a spritz to protect them from the elements, and they'll stay shipshape!

Mop up aluminum awnings. If your awnings are made of aluminum, a once-over with a sponge mop and a hose will make quick work of surface dirt. Follow this prewash with the DIY Ammonia Cleaner on page 4 to get rid of any deep-down dirt. If you've got big-time grunge on your hands, pick up some trisodium phosphate (TSP) at your local hardware store, and use it according to package directions. Whichever cleaner you use, don't forget to wear a pair of sturdy rubber gloves—they'll protect your hands from the cleaners, as well as any sharp awning edges. And keep your bright baby blues protected with a pair of safety glasses that'll stop any wayward drips.

Barbecue Grills

Clean when cool. Oh boy, those burgers sure were tasty. And since no one relishes the thought of cleaning up the mess on the grill after a leisurely summer cookout, many of us wait until just before the next cookout to do it. Fortunately, that's actually a safe time to clean, since the grill will be completely cool and you can't get burned. Just remember to allow yourself 10 minutes or so to tidy things up before you fire up the charcoal or press the igniter.

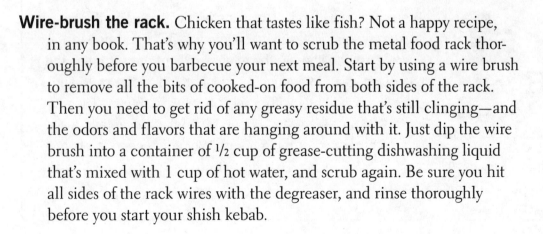

Wire-brush the rack. Chicken that tastes like fish? Not a happy recipe, in any book. That's why you'll want to scrub the metal food rack thoroughly before you barbecue your next meal. Start by using a wire brush to remove all the bits of cooked-on food from both sides of the rack. Then you need to get rid of any greasy residue that's still clinging—and the odors and flavors that are hanging around with it. Just dip the wire brush into a container of $1/2$ cup of grease-cutting dishwashing liquid that's mixed with 1 cup of hot water, and scrub again. Be sure you hit all sides of the rack wires with the degreaser, and rinse thoroughly before you start your shish kebab.

Don't get burned. Oh, no! There goes a shrimp, falling right off the barbie! And wouldn't you know it—it's landed near the gas burner that runs along the bottom of the grill. Not to worry—after the grill cools down, get out that wire brush and loosen up the bits, scoop them up with a damp paper towel, and deposit them into the nearest trash can. That way, your next meal won't be seasoned with the taste of burning leftovers, and you won't have sudden flare-ups from fallen food.

Recycle the ashes. Hickory chips aren't just for flavoring—the wood ashes make a great grill cleaner, too. So the next time you use hickory, mesquite, or any other wood to barbecue, put the cooled ashes to work by sprinkling a handful of 'em on the warm (not hot!) rack. Then scrub with a wet, soapy sponge or brush, and rinse thoroughly. Try this trick after your next campfire cookout to prep the metal rack for the next night's wienie roast. Now that's what I call being a good camper!

Give it a Soak. Rub-a-dub-dub, put that rack in the tub—and let dishwasher detergent do the work for you. You'll need a plastic tub that's big enough to hold the rack. Don't have one? Consider using your bathtub. Fill the tub with enough hot water to cover the rack, and mix in ¼ cup

Hocus Pocus

IT'S IN THE BAG

The easiest way to clean a grill starts with putting the greasy rack into a black plastic garbage bag. (Only a black bag will do because it will draw the intense rays of the sun.) Lay the bag down, pour in enough ammonia to cover the rack, and close the bag tightly with a twist tie. Leave the bag lying flat in the sun for two or three hours, then flip it over, and leave it for another two or three hours. When you open the bag, that grill rack will be clean as a whistle. Just rinse it off, dry it, and you'll be all set for your next barbecue.

Q. The flames in my gas grill burn yellow instead of bright blue. What's the problem?

A. Gunk, that's what! That telltale color change means that the burner holes are probably clogged with grease that's dripped down into the grill. The solution is to reach for the pipe cleaners. Those furry little wire stems are perfect for cleaning out the holes in the gas burner. Just poke a pipe cleaner into each hole, work it around, and pull it out. When the pipe cleaner gets dirty, switch to the other end; when both ends are grimy, get a new pipe cleaner. Pretty crafty idea, wouldn't you say?

The Great Clean-dini Speaks

of dishwasher detergent and ¼ cup of vinegar. Then submerge the rack and let it soak for an hour or so, until that rack is spankin' clean. Rinse it off, and immediately swab out the tub with lemon juice or vinegar to get rid of the greasy ring and any gunky residue.

Turn up the heat. When it comes to cleaning the inside of the grill, fire is your best friend. Leave the gas turned on or the coals burning after you take off the food, and close the lid. The heat will burn off the grease drippings and turn all the bits of food that slipped through the rack to ash. Turn the grill off after about 10 minutes, leave the lid closed, and keep everyone away from it until it cools down.

Dew you know? Here's another easy trick to make crud on the grill give up its grip—let the dew do it! Just set your cooled-down, dirty rack upside down in the grass, and let it rest there overnight. The dew will soften up that cooked-on residue, and with any luck, most of it will fall right off when you pick up the rack next morning. If any stubborn spots remain, they should come off easily with a few strokes of your wire grill brush.

Long live lava rocks. Ready to walk on a hot bed of coals? Me neither. But I will share my trick for keeping those lava rocks clean and long-lasting. Just fire 'em up every now and then for about 15 minutes so that any hidden drips or spills can burn off. Then when the grill and the rocks are thoroughly cool, use a scrub brush to remove any ashy residue.

Foil that dirty grill. Don't toss away the aluminum foil from your outdoor dinner—save it for a grill cleaner instead! After you've chowed down on your baked potato, crumple the foil wrapping into a ball, and use it to do a quick rubdown of the grill rack. This trick works best on a warm rack, but don't be too eager—wait until the grill is cool enough to touch.

Bathtubs and Showers

So long, soap scum! This quick fix will make that cloudy layer disappear from tub and tile in a jiffy. Just sprinkle a little baking soda on a damp sponge, rub away the cloudy film, and then rinse thoroughly to remove all traces of the residue. Scummy problem solved.

Make water spots vanish. Has hard water marred your pretty colored tub or tile with white spots? Then it's time for a real rubdown. Scour the spots off with a nonabrasive plastic scrubbie and plenty of white vinegar, then rinse thoroughly. But be careful when you're working on the tile: Full-strength vinegar can discolor or damage your grout, so scrub one small area of tile at a time, and rinse it quickly and thoroughly before you move on to the next. Follow up with the baking soda scrub above (see "So long, soap scum!"), and your tub and tile will shine.

Rejuvenate your tub. The next time you clean your old white porcelain or fiberglass tub, end with a good, long soak: Fill the tub with hot water, and drop in several denture-cleaning tablets. Let it sit overnight, rinse the tub out in the morning, and that porcelain will gleam.

Make your shower sparkle. Cleaning the shower tends to be the hardest job in the bathroom. But don't worry—if you follow my tips, it'll be a breeze. So gather up a few supplies, and take these steps to tackle that grimy tub and shower:

1. Spray the shower walls and glass shower doors with tile cleaner. Scrub the tiles and the grout between them with a tile brush. When you come to the tub faucets, clean them, too, using the tile brush and a toothbrush to get at the stubborn dirt.

2. Scrub the shower doors with a nonabrasive plastic scrubbie.

3. Use a toothbrush and an all-purpose spray cleaner to get the grime off the tracks of the shower door.

4. Scrub the bottom and sides of the tub, using the tile brush and the right product for your type of tub. Clean the joint where the tub meets the shower wall with the toothbrush.

5. Rinse the shower walls and doors thoroughly, then rinse the tub. Dry the faucets with a soft, clean cloth to make them shine.

6. Clean the outside of the shower doors and the outside of the tub with the all-purpose spray cleaner.

7. Give yourself a big pat on the back. The hardest job is done!

Hocus Pocus

LET IT POUR

Has your showerhead gone from the bathroom version of Niagara Falls to a feeble trickle? Hard-water deposits are probably clogging the holes. To keep your shower flowing freely, fill your sink with hot water and add a couple of denture-cleaning tablets. Then unscrew the showerhead and soak it in the mix for a couple of hours. Rinse it well, screw it back in place, and you'll enjoy a full-force shower again.

Powerful Potions

All-Purpose Cleaner

This fast-acting formula makes it as easy as pie to keep your tub, shower, and tile in tip-top shape.

- **½ cup of vinegar**
- **1 tbsp. of dishwashing liquid**
- **1 tbsp. of borax**
- **3 cups of hot water**

Mix all of the ingredients in a handheld sprayer bottle, and give it a good shake. When you're ready to tackle that tub or shower, just spray it down, and wipe the cleaner (and the crud) away.

Degrease the tub. Ready for a nice relaxing bath? Go ahead, pour in that scented bath oil. It'll smell wonderful and leave your skin silky smooth—but it'll also slick down the tub in the process. So you'll need to wipe down the tub after your bath with my grease-cutting All-Purpose Cleaner at left. Lemon juice will do the trick, too—just pour a liberal amount on a sponge, and wipe away the oily film. Rinse thoroughly, and your nonslip tub will be ready for the next bather's relaxing soak.

Spotless! Remove stubborn water spots on your chrome faucet by rubbing it with a fresh-cut lemon half, letting the juice soak in for a few minutes before you rinse it with fresh water. Then go ahead, take a great big sniff—now that's the smell of clean! And to make that shine last longer, wipe the faucet with a dab of baby oil on a soft cloth. That way, the water will bead up on the thin film of oil instead of on the metal, and any spots that do show up will be easy to wipe away.

From fridge to faucet. Believe it or not, a plain old ordinary bottle of ketchup will work wonders to clean brass or bronze faucets. Just squirt a big dab onto a dry cloth, and rub it over the faucet until all of the grime is gone. Rinse the faucet, buff it dry, and then put that big red bottle back in the kitchen until next time. And don't blame me if you suddenly get a hankering for a nice juicy burger and a pile of fries…with plenty of ketchup, of course!

Q. I can't get rid of the mildew in my bathroom. I swab it with a bleach solution, and a week later, it's back again. Is there anything else I can do?

A. Keeping your house on the dry side is the only way to win the war against mildew. To dry things out a little, try these battle-tested tips and tricks:

★ Use a bathroom ventilation fan or dehumidifier. Turn on the fan before you step into the shower or take a steamy bath, and let it run until the bathroom air loses all of its extra humidity.

★ Set a pan of unscented clay cat litter or silica gel on a closet shelf. Or fill the foot of an old pair of panty hose with the litter, knot the panty hose at the ankle, and cut off the extra part above the knot. Then put this nylon sack on a shelf.

★ Avoid grouping houseplants together in the room; the water vapor released by their foliage and the soil may encourage mildew to form on nearby surfaces.

★ If mildew and mold are common problems in your house, try drying out the air with a large-capacity dehumidifier.

The Great Clean-dini Speaks

Buff up the brass. If you liked playing in mud as much as I did as a kid, you'll get a kick out of this homemade brass polish. Just mix ½ teaspoon of salt into ½ cup of vinegar, and slowly stir in enough flour to make a gloppy paste. Now comes the fun part: Slather the stuff onto those dingy brass faucets, and then polish away—you'll actually see the brass get brighter! Just be sure to rinse the polish off while it's still wet, and use a soft brush to get every trace of white stuff out of all the nooks and crannies because that flour paste will dry hard as a rock.

Preventive maintenance. Soap scum is the bane of many a bathroom. So keep a cellulose sponge handy, and use it to wipe out the tub after you bathe. It takes just a minute or two, but it'll cut down big-time on soap scum. Keep a squeegee or a chamois nearby, too, so that you can wipe off the walls and glass shower doors when you're finished. Then stash the tools in a wire basket that hangs over the showerhead, and they'll be ready when you are.

Polish the walls. Even though oily residue can be a slippery subject in the bathtub, it's a solution to soap scum on shower walls. A very light layer of oil will actually slow down the formation of stubborn scum. Try a liquid lemon furniture polish for a pleasantly scented preventive—just pour a small amount on a soft, dry cloth, and lightly rub it over the shower walls in a circular motion.

Nix the abrasives. Once upon a time, we reached for a can of powdered cleanser and a steel wool pad when the tub needed scouring. But today's abrasive cleansers and pads can easily scratch your tub's surface, or the walls of a fiberglass shower surround. Then dirt can collect in the scratches, making your next cleanup even harder. What's more—the scratches themselves dull the tub's shine. So skip the heavy-duty scouring powder, and use liquid nonscratch products instead. If you need to get tough, try the gentlest of abrasives, such as Bon Ami® cleanser or baking soda applied with a nonabrasive plastic scrubbie.

Bleach away mold. If unsightly black mold has made itself at home in the grout around your tub, just take a tip from "peroxide blondes," and bleach the black away with hydrogen peroxide. Mix ½ cup of it with 1 cup of water in a handheld sprayer bottle, and spritz away. Wait about an hour or so for the peroxide to do its stuff, then scrub off the residue with a plastic scouring pad. Oh, and don't be tempted to spray your lovely locks unless you're a fan of brassy orange hair—household hydrogen peroxide is only a 3 percent concentration of this bleach; hair salons use a much stronger version.

Hard-water hang-up? Fasten a plastic bag of vinegar around a clogged showerhead, and those holes will open up like magic—and you won't even have to unscrew the showerhead! First, stretch a rubber band over the showerhead, and let it rest loosely on the neck. Then, pour some vinegar into a plastic bag, and slip the bag over the showerhead. Fasten the bag to the showerhead neck with the rubber band, and let the vinegar dissolve the hard-water deposits with its own natural acid. After an hour, remove the bag, step out of the way, and turn the shower on full blast.

The shower chamois. Super soft and absorbent chamois (both leather and synthetic versions) makes a perfect cleaning aid because it soaks up water in two shakes of a lamb's tail. Just wipe down the wet walls of the shower and tub to remove soap residue and hard-water spots.

Powerful Potions

Daily Shower Spray

Preventing dirt from building up sure beats scrubbing it off later, so use this spray after your daily shower to ward off the scum on the walls and in the tub. It'll make your next full-scale cleaning way easier!

- **½ cup of hydrogen peroxide**
- **½ cup of rubbing alcohol**
- **2 tsp. of spot-free liquid dishwasher detergent**
- **A few drops of grease-cutting dishwashing liquid**
- **3 cups of water**

Mix all of the ingredients in a handheld sprayer bottle with a "mist" or fine setting on the nozzle, and shake to combine. Then park this miracle mixture right on the tub, where it will be handy after your daily shower. Once you're fresh and clean yourself, take a minute to mist the walls of the shower, so that pesky soap scum never gets a chance to settle in. Hard-water spots will be foiled, too, because this solution dries fast and streak-free.

Bedrooms
(See also Bedspreads, Blankets, and Comforters)

Conquer the clutter. Just how cluttered is your bedroom? Are there clothes on the chair? Stray doodads on the dresser? A pile of receipts on the night table? I thought so! Bedrooms have a habit of collecting clutter, probably because they're out of sight and out of mind most of the time. So before you start cleaning, put things away—hang up clean clothes, put dirty laundry in the hamper, and clear off the tops of dressers and nightstands. Once the clutter is under control, then you can dig in.

Air it out. Open the windows at least once a week, so your bedroom smells like fresh air instead of stale socks. Even when it's frigid outside, cracking a window open for a few minutes can bring in a breath of the great outdoors—and that's the best air freshener there is. For a stronger treatment, set a saucer of cedar shavings or dried lavender on top of the dresser. Stir the contents every now and then to release more of the pleasant aroma.

Dry before wet. It's easier to deal with loose, dry dirt than it is to clean up wet grime. So sweep, vacuum, and dust before you reach for a wet sponge or a spray bottle. Sometimes, particularly in lightly used rooms like bedrooms, you'll find that things look so good after a quick once-over with a dry cloth that you don't even need to wipe them down with a wet cleaner. And that's a major time-saver!

Away with allergens. Are you sneezing and wheezing in your bedroom? If so, then it's time to get rid of allergy-aggravating dust, dander, and dust mites from your mattress and box spring. All you need to do is give them a good going-over with your vacuum cleaner about once a month. Start by sprinkling some baking soda on each of them about 30 minutes before vacuuming to freshen things up. Use the upholstery brush attachment to lift the dirt, and spend extra time on the nooks and crannies along the seams, where those nasty little troublemakers like to hide.

Bedspreads, Blankets, and Comforters (See also Quilts)

Dust 'em off. To lengthen the time between laundering, vacuum your bedclothes with a duster brush every month or so. A good going-over removes any dust, dirt, and dry skin, as well as those devilish little dust mites that can cause allergic reactions. Then when you do launder the covers, use only mild soap and cool water and nix the scented fabric softeners, which can also cause allergic reactions.

Room to move. Most home washers and dryers are too small to accommodate a big bedspread or comforter, so the next time your bedclothes need cleaning, cart them to the local Laundromat and use its extra-large machines. (An overcrowded washer won't clean very well, and the wet weight can be hard on both your washer and dryer.) Add a couple of towels to the load for balance, and set the water at the highest level. Your bed coverings will get cleaner and they'll dry fluffier and faster when they have space to spare.

Grandma Putt's Magical Methods

If your bedclothes are just plain tired (and not soiled), give them a new lease on life with a good dose of fresh air. Simply hang them over a clothesline on a nice windy day, or borrow a trick from my Grandma Putt and air them out of a second-story window. Be sure to pick a breezy day that's not too windy because you don't want your bedspread or blanket to go sailing off like a kite! Drape your bedclothes over a windowsill on the shady side of your house, and close the window to anchor them in place. An hour or so in the great outdoors will blow away all that dustiness and mustiness, leaving your bedspread or blanket smelling as clean and fresh as the morning sunshine!

Soak away dirt. Once a big, bulky bedspread or comforter gets twisted into a jumble in the washing machine, it's hard for your detergent to do its job. So give your laundry soap a helping hand by letting your bed-clothes soak for about 10 minutes before you begin the wash cycle. That way, you can use a shorter wash cycle, which saves wear and tear on the stitching, but still does a good job of cleaning.

Do not remove this label! Good blankets cost a bundle, but they can last a lifetime—unless you wash and dry a wool one by mistake and it ends up a shrunken wreck. So head off those nasty surprises by keeping the labels attached to your blankets and other bedclothes—and remember to always read that label before you try cleaning the covers!

Fluff and tumble. When your comforter is ready for the dryer, toss in a couple of new tennis balls or clean canvas tennis shoes to bump along for the ride and keep the filling from matting. And here's another trick: About halfway through the drying cycle, remove the comforter and shake it out to fluff up the filling so it'll dry faster and more evenly.

Bicycles

Heavy-duty dirt removal. Kids these days! I don't think they even know what putting playing cards in their bicycle spokes is all about. But before you show them how to clothespin those cards on, why not teach 'em how to get their bikes good and clean? Start by knocking off any dirt under the fenders and on the tires with a good stiff brush.

Sponge away. This is the part of the job your kids or grandkids will enjoy the most! Squirt some dishwashing liquid into a bucket of warm water, and dip a big, soft sponge into it. Start washing the bike, sploshing the soapy sponge over every inch. Then rinse with a garden hose and let it drip dry, or take it for a quick spin to blow the water off.

Oil it up. After you wash the dirt off the bike, lubricate the chain with a few squirts of WD-40®, using the applicator to aim the oily stuff directly onto the chain. Spin the pedals a few times, or take the bike out for a quick jaunt to work the WD-40 along the entire length of the chain.

Wax on, wax off. Last, but not least, finish the cleanup by waxing your bike to a shine. Dab a little bike or car wax on a soft rag, and rub it on the frame and fenders in small circles. Buff with a clean, dry cloth, and you're ready to go show off that shine as you ride up and down the block.

Powerful Potions

Kids' Bike Wax

Here's a quick and easy way for kids to make their bikes nice and shiny.

3 sheets of wax paper, about 12 inches long
Soft cleaning cloth

Fold up each sheet of wax paper into a pad. Hold the pad in your palm, and rub it back and forth along the bike's frame, fenders, and handlebars (but not the handgrips). When the wax wears off the surface of the paper, flip it over and use the other side. Finally, polish the waxed parts of the bike with the soft cloth until they shine like the sun.

Birdbaths and Bird Feeders

Banish algae with bleach. You need to kill all traces of algae when you clean your birdbath, so that any lingering bits don't spring back to life when you refill it with water. Start by preparing a solution of ¼ cup of bleach in a gallon of water. Dip a sponge into the mix after you've scrubbed the birdbath, and wipe every inch of it—including the rim and outside areas. Rinse thoroughly, until you can't catch even a faint whiff of bleach, and then refill your algae-free birdbath with fresh, clean water.

Shady setup. Slimy birdbaths are no use to birds, but skeeters sure love them! So keep things clean with a daily scrubbing in summer, when warm temperatures encourage algae to grow. And since algae need sun-

The Great Clean-dini Speaks

Q. What's the best way to clean nectar feeders?

A. A quick rinse may be all your feeder needs before refilling, if birds are emptying it every few days. I add a drop of dishwashing liquid and shake it up, then rinse it several times to make sure every trace of the soap is gone. If your feeder needs further attention—maybe there's scum, black gunk, or dead insects trapped inside of the reservoir—you'll need to disassemble it to do a thorough job. Here's how to get a dirty feeder squeaky clean:

★ To dislodge deposits within the bottle, start by filling it with warm water and a few drops of dishwashing liquid. Let it sit for about half an hour. Then empty the feeder, and drop a few dozen grains of uncooked white rice into the bottle, followed by an inch or two of water. Cover the opening with your hand, and shake, shake, shake, as fast as you can! The friction of the rice grains will help scrub off the scum. If stubborn spots remain, dump out the rice and water, let the bottle soak in warm, sudsy water, then repeat the rice-shaking operation. When the bottle is nice and clean, rinse it thoroughly before refilling it.

★ Get yourself a pack of good old-fashioned pipe cleaners from a craft store—they make ideal tools for getting the gunk out of feeder openings. Just poke them through until the holes are perfectly clean. Wash the pipe cleaners by rubbing a bit of dishwashing liquid into them with your fingers, so you can reuse them for several go-rounds.

light to grow fast, moving your birdbath to a shady spot can also help keep the green stuff in check. A simple move may allow you to skip a day or two between scrubbings.

Lord of the rings. To keep your birdbath in tip-top shape, add a teaspoon of apple cider vinegar to the water when you refill it. Birds don't seem to mind the taste, and it appears to slow down fast-growing algae. Plus, it'll help prevent "ring around the birdbath"—those white lines of dried minerals that form inside the basin as the water evaporates.

Penny for your thoughts. Some folks swear that copper pennies slow down the growth of algae, so why not give it a try? Just toss three pennies into your birdbath after you clean and refill it—and don't forget to make a wish—for no more algae!

Less mess. Feeding birds is a lot of fun, but boy, those empty shells can pile up! The solution to reducing the mess is to fill your feeders with hulled sunflower chips, which leave no waste behind. Or opt for millet and niger seed, which have lightweight shells that blow away in the breeze.

Cover it up. I would never stoop to sweeping dirt under the rug, but I'm not above hiding the mess under my feeders! A layer of wood chips or bark mulch will instantly make the area look nice and tidy, and it's easier than shoveling up the shells. The mulch will also prevent most weeds from sprouting, although a few sunflower seeds will probably manage to work their way through it. Let them grow; they won't get very big, and the cheery yellow flowers will beckon a bevy of goldfinches.

Seed-catching saucer. No matter how careful you are, your tube feeder is destined to be a seed spiller. Birds will sometimes pull out extra seeds as they feed, which then fall to the ground. Catch those spills, and you'll save seeds and add more feeding space at the same time. Here's how to do it: Buy a clear plastic plant saucer at a discount or home-supply store or garden center. These thin, lightweight saucers are remarkably

Hocus Pocus

CRYSTAL-CLEAR BINOCS

An extra-powerful set of eyes is just the ticket for watching birds at your feeders, but binocular lenses can get mighty grimy with frequent handling. Don't be tempted to use your shirttail to shine them up—you can scratch the lenses or rub off the special coatings on the glass. Instead, wipe them very gently with lens tissue and lens-cleaning fluid.

inexpensive. Glue the saucer to the bottom of the tube feeder. An all-purpose glue such as Aleene's Tacky Glue® should do the trick. That's all there is to it. Now, dropped seeds will fall into the saucer, where finches can perch on the rim to retrieve them with no muss and no fuss.

Put a stop to spillage. Ever notice how the level of seed in your tube feeder sometimes takes a sudden dive? The likely culprit could be whistling over your shoulder right now. That's right—wind can blow light-weight tube feeders willy-nilly, causing the seeds to spill out of the feeding holes faster than you can say "Whoa!" To stop seed spillage in stiff breezes, add some weight to your tube feeder. Before you fill it, simply drop in some small but heavy stones to just below the first feeding hole. The extra weight will add stability.

Cleanliness counts. Germs are a big concern at bird feeders because birds can spread disease like wildfire when they're all crowded together. So once a month, scrape out all of the seed, and blast the feeder with water to dislodge as much dirt and debris as possible. Then scrub it well with a disinfectant solution of ¾ cup of bleach to 1 gallon of water. And give your tube feeders a bleach treatment in the kitchen sink: Disassemble the feeder, cover the pieces with warm water, add a capful of bleach, and let the whole thing soak for about an hour. Use a bottle brush to get off any stubborn dirt. Then rinse the feeder thoroughly until there's no scent of bleach, and let it dry before you refill it.

Blenders

Going to pieces. Most blenders are built to come apart pretty easily, so make sure you clean all of the parts thoroughly, including the cracks and crevices. Just unscrew the bottom from the base of the machine—careful with those blades!—and separate the parts. Wash each one in soapy water, along with the lid and the blender jar. When you're done, set the pieces on a double thickness of paper towels on your counter, so you don't lose track of them. When everything is dry, put it all back together, and you're good to go!

Whirlwind clean. If you'd rather not get up close and personal with those sharp blades, let your blender clean itself. Here's how: Simply put a few drops of dishwashing liquid in the blender jar, add hot water to the jar until it's about one-third full, throw in half a lemon (if available), and run the machine on high speed for 20 to 30 seconds. Finish up by giving the jar a once-over with a soapy cloth, then rinse it thoroughly and let it air-dry.

Finger-savin' suds. If the blender blades are really caked with dried-on food, start with the "Whirlwind clean" above—but instead of rinsing that soapy lemon water down the drain, let it soak in the blender for about 15 minutes. Follow up with another 30-second burst of blending, give it a rinse, then remove and wash the jar. The caked-on crud will disappear, and your fingers won't have to get anywhere near those scary blades!

Odor eliminator. Whipping up a batch of garlicky pesto (or other odor-iferous delights) in a blender can leave the jar smelling less than fresh—especially if you don't wash it out right away. To get rid of any lingering odors, just blend ½ cup of baking soda and ½ cup of water in the jar, let it sit for about 10 minutes, then wash as usual. Keep following these simple steps and you'll never have a garlicky milkshake again.

Icy clean. When it comes to cleaning blenders, vinegar can't be beat, especially if you give it an extra kick of cleaning power. How? Add ice cubes! Just put a few inches of water in the blender, add a healthy splash of vinegar and a bit of dishwashing liquid to cut the grease, then drop in a handful of ice cubes and let 'er rip. When the clunking and grinding stop, your blender will be ready to rinse clean.

Open wide. If you add a toothbrush to your kitchen utensil lineup, cleaning those blender blades will be a snap. Just put a drop of dishwashing liquid on the wet toothbrush and scrub over, under, and around the blades until they're shining like new.

Blinds

Give dust the brush-off. You can make fast work of dusting most blinds by using your vacuum cleaner (with the brush attachment) to power your way through the job. Start by pulling the blinds nearly closed, and run the brush across the slats (not up and down) to suck up the surface dust in a hurry. A quick once-over every week or two is all it takes to keep light dirt from turning into a heavy chore!

Wild and woolly. For my money, thick, fluffy lamb's wool—the real stuff, not some synthetic wannabe—can't be beat. It picks up dust like a magnet, and it swoops blinds clean like nobody's business. So grab a duster and simply wipe away that dirt with a few fast, sideways strokes. When the wool gets too dusty for dirt to stick, take it outside and roll the handle quick-like-a-bunny between your palms to dislodge the dust and make it fly away fast.

Don't get unhinged. The slats of vertical blinds are attached to the frame by hooks at the top, so be sure to brush the slats down and not up. That way, you won't accidentally unhook the slats and send them crashing to the floor. A lamb's wool duster is perfect for verticals because it can reach the full surface of each slat. Just be sure to open the blinds first.

Freshen fabric blinds. There's no need to take down fabric blinds or shades to clean them. You can do it in place with a magic tool called a dry sponge, which is a foam latex pad that's available at most hardware and paint stores. To use one, close the blind or shade, and rub the dry sponge across it in short, even strokes to gobble up that dust and grime. When the sponge gets dirty, just rinse it out, give it a good squeeze, and let it air-dry for the next go-round.

Micro clean. Microfiber dust cloths work great to spruce up pleated fabric shades because you can cover big areas in a hurry. Wet the cloth, wring it out so that it's barely damp, and swipe it across the pulled-down shade.

The Great Clean-dini Speaks

Q. My blinds are a real mess, and dusting them just seems to smear the dirt around. What can I do?

A. Sounds like you've got a greasy buildup on your blinds—a common occurrence, especially if they're near the kitchen, where grease molecules go airborne. When metal or vinyl blinds are really grimy, the easiest solution is to take them down and scrub them thoroughly outside, where you don't have to worry about drips and spills from wet cleaners. To cut the grease, put a few drops of dishwashing liquid in a bucket of water, and give both sides of those dirty slats a good going-over with a soft cloth. Spray the soap off with your garden hose, and then repeat the scrubbing—but this time, use a few drops of liquid dishwasher detergent in a bucket of fresh water. Finally, rinse one last time, and drape the blinds over the back of a lawn chair to dry.

Major trick for mini blinds. If your bathroom mini blinds are a real mess, reach for a can of foaming bathtub cleaner and spray away, so those scrubbing bubbles can lift off the crud. Wipe the surface with a damp sponge, then pull the cord to reverse the slats, and do it again. Just be careful where you spray that stuff—be sure to keep it on the blinds and away from any painted or wood surfaces. Oh, and if those pull cords are dirty, too (and they probably are), give them a shot of shaving cream and a rubdown with a damp sponge to freshen them up.

Bloodstains

Always start fresh. The hemoglobin in blood has a nasty trick up its sleeve—it chemically binds to fabric as it dries, making it even harder to remove. So you've got to work on it right away. If you don't have much time, soak the stain with cold water until you can give it more attention.

The cold-water cure. If the blood is still wet, blot up what you can, then simply hold the area under cold running water while you rub the stain away. For older stains or dried blood, soak the item in cold water for several hours, and rinse it clean. Remember, never use hot water on bloodstains; it will cook the proteins in the blood and set the stain, making it nearly impossible to remove.

Toothpaste touch-up. You can give bloodstains the brush-off by scrubbing them with non-gel toothpaste. Here's how: Just wet the fabric with cold water, squeeze out some paste on the spot, and rub the fabric with—what else?—a clean toothbrush. Then rinse the area thoroughly.

Lather, rinse, repeat. A dab of shampoo works wonders on bloodstains, and it won't harm washable fabric. Just soak the stain first in cold water, then squirt on a bit of regular shampoo (not one with a built-in conditioner). Lather up the area while you rub gently, then rinse and repeat.

Ammonia chaser. Hand washing will make most bloodstains vanish, but if you still see a trace of that stubborn stain after you rinse the item, just pour a little ammonia onto the spot. Ammonia is safe for cotton and most synthetic fabrics, but don't try this trick on delicate fabrics or on silk, batiks, or that tie-dyed T-shirt—it might damage the fibers or discolor the dye.

Bleach in a bag. Here's a dandy way to get bloodstains out of a small item. Pour some hydrogen peroxide into a large ziplock plastic bag, and then slip the stained item into it. Seal it up, and let the gentle bleach of the peroxide do its stuff for about 20 minutes. Squish the bag around a few times to speed up the action, then fish out the item, and rinse it thoroughly under cold running water. That stain should vanish lickety-split.

Powerful Potions

Bloodstain Pretreater

Before you toss those sheets or clothes into the washing machine, get a head start on dissolving stubborn bloodstains with this quick fix.

1 cup of hydrogen peroxide
1 tsp. of laundry detergent

Mix the peroxide and detergent in a small bowl, dip in a clean, dry sponge, and blot the mixture onto the bloodstain. Give it about 10 minutes to penetrate the stain, and then launder as usual. And make sure you turn that dial to "cold" for the wash and rinse cycles!

Scrubbing bubbles. Let the foaming action of hydrogen peroxide lift bloodstains out of white clothes or sheets. First, rinse the stain with cold water. Then hold the fabric over the sink, and pour peroxide directly onto the stain. When it stops fizzing, rinse thoroughly, then launder in cold water.

Carpet cleanup. Blood on the Berber? Just grab a can of Barbasol® shaving cream, and spray the foam all over those darned spots. Rub the cream in with your fingers, and wipe it up with a damp cloth. A close shave? Not when you know a little cleaning magic!

A grain of salt. If you've got dried blood on your carpet, lift it out with this nifty two-step trick. First, rewet the stain by spritzing it with cold water from a clean handheld sprayer bottle (but don't soak the carpet). Then pour table salt directly onto the stain, and watch the blood soak right up into it. Scrape up most of the dirty salt with a teaspoon, and then vacuum the rest away. There's no muss, no fuss, and no hassle!

Spit on it! If you don't have the usual arsenal of bloodstain-busting weapons handy, as a last resort you can always spit on the stain (no cursing allowed!). The idea is to try to dilute it as much as possible. Spittle contains enzymes that do a fairly good job of breaking down the proteins in blood, which should make the stain easier to remove later during a normal washing cycle.

Books and Bookshelves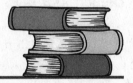

Floors first. Want to cut down on dusting your books and bookshelves? It's easy—just vacuum the floor more often! Carpet dust goes airborne every time you walk across the room, so if you keep the dirt out from underfoot, it can't settle on the shelves. Just do a weekly deep cleaning of those rugs using the strongest suction your vacuum can summon, and your shelves and spines will stay clean longer.

Step back. Use a clean, dry dust cloth to gently wipe down all sides of each book, including the edges of the pages. And remember, don't stand in front of the bookshelf to clean your collection, or you'll send dust flying right back onto those nice clean shelves!

Freshen 'em up. If your classics have "aged" real well and developed a musty smell in the process, you can freshen 'em up in one of several ways. The quickest way is to stick several scented dryer sheets between the pages, leaving them in place for two to three days (or longer, depending on the smell). Or you can place the book in a paper bag that's got a handful of baking soda, cat litter, or cedar chips in the bottom of it, and leave the book in there for a week or so. That should do the trick.

Magnetic attraction. Microfiber dust cloths beat a ragbag remnant by a mile, but a "magnetic" dust cloth works even better! The secret is in the fabric—it has a permanent electrostatic charge that actually attracts dust, causing it to jump right onto the cloth and stick tight. Just run the cloth down the edges of each book, and it'll lift the dust right off the paper.

Go deep. You should dig down to the bare bones of your bookshelves at least once every six months or so, removing all of the books so you can do a really thorough job of cleaning. After you empty the shelves, wipe them clean using a soft cloth with a little polish for wood, a damp cloth with a rust inhibitor for metal, or a plain, damp cloth with a gentle cleaner for hard vinyl shelves. Dry the shelves with a clean cloth and then, for good measure, let them air-dry for several hours, just to make sure there's no trace of moisture lurking in the corners. When the shelves are ready and waiting, refill 'em, one tome at a time.

Q. Got any tricks up your sleeve for making fast work of dusting my books? My feather duster doesn't seem to do a very good job.

A. Boy, do I ever! For a speedy solution, nothing beats your trusty vacuum cleaner. Just use the brush attachment, and that dust on your books will be history in a hurry. Run it over the shelves in front of the books, too. Then switch to the crevice tool, and run it along the bottom edge of those volumes where they meet the shelf. Your collection will be spiffy clean in no time flat!

The Great Clean-dini Speaks

Grandma Putt's Magical Methods

Clean a book with white bread? That's how my Grandma Putt used to clean the pages of her dog-eared Bible that was handed down from her grandmother. Every six months or so, she'd grab a piece of fresh white bread from the kitchen, sit down, and give the page edges the once-over to keep them in tip-top shape.

Dirty books. Are the covers of your favorite Jerry Baker books getting a little grungy? Just grab a clean, damp sponge or a Clorox® wipe, gently rub off that grime, and then follow up with a dry paper towel. This easy cleanup works great on almost any book with a shiny cover, even on paperbacks and dust jackets. But be sure to work carefully—you don't want to dampen any unprotected paper.

Order, please? Putting your books back in the right order can take a whole lot longer than cleaning them—if you mix them up when you're taking them down! Here's how to keep it all straight: After you clean each book, simply refill the shelf in the opposite direction from which you emptied it. Just remember that the last book you removed should be the first one that goes back into its place.

Brass and Bronze

Down with dull. Brass and bronze tarnish like an old penny, and no wonder—both of these alloys include a hefty helping of copper, which oxidizes when it hits the air. So manufacturers slap on a protective coat of lacquer before the brass or bronze leaves the factory. Unless your object is an antique—or a heavily used doorknob—that dullness is probably just dirty lacquer. Before you reach for the cleaning polish, try a simple rubdown with a soft, dry cloth to bring on the shine.

Cleaners from cows. Pew-ee, that milk sure smells sour! But wait, don't pour it down the drain—fill a bowl with it instead, and use it to soak the tarnish right off your brass or bronze. In just a minute or two, the mild acid in sour milk will dissolve the dirt. Rinse the milk off thoroughly, and dry the metal with a microfiber cleaning cloth. Or you can try a coating of unflavored yogurt to counteract that grime: Just wipe it on, wait about a minute or so, rinse it off with plenty of water, and buff until dry.

Tarnish-fighting toothpaste. Plain old scrubbing can work wonders on brass and bronze, especially if you use this terrific toothpaste trick. Just squeeze a big squiggle of non-gel toothpaste onto an old, soft tooth-brush, and dig in to that tartar—I mean, tarnish!

Getting down to brass tacks. My No-Scrub Brass and Bronze Cleaner on page 38 is just the ticket for removing tarnish from these metals—but how do you keep that pesky stuff from coming back? Just rub on a bit of olive oil or mineral oil with a soft cloth. And don't be afraid to put some muscle into it—applying it in fast, hard circles will really brighten that brass, and the thinnest film of oil is all you need to fend off future tarnish. Or try a treated yellow dust cloth, which is a nonwoven fabric that has a tiny amount of mineral oil built right in to attract dust as you wipe, leaving a nice thin layer of protection behind.

Hocus Pocus

BRASS OR BRONZE?

Are those brass can-dleholders you picked up at the local flea market really brass, or are they bronze? Here's how to tell: Brass, which is an alloy of copper and zinc, is a warmer, deeper yellow metal than bronze, which is usually a mixture of copper and tin. So if those decorative objects have a cooler hue, they're probably bronze. Inexpensive "brass" decorative objects, like pierced votive candleholders, are often made of bronze. Luckily, the cleaning solutions are the same for both metals.

Powerful Potions

No-Scrub Brass and Bronze Cleaner

If your metal is looking mighty dingy, just slather on this magic mixture to make it shine.

- 1 tsp. of salt
- 1 cup of white vinegar
- 1 cup of flour

Mix the salt into the vinegar until it dissolves, then stir in the flour until you have a smooth, thick paste. Sponge it onto the brass or bronze and let it sit—no elbow grease required! Wait about 15 to 30 minutes, depending on how tarnished the metal is, then simply rinse the stuff off with warm water, and buff with a soft, dry cloth to bring out that gleam.

Top brass. A mellow glow is part of the charm of antique brass, so don't scrub away the patina along with the crud. Instead of using an abrasive cleaner, give your brass a bath and a buff. Here's how: First, wash the object in hot, soapy water to get off the grime and any old wax. Rinse and dry thoroughly, and then remove any deeper dirt by rubbing the brass with a soft cloth moistened with boiled linseed oil. When the piece is nice and clean, buff it with a soft, dry cloth.

Pour on the sauce. A splash of Worcestershire sauce or a blob of tomato ketchup is just the ticket for livening up that dull metal. Simply rub it vigorously over the surface with a dry cloth, until the mildly acidic sauce cuts through the crud.

For more stubborn grime, coat the surface with another good dollop, and let it sit for a minute or two before you buff it off. Still not as bright as you'd like? All you need to do is slather on more of the sauce, and wait a few minutes longer before you rub it to a gleaming shine.

Now you're cookin'! Burp! 'Scuse me, it's just the onions talking. And that acid is exactly why those tummy troublemakers make such a great brass cleaner! Just put 2 inches of chopped onions into a small saucepan, add water until the onions are covered, and bring the mixture to a boil.

Reduce the heat, let your "cleaning soup" simmer for about two hours, then drain the contents of the pan through a colander to collect the liquid. When you're ready to clean your brass, just pour some of that onion juice onto a soft, clean cloth and rub away. And don't forget to rinse thoroughly until all the onion smell is gone.

Wood ash wipe. Always keep the word *gentle* on your mind when you're cleaning brass or bronze because it's all too easy to scratch the soft surface of these coppery metals. So put away that harsh scouring powder, and give mildly abrasive wood ashes a try. Simply sprinkle a soft cloth with powdery wood ashes—no charcoal chunks or splinters, please!—and add a little elbow grease to make that dullness disappear in a flash.

Aging gracefully. Unlacquered bronze darkens over time, giving bronze sculptures a mellow, aged look that's prized by art collectors. But that doesn't mean you can rest on your laurels—dirt and grime can actually eat into the surface of bronze. So dust your unlacquered pieces regularly, and be sure to get the crud out of crevices with a soft brush.

The Great Clean-dini Speaks

Q. A neighbor of mine who was in the Navy years ago told me about something called "bug juice" that was used to shine the brass on his ship. Where can I get some of this stuff?

A. Just snitch the fixings from the kid at the Kool-Aid® stand down the street! The one and only bug juice was the military's own brand, but you can make a home-made version with any unsweetened instant drink mix that contains citric acid. Just mix a 13-ounce packet with 1¼ tablespoons of water, rub the juice in with a dry cloth, and rinse with fresh water. There you have it—military magic!

Rx for ailing bronze. Uh-oh—could those patches of light green spots be the telltale signs of "bronze disease"? Sure could, especially if you notice the symptoms on bronze in the bathroom, where moisture is a main cause of the ailment. You can stop it in its tracks by pouring boiling distilled water over the bronze several times, which will halt the chemical reaction that's causing the problem.

A little dab'll do you. Too much of a good thing can lead to big problems with brass and bronze, so if you decide to use a store-bought polish, be sure to apply only a tiny bit. Otherwise, you'll end up with a greasy film that shows every last fingerprint and dulls the metal. And be sure to buff that stuff like you'd spit-shine a shoe, so the polish hardens into the thinnest possible layer of protection—which is exactly what you're after!

Bright idea. Got a brass planter, platter, or other big polishing job ahead of you? Then use a lemon as your scrubbie! Just pour some salt into a small bowl, cut a fresh lemon in half, and press the cut side of the lemon into the salt. Now grab that salty lemon, hold it salt side down, and scrub-a-dub-dub. Finish the job with a thorough rinse.

Brick

So long, salt! Ever notice white residue on your brick wall or patio? If you licked your finger, dabbed it against the white stuff, and took a taste, you'd find that it's salt. Clay—which is what bricks are made from—often includes some natural salt, and rain or a nearby sprinkler can leach it out, bringing it to the surface. To get rid of this problem, just spray it away with a good stiff blast from your garden hose.

Stains be gone. For stubborn stains on brick that won't come off with plain old water, mix ½ cup of ammonia in a gallon of water and scrub the area with a stiff-bristled brush. Rinse well, and you should be all set.

Fireplace freshener. If the brick around your fireplace has turned black from soot, it's time to get to work. First, move all of the furniture out of the way and protect your carpets and the surrounding areas with plastic drop cloths. Then mix ½ cup of Spic and Span® or ½ cup of trisodium phosphate (TSP) in a gallon of water, and give the brick a good scrubbing with a stiff-bristled brush. Or you can mix ½ cup of liquid soap and ½ cup of salt, spread it on the brick, let it sit for about 15 minutes, and then carefully scrub (don't splatter) until the black is gone. Rinse thoroughly afterward, and let the brick air-dry.

Slip 'n' slide. Moss or algae can make your brick walk more slippery than all get out, especially when it's wet. Spray the moss with a mix of 1 part household bleach to 2 parts water. When the moss turns white in about a week, pull on a pair of rubber gloves and remove it with a stiff-bristled brush and your garden hose. There—now you're back on safe footing!

Leave pressure washing to the pros. Sometimes it just doesn't pay to DIY—and pressure washing a brick house or wall is one of those times. Why? Because it's easy to make the wall look worse, or to damage the bricks or mortar. So when you have a really big job, call in the pros.

Q. Help! Barbecuing has left grease stains on my new brick patio. How can I get them out?

A. Don't panic—the solution is right under your kitchen sink. Just use a grease-cutting dishwashing liquid to break up that stain. Here's how: Mix 2 tablespoons of dishwashing liquid with 4 tablespoons of water, and pour it on the stain, making sure that all of the grease spot is covered. Give it about 10 minutes to soak in. Then scrub the area with a stiff-bristled brush, and rinse well.

The Great Clean-dini Speaks

Burn Marks

Skin deep. To remove a burn mark that has penetrated the finish on your wooden furniture but not the wood itself, just wrap a small piece of extra-fine steel wool around your finger, and use it to carefully sand out the stain. Brush away the dust, apply a coat of wax or furniture polish to the surface, and the mark will hardly be noticeable.

Mark out burns. Got a cigarette burn on your coffee table or hardwood floor? Apply a paste made of equal parts of vinegar and baking soda to the mark, and use a pencil eraser to rub it in. Wipe the residue off with

Hocus
Pocus

FORMICA® FIRST AID

Formica countertop burn marks can be impossible to totally remove because anything you use to scrub them away may also remove the counter's finish. So before you resort to covering that mark with a cutting board, give these tricks a try:

★ Squeeze out some non-gel toothpaste on the mark, and scrub the stain away with an old toothbrush.

★ Sprinkle a little baking soda on the stain, and scrub it with a nonabrasive plastic scrubbie until the mark vanishes.

★ Rub the spot with a Mr. Clean® Magic Eraser®.

★ Gently scrape off the brown part of the burn with a paring knife or razor blade, working very carefully. Now the burn won't be so obvious.

★ If the burn mark is small, sand out the dark spot with very fine steel wool, wipe away the dust, and then apply a thin coat of nail polish—in a matching shade, of course!

a damp sponge, and let the spot dry thoroughly. Then use a wood-stain "marker" to color the spot until it blends right in. These nifty pens come in a wide range of colors and shades.

Carpet cleanup. To counteract a carpet burn, start by rubbing off as much of the blackened residue as you can with your fingers. If the fibers are sizzled or melted, snip off the worst of the damage with a pair of manicure scissors—but don't take off too much, or you'll end up with a bald spot in your rug. Then use your fingers to comb the neighboring fibers over the spot. You may be able to stop right there, but if the burn is big or deep, you'll need to call a carpet repair service, or do a patch job.

That sinking feeling. Burn marks can be mighty upsetting, so when your curling iron leaves its calling card in your bathroom sink, just reach for the Alka-Seltzer®. Not for your stomach—for the stain! Just wet a tablet of the fizzy stuff and rub it on the burn mark until the stain disappears.

Butcher Block

A new season. Stinky onions, soaked-in stains, and bugaboo germs—you can stop them all in their tracks by seasoning your new butcher block before you use it. Simply heat up a food-grade mineral oil (which won't turn rancid like vegetable oils can), apply with a soft cloth in the direction of the grain, and wait for it to soak in. Repeat the process four or five times, until the wood won't absorb any more oil. Finish by wiping off any excess oil with a clean, dry cloth.

Regular renewal. Oil not only protects against germs and odors, it also prevents your butcher block from drying out and splitting. Whenever the wood looks pale and dry, give it another coat of mineral oil, and it'll stay in great shape.

Keep it clean. Be sure to clean your butcher block after every use, so nasty bacteria don't start multiplying like rabbits. Just wipe off the loose crumbs, scrape off any gunk, and finish up by swiping the surface with a mild dishwashing liquid solution. Then wipe the block with full-strength white vinegar—its mild acid is mighty tough on germs.

Bee smart. If you're like most folks, you probably use your butcher block for everything from cutting up chicken to chopping tomatoes. To keep that ol' block looking like new, try this trick: Shave about $1/2$ teaspoon of beeswax into a cup of mineral oil, and microwave the mix on "high" for about 45 seconds to melt the wax. Stir the mixture, pour some on your butcher block, and rub it in while it's still warm. It'll help keep liquids from soaking in before you can wipe them away. Now that's what I call bee-ing smart!

Cabinets

Cut the grease. If your kitchen cabinets are starting to feel a little sticky, then you've got a greasy buildup. The oily residue from cooking can quickly dull even the brightest cabinet's shine, so you need to wipe down those doors at least once a month. The simplest solution? Just use a damp sponge with a dab of grease-cutting dishwashing liquid or Murphy® Oil Soap on it. Rinse with a clean, damp sponge, and dry with a lint-free microfiber cloth to make the finish look as good as new.

You can handle it. For regular cleaning of cabinet hardware, depend on a damp Mr. Clean® Magic Eraser® to do the job. Just wipe over, under, and around your cabinet handles, drawer pulls, and hinges, making sure to swab out all of those dirt-collecting crevices. Handle that hardware cleaning at least once a month, and you'll be able to easily wipe off that PB&J or cookie dough with a damp cloth in between times.

Powerful Potions

High-Powered Handle Cleaner

Plain soap and water will do the trick on most cabinet door handles, but if yours are really grimy, call on the magic power of this mixture to make that crud vanish in a jiffy.

3 parts ammonia

1 part vinegar

Mix the ammonia and vinegar in a handheld sprayer bottle. Then spray some of the mix on a damp microfiber cleaning cloth, and give your cabinet handles and knobs a thorough wipedown, working on them one at a time. Remember to reach inside any hollowed-out handles (where greasy residue can hide), and rinse off each handle with a clean, damp cloth before you move on to the next one. Don't forget to keep a clean, dry cloth or paper towel within easy reach—that way, you can catch any runaway drips, so they don't leave streaks on the cabinet doors.

Total rejuvenation. Have your cabinets been neglected for far too long? If so, then here's the most efficient way to get them back in shape:

1. Start by removing all of the handles and knobs from the cabinets and drawers—trust me, taking those screws out now will be faster in the long run than cleaning each knob individually.

2. Set the screws aside, and put the hardware in a sink filled with hot water and a few squirts of grease-cutting dishwashing liquid.

3. Let the soap soak away the grime while you clean the cabinet surfaces, a task that's much easier without having the handles in place to work around.

4. Wash each handle with a sponge, rinse, and dry with a soft cloth.

5. Reattach the handles, and your once-grungy cabinets will have a new lease on life.

Welcome to the club! Fizzy club soda breaks right through that dull, greasy buildup on cabinet surfaces. So the next time you have a little extra left in the bottle, don't let it go flat in the fridge! Instead, use it to dampen a cleaning cloth and wipe the grime away.

Raid the laundry. To coax stubborn cabinet crud into giving up its grip, grab a can of Spray 'n Wash® stain remover from your laundry room, and give the surfaces a spritz. Wait about a minute or so to let the foam do its stuff, and finish up by wiping off the stain remover and the greasy dirt with a damp sponge. If your cabinets are made of wood, play it safe and test this technique in an inconspicuous place first to make sure it doesn't affect that beautiful finish.

Candleholders and Candle Wax

Nonstick coating. If you pretreat your candleholder by lightly spraying the inside of it with vegetable oil before you set the candle in, any wax that hardens will slide right out. Or you can wipe the inside beforehand with a dab of mineral oil on a dry cloth for quick and easy cleanup.

Puddle of prevention. Ever pick up a votive candleholder at a garage sale? Chances are that it had a puddle of hardened wax glued to the bottom of it. Not to worry—it's not hard to get that glob out (see The Great Clean-dini Speaks on page 48), but it makes even more sense to prevent it in the first place. Here's how: Just pour about ¼ inch of water into the bottom of your votive candleholder before you set the candle in. The wax will harden on top of the water, instead of getting stuck to the holder. That way, it's a snap to remove.

3, 2, 1, liftoff! If you hate wrestling old candle stubs out of that classy chandelier or candelabra, the next time you need to replace the candles, put a drop of dishwashing liquid in the bottom of each empty candle cup. The soapy film will make it easy to remove the old wax and lift out the stub later.

Blot the bricks. If candles on the mantel have made a mess by dripping onto your brick fireplace, start the cleanup by scraping off as much wax as you can with a flat-bladed knife. Then call on your clothes iron to coax away the rest of the mess. Here's how: Hold a folded cotton cloth against the wax, and press the hot iron against it while you count to 10. Lift off the cloth, and refold it so that a fresh part is against the wax—and against the iron—and repeat until the wax is gone.

Soot solution. Flickering candlelight sure makes everything look beautiful—but the soot it leaves behind isn't so pretty! For a swift solution to this unsightly mess, wipe that hurricane chimney or votive holder clean as a whistle with a used dryer sheet. And remember to keep that wick trimmed—$1/8$ inch is all you need—so that it's less likely to blacken things up the next time.

Hocus Pocus

CANDLE DISASTER CLEANUP

Oh, no—your favorite candle spilled wax all over the carpet! Now what? Easy—just grab your clothes iron and a brown paper grocery bag, and get ready to make it disappear. Here's how: Put the iron on its lowest setting, rip open that grocery bag, lay it over the stain, and set the iron on top of it. After a few seconds, move the bag to another spot, and repeat the treatment until all of the wax is gone. You'll see the wax start to soak into the brown paper almost right away, and in as little as 10 minutes (depending on the size of the spill), your cleanup will be complete. Even colored wax comes right up with this trick! And it works for clothes and upholstery, too. If you don't have a paper bag, use paper towels instead; it'll take a little longer, but they work just as well.

A warm bath. You can soften up a hardened layer of old wax with a little warm water. Just set your glass or metal votive holder or candle plate in a bowl of very warm water, and let it soak for a bit. Hot water from the tap should be warm enough to do the trick.

Gleaming glass. Cleaning up crystal candlesticks is a breeze if you give them the freeze-pop treatment first (see The Great Clean-dini Speaks below), then follow up with a nonscratch silicone cleaner to pry up the edges of those waxy drips before you lift them away. And for a sparkling finish, wipe the candlestick down with a little vinegar.

Treat with heat. If you don't have room in your freezer for that nine-armed candelabra (see The Great Clean-dini Speaks below), it's no problem! Just heat things up instead by giving it a blast of hot air from a hair dryer. Once the hardened wax is softened up—a few seconds is all it should take—simply use your fingers to roll it away.

The Great Clean-dini Speaks

Q. Do you have any simple shortcuts for getting old wax out of my candleholders? It takes me forever to dig it out or scrape it off.

A. Please, put down that butter knife—there's no need to dig out old wax when you can use my "freeze-pop" trick. Simply put that glopped-up candleholder into the freezer for about 15 minutes or so. Then turn the holder upside down and slap its bottom with your hand, and the wax will pop right out. If any stubborn bits remain, they'll be a cinch to lift off with your fingernail. This secret works like a charm on any kind of candleholder—wood, glass, silver, brass, bronze, or what have you. So clear a space in that freezer, and get ready to make your own freeze-pops.

Can Openers

Overdue cleanup. To clean a really disgusting handheld or electric can opener, fold a paper towel into thirds, making a long pad out of it. Put an edge of the pad into the can opener's blades, or "teeth," and close the handles to grip it tightly. Now turn the knob or push the button and slice away, as if you were opening a can. You'll see a trail of nasty grime on the paper towel as the blades work themselves clean. Toss the evidence in the trash when you're finished, then resolve to do a better job of cleaning those blades after every use.

Look, Ma—no hands! I like my fingertips far too much to get them anywhere near those super-sharp blades. So when it's can opener cleaning time, I simply unplug my opener, remove the top part, and pop it into the silverware basket in my dishwasher, without ever touching the blades. That way, it comes out clean and shining, and my fingers stay safe.

Brush up the blades. What's by far and away my favorite cleaning tool for just about any job around the house? It's gotta be an old toothbrush because nothing works better at scrubbing dirt out of tight quarters! So when your can opener needs some serious cleaning, reach for a toothbrush. Dip the brush into some full-strength vinegar, and go to town scrubbing those crusty old blades.

Grandma Putt's Magical Methods

Moisture can make can opener blades rust fast, and getting that darn rust off is way harder than preventing it in the first place. So try a little bit of my Grandma Putt's magic: After you wipe the blades clean, crumple up a piece of old-fashioned wax paper, and slice into it with your opener. The can opener teeth will get coated with a thin layer of wax that stops moisture in its tracks, so that rust can't settle on the metal.

Wiggle away dirt. Cleaning an electric can opener is easy if you keep a few pipe cleaners in your kitchen junk drawer. After each time that you use your can opener, simply wiggle a pipe cleaner between the blades, and wipe off the dirt around the cutting wheels. Rinse well and you're good to go!

Give rust the brush. For a great nontoxic solution to cleaning rusty can opener blades, mix up a paste of baking soda with a bit of water, then slather it on, and let it sit for at least a day. Scrub the rust off with an old toothbrush or nailbrush, rinse thoroughly, and your blades will be ready to roll like new.

Carpets (See also Rugs)

Double the doormats. What's the best way to keep dirt out of your carpets? Why, that's simple—don't bring it in! Make cleaning double quick by placing a doormat outside for folks to wipe their feet on, and another one inside, to catch the rest of the crud. Make that inside doormat a floor mat that's long enough to take two or three strides on, so it grabs even more dirt. Mats made from polypropylene are great for this dirty job—just shake them off frequently, or vacuum up the crud they catch. And when they get really dingy, take 'em outside and hose 'em off.

Join the Japanese. Just about anything could be on the bottom of your shoes—and rubbing off on your rugs! Save your carpets from wear and tear by training your family and friends to take off those dirt collectors when they step inside, like they do in Japan. Just keep a shoe rack with a few pairs of inexpensive, one-size-fits-most spa slippers inside the door, where folks can trade their street shoes for house slippers. Soon everyone will pick up the habit—and you won't be picking up nearly as much dirt.

Powerful Potions

Two-Step Carpet Cleaner

Lift muddy footprints and other stains out of your carpet with this quick and easy recipe. Just mix up the amount you need for the job at hand; this recipe is plenty for a stain about the size of a single adult footprint.

2 tbsp. of dishwashing liquid

½ cup of warm water

White vinegar

Mix the dishwashing liquid and warm water gently so that the solution isn't too sudsy, and dab it sparingly onto the stain using a sponge or a cleaning cloth; do not rub! Wait a few minutes, then lay a clean, dry cloth on the area, and blot up the soap solution.

Now for the power boost: Pour a little white vinegar onto the stain, and blot again with a dry cloth. Then sponge on the soap solution again, blot with a cloth as before, and rinse by sponging with plain water. Blot with a cloth to remove as much moisture as possible, let the carpet dry, and then fluff up the fibers with your fingers to make it look good as new.

Blot with rubbing alcohol. To quickly remove most carpet stains, pour a little rubbing alcohol onto a dry white cloth, gently blot the spot, and wipe the stain away. Always test this trick first on a hidden area of your carpet to make sure it doesn't lift the color along with the stain.

Out with the ink. As soon as you spot an ink stain on your carpet, get to work because the longer you wait, the harder it is to remove. First, blot up whatever you can with a paper towel. Next, sprinkle the stain with some cream of tartar, add a few drops of fresh lemon juice, and blot some more with a damp cloth, adding a gentle wipe-and-lift motion. Be sure to fold the cloth as you work, so you're always using a clean side. Finally, vacuum up the cream of tartar, and you can write that stain off!

Wipe 'em away, baby! For a really fast fix when nothing else is available, grab a baby wipe when something spills on your carpet, and wipe that stain away. The alcohol and very gentle soap in the wipe will remove most food stains or smears, and the cloth has just the right amount of moisture to remove the stain without soaking the carpet.

Stuck in the mud? It's way easier to vacuum up dried mud than it is to wipe up the wet stuff, so start by blotting up what you can with paper towels, and let it dry. When the mud is nice and crusty, scrape off as much as possible with an old credit card or butter knife, and use your vacuum to suck up the clods and dust. Wiggle the rug fibers with your fingers to loosen any stubborn bits that are stuck deep down in the pile, and vacuum again. Finally, remove any lingering traces with my Two-Step Carpet Cleaner on page 51.

Freshen up. Smoke, pets, kids, and daily life can all contribute to making your carpet smell stale—or even worse. And unfortunately, store-bought carpet fresheners will only mask the smell for a while, not eliminate it. What you need is an odor neutralizer, and I've got just the tickets! Here are several of my favorite ways to get your carpet smelling fresh as a summer's breeze again:

★ Sprinkle baking soda over the entire carpet, leave it in place for at least an hour to absorb and neutralize odors, and then vacuum it up.

★ Mix 1 part powdered borax (giddyup, mules!) with 2 parts cornmeal, and use a flour sifter to sprinkle it all over your carpet. Wait about an hour to let it do its stuff, and vacuum it away.

★ To enjoy a fresh scent, add a drop of essential oil—lemon, lavender, or whatever you like—to 2 cups of baking soda, and mix it up thoroughly before you sprinkle it on your carpet.

★ Fill a handheld sprayer bottle with 1 part liquid fabric softener and 6 parts water, and mist the carpet—very lightly!—after you use the baking soda or borax treatment described above.

Make your carpet smile. You can put the bleaching action of denture-cleaning tablets to work on carpet stains by dissolving a tablet in a cup of water, and using that mix to sponge the stain away. Just be certain to test it first in an inconspicuous spot to make sure it's safe for your carpet.

Easy does it. For a safe way to remove most carpet stains, use a mixture of $\frac{1}{2}$ teaspoon of dishwashing liquid and 1 cup of warm water. Dab a clean cloth into the mixture, and apply it to the stain with a blot-and-lift motion. Avoid the urge to rub vigorously—that will only drive the stain in deeper. Instead, be patient and use a gentle touch, even if you have to repeat the process a few times. When the stain is gone, gently sponge the spot with 3 teaspoons of white vinegar in 1 cup of water, and blot away the moisture with paper towels. Let your clean carpet air-dry completely, and then fluff up those fibers with your vacuum cleaner.

Mix your drinks. When a glass of red wine gets a little bit tipsy—uh-oh, there it goes, right on the rug!—pour a bit of club soda on the stain, and let it go to town. After the soda has fizzed away for about 30 seconds, blot the stain and the soda with paper towels.

Grandma Putt's Magical Methods

When my Grandma Putt wanted to make her wall-to-wall carpet smell extra good, she borrowed a magic ingredient from her spice rack—and added a pinch of cinnamon to her homemade carpet freshener. To spice things up yourself, mix $\frac{1}{8}$ teaspoon of cinnamon with 1 cup of baking soda, sprinkle it lightly over your dry carpet, and wait about half an hour so the scent can soak in before you vacuum it up. The fine cinnamon dust can leave a stain if you grind it into the fibers, so don't walk on the mixture, and don't use this trick on white or pale carpets. For those, try light-colored powdered ginger instead of the darker-colored cinnamon.

Foam vs. food. You can also make red wine and other food stains vanish by covering them with a shot of shaving cream. Let the foam sit for 15 minutes or so, wipe it away with a damp sponge, and blot your carpet dry. If you don't have any shaving cream, try a foaming bathroom cleaner—but test it first in a hidden spot to make sure it's safe for your carpet.

Vinegar to the rescue. Don't make a sour face at that carpet stain—just reach for the vinegar to make your carpet look sweet again! Here's how: Mix 1/3 cup of white vinegar with 2/3 cup of warm water, sponge it on the stain, and blot with a clean, dry cloth. You may need to repeat the process a few times, but it'll be well worth the effort.

Salt for soot. If fireplace soot sullies the carpet near your hearth, don't get all burned up about it. Simply sprinkle those black spots with plenty of salt, let it sit for at least half an hour to absorb the stain, and vacuum your troubles away.

The Great Clean-dini Speaks

Q. My carpet looks great after I shampoo it, but it seems to get dirty even faster afterward. Should I have it professionally cleaned?

A. It's not your imagination—DIY shampooing can leave a sticky residue that attracts dirt like a magnet. But before you call in the pros, try this solution: Instead of filling the shampooer with soapy stuff, fill it with water and vinegar, using 1 cup of white vinegar for every 2½ gallons of water. Then "shampoo" your carpet, and let the vinegar lift out the old soap that's built up on the fibers. Empty the reservoir and refill it with warm water, and make another pass to make sure all of the soapy residue is gone. Your carpet will be clean and soft—and it won't be a dirt magnet anymore!

Powder power. Dropped a piece of pizza facedown in the family room? Just sprinkle some baking soda or cornstarch on that greasy stain, let it soak up the oil overnight, and vacuum.

Last resort. Got a tough stain that just won't give up its grip? Pour a small amount of hydrogen peroxide onto that stubborn spot, let it fizz, and blot it up with a clean, dry cloth or paper towel. Repeat until the stain is gone. Test it first in a hidden spot to make sure your carpet can take the treatment.

Hocus Pocus

BREATHE DEEPLY

Baking soda, borax, and other powdery odor-soaker-uppers can irritate your lungs and bring on a coughing fit. So play it safe by wearing a disposable dust-filter mask whenever you're using a mixture with one of these substances. And to be on the even safer side, keep your kids and pets out of the room until well after you've vacuumed up the powder.

Cast Iron

Keep rust away. Water makes cast iron rust so fast, you can almost watch it happen. So keep wet cloths and sponges away from any iron fixtures you want to remain rust-free. That means no spray-on cleaners, either! Instead, use a dry microfiber cleaning cloth to wipe off dust and dirt.

Navy know-how. Got rust? Then get some naval jelly! This gel is available at most hardware stores, and it's great for removing serious rust from cast-iron outdoor furniture, fireplace surrounds, old cookstoves, and other hard cases. After the rust is gone, apply a coat of stove polish to keep the moisture out and blacken the bare metal. And by the way, if you're wondering why your cast-iron garden ornaments stay rust-free, it's because they were given a protective powder coating at the factory.

Salty scrub. To remove those stuck-on bacon bits or other crusty food remnants from the bottom of your pan, just pour about a teaspoon of coarse kosher salt into the pan while it's still warm, and scour the crud away with a nonabrasive plastic scrubbie. Wipe it with a light coating of vegetable oil, and you're good to go!

The original nonstick. Nowadays, most new cast-iron pans are preseasoned, but it's still essential to know how to season them just in case you do burn something. Here's how to create that nonstick coating from scratch:

1. Cover the lower rack of your oven with aluminum foil, and preheat the oven to 400°F.

2. Scrub your pan with a stiff plastic brush and warm, soapy water; dry it with a paper towel.

3. Rub the pan—inside and out, including the handle—with lard or vegetable oil, and place the pan upside down on the top rack of your oven. Set the timer for an hour.

4. Run the oven fan and open a window because the oil will drip and smoke for about 20 minutes. After an hour, turn the oven off, remove the piping hot pan—very carefully!—and set it on the stove to cool.

5. Wipe the cooled skillet with a paper towel to remove any extra oil.

6. For a darker, more nonstick coating, repeat the process; three coats will leave it nice and slick and shiny black.

Coke® soak. To restore an old, rusted, greasy iron skillet to its prime, set it in a plastic tub and pour enough Coca-Cola® in to completely cover it—about three 2-liter bottles should be plenty. Let it soak overnight to loosen the gunk, and then give it a good going-over with a stiff plastic brush. Wash the pan with warm, soapy water, pat it dry, and it's ready to be reseasoned (see "The original nonstick" above).

Definitely dry. Hand drying may leave your cast-iron cookware looking dry—but sneaky moisture may still be lingering, ready to come out of hiding and speckle your skillet with rust spots. So the next time you rinse out your pan, set it on the stove afterward and heat it up for a few minutes to ensure that every last bit of moisture evaporates. And don't worry about damaging the empty pan on a hot burner—the heat treatment will only improve the seasoning.

Light cleaning. There's nothing better than a cast-iron skillet for fixing up a batch of flapjacks on a Saturday morning. The heavy metal lets you cook over high heat, while the slick black surface keeps foods from sticking. To preserve that priceless finish, use a light touch whenever you clean the pan. Many folks swear by simply wiping out the pan with a paper towel, but you can also wash a well-seasoned pan with a sudsy sponge, dry it immediately and thoroughly, and finish up by applying a light coat of vegetable oil.

Banish burned-on food. Burned potatoes stuck to that cast-iron skillet or Dutch oven? Instead of soaking or sudsing the pan, just scrub away the burned-on food with a wooden spoon. And don't worry—you won't hurt a well-seasoned finish. Or you can simmer an inch or so of water in the pan for several minutes to loosen the food, and then scoop off the remains with a sturdy spatula. Finish the job by wiping the inside of the pan with vegetable oil, and heating it up to renew the slick cooking surface.

Grandma Putt's Magical Methods

Cast iron can really take the heat, so my Grandma Putt used her old noggin and stored her skillet in the oven—and kept it there whenever she baked something! The heat only makes the finish harder, plus it stops the growth of any bacteria that might be lurking about. And since the oven is nice and dry, even when it's not cooking, your pan will stay rust-free.

CDs and CD Players

Baby your CDs. Skip, crackle, and pop—dirty CDs can make all kinds of distressing sounds, or they can simply refuse to play at all. If your CDs get a little dirty, you can shine 'em up with a drop of baby shampoo mixed with a little warm water. Just dip in a soft cloth, hold the CD by its edges and center hole, and wipe it clean from the inside out. And here's the real trick—wipe in straight lines across the disc, not around in circles. You're aiming to wipe that dirt right off the edge, not grind it into the grooves. Follow up by drying the CD thoroughly before you stow it away.

Gone without a trace. Your hands may be clean, but if you touch the shiny side of a CD, the oils in your fingertips will leave their mark behind. There's no need to wear white gloves—simply wipe off those prints with a soft cloth moistened with a little rubbing alcohol. And next time, remember to keep your cotton-pickin' mitts off!

Toothpaste touch-up. For thoroughly filthy CDs (like that one with the melted chocolate hardened onto it), put a dab of toothpaste on a microfiber cloth. Wipe the paste all over the playing surface of the disc using gentle strokes, and wipe across the disc, not in circles. Then rinse off the paste, dry the disc with a clean microfiber cloth, and pop it into the player. Now, that's what I call good clean sound!

H_2O, only better. Even with those handy-dandy cup holders in today's cars, spills can happen. But I've got just the solution for sticky stuff on your CDs: Wipe the disc with distilled water, which is available at any roadside convenience store, and polish it dry with a soft cloth. Distilled water won't spot or scratch the CD with hard-water deposits like tap water or bottled mineral water can do.

Noninvasive cleaning. Cleaning those delicate parts inside of your CD player is best left to the pros, who know just which parts they can fiddle with. But by regularly using a laser lens-cleaning disc, you may never need anyone to get up close and personal with the innards of your CD player. Every week or so, or whenever your CD player starts acting balky, pop in the cleaning disc, and let it gently scrub the lens clean.

Blow dirt away. Car CD players can get even dirtier than home models, so if yours starts hopping, skipping, jumping, or otherwise getting temperamental, use compressed air to clean it out. Start by removing the CD player from the car and taking the cover off to expose the inner workings. Then blow out any debris that may have settled in all those nooks and crannies with short blasts of compressed air.

Double up! When you notice scratches on one of your CDs, burn a copy of it as insurance in case those marks eventually make it unplayable. But don't toss the damaged disc! If you can't see through the scratches when you hold it up to the light, it's only the protective lacquer that's damaged, not the info on the disc. Try my "Toothpaste touch-up" trick at left to smooth the surface, then keep that CD for backup.

Ceilings

Cobwebs come first. Cobwebs certainly collect a lot of dust. So before you actually start cleaning, you need to get rid of them, or you'll end up with dirty smears on the ceiling. Plus, they have a nasty habit of sticking like glue when you try to sweep them away. So outwit those creepy webs by using your vacuum cleaner to clear them away.

Vacuum the vents. Heating and air-conditioning vents are natural-born dust magnets, so before you tackle the ceiling, you also need to vacuum those vents. Use the dusting attachment or the upholstery brush to remove the dirt that collects on the grid or louvers. And if you need more backbone in that floppy vacuum hose, tape it to a broom handle to improve your aim.

Disposable dusters. If your ceiling is smooth, you'll have an easier go at it by using a disposable duster to whisk the dirt away. Stuff will stick like magic to those static-charged fluffy fibers, and the light weight makes it a breeze to handle. And while you're working your way across the bottom of the upper story, don't forget to swab the dust off your ceiling fixtures, too.

Grandma Putt's Magical Methods

Washing a ceiling can be a real chore, but my Grandma Putt had a couple of neat tricks for cutting the job down to size. First, she used the two-bucket system—the cleaning solution went into one bucket, and clean water in the other. That way, she could rinse out her sponge as often as she wanted without trekking back to the sink or dirtying the cleaning solution—because frequent rinsing means a streak-free job! Plus, she made sure to dip only about one-third of the sponge into the cleaner to prevent drips from running down her arm, or streaking the walls. Now that's what I call good old commonsense cleaning magic!

Give dirt the brush-off. A good dusting is often all the cleaning a ceiling needs because, let's face it, spills and mud just don't fall upward. So if you use a long-handled lamb's wool or synthetic fabric duster, you can take care of this chore in a few minutes flat. Start in the corners, and then swipe across the surface in a straight line, overlapping as you go. Even if you can't see any dust—it's there, all right, and any spots you skip will be noticeable when the rest of the ceiling is clean.

Tools with reach. There's no need to buy a special ceiling duster because you already have a perfectly good cleaning tool sitting right in your utility room closet—yes, indeedy, it's a broom! Use one with soft, plastic bristles to avoid scratching the surface, or fasten an old flannel shirt over your corn broom, and sweep that dirt away. Just be sure you remove the shirt's buttons first, so you don't scratch the ceiling as you're getting rid of the grunge.

A wash that works. Sometimes dusting the ceiling isn't enough, especially in kitchens, where cooking can leave a dark, sticky, and greasy residue. When it's time to get tough, reach for the trisodium phosphate (TSP) or Spic and Span® (which just so happens to have TSP as a main ingredient), and wash the grime away. A sponge mop is the perfect tool for this job—upside down, of course! And be sure to wear goggles, rubber gloves, and a scarf over your head to keep those drips away. Just remember, use a wet cleaner only on ceilings that won't soak up the water; getting acoustic tiles wet is a definite no-no!

Fancy finishes. Ceilings made of wood, metal, or leather (or their faux cousins) are made to show off, so keep them shining like new with a weekly dusting. An electrostatic duster, such as those made by Swiffer®, locks the dust onto its fibers, so the dirt doesn't fly away or resettle in the raised design. Keep in mind, though, that if your ceiling has any sharp edges, they might just catch on the duster, leaving telltale threads or shreds behind. If that's the case, use the dusting attachment of your vacuum cleaner for a quick touch-up.

Chewing Gum

Good-bye, gumshoe. Say "so long" to sticky shoe soles by putting them in the deep freeze. Simply pop the shoe into a plastic grocery bag, press the bag against the gooey gum, and set it in your freezer for about two hours. Pull the bag away from the shoe, and the mess will lift right off with it.

Don't pull your hair out! To get gum out of those lovely locks, work a dab of peanut butter in until the gum simply slides right off. Or soak the strands in a glass of Coca-Cola® for about 10 minutes to coax the gum into giving up its grip. If you can't dip the strands, saturate a paper towel with Coke® and lay it in place. Remember—Coke refreshes you best!

The big chill. Got gum on your clothes? Here's a solution for any fabric: Put a few ice cubes in a ziplock plastic bag, hold them against the gum for several minutes, and pick off the frozen gum. If the wad is still pliable deep down, repeat the treatment. Or you can put your sticky clothes in the freezer, wait a couple of hours, and then flick off the gum with a dull knife. You'll have no more double bubble trouble!

Hocus Pocus

ICY BREATH

A blast from a can of compressed air will freeze gum in a jiffy, so you can easily lift that once-sticky stuff from clothes, carpets—or your hair. But be careful with canned air—it's mighty powerful. Not only can that high-pressure blast make you say "Ouch!" when it hits you, it can even burn your skin like frostbite if you're not careful. So take the sticky shirt or shoe off before you blast it, or get a steady-handed helper to aim the can while you hold your gummy hair away from your head. Then double-check which way the nozzle is pointing—before you push the button.

Soap and salt. Here's a nifty little trick to remove pesky chewing gum from most washable fabrics if "The big chill" at left doesn't work. Just squirt some dishwashing liquid on the spot, and then pour about a teaspoon of table salt on it. Rub the fabric against itself, and presto— the goo will be gone!

Slippery slope. Grease and oil will loosen up gum—but beware because they can leave a worse stain behind. So a word of advice: Try my other tricks before you resort to applying vegetable oil, cooking spray, peanut butter, WD-40®, or any other oily substance to that stuck-on, stubborn mess. Or save these slippery solutions for materials (like shiny plastic) that won't get stained by grease.

China and Porcelain

Catch the dust. A microfiber cleaning cloth is your best bet for dusting your precious china and porcelain because the dirt particles will stick to the fibers, and the cloth won't scratch the glaze. So give your collection a quick wipe-down once a week. And if you want to really cut down on your caretaking chores, consider keeping your pieces inside a glass display case.

Hand wash. Paints and glazes on china can be delicate, especially if the piece is old. So unless your collection is specifically marked as dishwasher safe, always wash your china by hand. Fill your sink with lukewarm water and a squirt of dishwashing liquid, and sponge off the pieces, one at a time. Rinse each one with lukewarm water as you finish it, and set it aside on a padded surface to dry. And remember, use water that's only mildly warm: A sudden dunk in hot water or a rinse in icy cold water can cause china to really crack up—and that's no laughing matter!

Handle with care. When you're washing those one-of-a-kind china and porcelain items, be sure to wash just one piece at a time, and don't be tempted to put them all in the sink at once for a nice long soak. Why? Because it's hard to see what you're doing in soapy water, and it's also very easy to upset the applecart—and if you accidentally bump a saucer against a cup, that could be the end of your Ming Dynasty!

After the bath. Once you're done washing, set aside your china to air-dry on several layers of paper towels or a bath towel, and then hand dry each piece with a soft, clean cloth. If you're cleaning old porcelain or china, be extra gentle and pat the surface dry instead of wiping it, so you don't damage the glaze. Then when you're stacking your china away for storage, place a paper coffee filter between each piece for added protection against chipping and scratching.

Lift off paint speckles. Porcelain figurines have an unfortunate habit of picking up tiny speckles of paint when you redo the living room, thanks to the overspray from a too-close paint roller. So if you see that your figurines have developed paint "freckles," use your fingernail to scrape them off, or coax them away with a bit of orange oil or a goo remover like Goof Off® on a paper towel.

Tea for two. A dainty tea set isn't nearly so appetizing when it's darkened with unsightly tea stains. So here's a neat trick for getting rid of the discoloration without damaging your china: Set your teacups in a dishpan, and fill each one to the brim with a solution of 1 part white vinegar and 1 part water. If your saucers are also stained, set them in a large bowl full of the vinegar/water mix. Let the pieces soak overnight, and then wipe the stains away with a soft cloth the next morning. Finish up by rinsing each piece until there's no telltale trace of vinegar left, and dry them with a soft, clean cloth.

Stones for stains. If your china won't come clean with hand washing or a vinegar soak, try this trick: Use a soft pumice stone to scrub away the stains. You'll find pumice stones in the bath-and-beauty aisle of your local supermarket. Hold the piece under running water, wet the stone, and rub it very gently over the china. You can also get the same gentle abrasive action by mixing 1 tablespoon of white vinegar with 1 tablespoon of table salt, and rubbing the stain away with a nylon brush or nonabrasive plastic scrubbie. And remember, don't try these tricks on antique porcelain or china because even a gentle abrasive can easily scratch the surface.

I'm a little teapot... And boy, oh boy, am I full of tea stains! To get your teapot looking like new again, drop two denture-cleaning tablets into it, fill it to the brim with boiling water (so the spout is filled, too), and let the stains soak away. (If you clean stained teacups at the same time, use only a quarter of a denture-cleaning tablet per teacup of water.) Check the pot in an hour, and if the stains persist, empty the pot and repeat the treatment. Another alternative is to let the filled pot sit overnight. When the stains are gone, wash the pot inside and out with soapy water, rinse it clean, and set the pot upside down to air-dry. Tea stains in an antique teapot call for special treatment, so "let your fingers do the walking" and phone a china-restoration expert for help.

Grandma Putt's Magical Methods

My Grandma Putt's knickknacks got the kid-glove treatment when it came time to give them a bath. First, she padded the sink—including the front edge and the drain board—with a bath towel in case of any soapy slips. Lightweight rubber or foam mats, including washable foam placemats, work great, too. For Grandma's final trick, she made sure to pad the faucet by using rubber bands to hold a big sponge or hand towel in place. That way, there was no school of hard knocks for her delicate china.

Chrome

Foil that grime. Use an aluminum foil scrubbing pad and white vinegar to bring the shine back to cruddy chrome. Here's how: Just fold up a piece of aluminum foil into a pad about the size of an index card, so that it's easy to handle. Dip the pad into a bowl of white vinegar, and scrub away, using moderate pressure. Frequently add more vinegar, so the surface is eventually sopping wet. Wipe off the residue every now and then with a damp sponge or cloth, and before long, you'll be able to see your smiling face again!

Hard-water help. Hard-water spots will vanish from chrome faucets and fixtures quicker than you can say "Alakazam!" if you wipe them down with a cloth dipped in white vinegar. Scrub any stubborn spots with an old toothbrush dipped in vinegar. For extra tough cases, lay the cloth over the metal, pour on the vinegar, and wait an hour so the acid in the vinegar can loosen the deposit. Then wipe away all traces of the residue, and finish up by polishing the fixture with a dab of mineral oil or car wax for easier cleanup next time.

Rust remedy. Got a rusty car bumper or golf club handles? Crumple a piece of heavy-duty aluminum foil, shiny side out, moisten it with water, and rub it briskly over the spots until they're gone.

OUT OF THE DRYER...

You'll save a whole bunch of money if you stop tossing your used fabric-softener sheets in the trash, and start recycling them into polishing cloths. The soft, spun fabric won't scratch your chrome, and the tiny bit of fatty acid that works as a fabric softener in the sheets will polish away dirt, grime, and even soap scum, while leaving the chrome sparkling clean.

Hocus Pocus

Coke® or Pepsi®? It doesn't matter because either one will do the trick when it comes to cleaning chrome. Just pour some cola onto a dry cloth—or a ball of aluminum foil— and rub your chrome clean. Keep in mind that these are sticky liquids, so be sure to rinse the area thoroughly with plenty of fresh water after you clean the chrome, and wipe up any drips or spatters before the neighborhood ants come running.

Shiny appliances. You can wipe away greasy fingerprints, oily smudges, and most minor spills on your toaster, blender, and other chrome appliances with any of these handy household helpers:

★ Apple cider or white vinegar

★ Club soda or seltzer water

★ Rubbing alcohol

★ A solution of 1 part ammonia to 16 parts water

Oil up. Both baby oil and mineral oil do a fine job of removing dirt from chrome; plus, they leave behind a dazzling shine. Just pour a bit of oil onto a soft cloth, apply a little elbow grease, and you'll be good to go!

Clothes
(See also Fabrics; Grease Stains; and other stains by name)

Get the stains out first. You should always pretreat stains before you launder your clothes because warm water and dryer heat can make those marks a permanent feature of the landscape. A stain-remover pen or spray will take care of most culprits, but you can also use common household products to make them vanish. Read on to learn how to get your clothes spot-free before you suds them up. And if you need more cleaning magic, turn to the entries on specific stains for more of my fabulous fix-it tips.

Keep your cool. Modern laundry detergents and stain removers do a great job of removing the "souvenirs" from last week's dinner, but keep those clothes away from heat until you know the stain is gone. That means wash and rinse the item in cold water and air-dry it—because even the lowest dryer setting is hot enough to set a stain. And keep the iron away, too.

Black triangle = red flag. Care labels on clothes are a great idea, but some of those symbols—like that solid black triangle with a line through it—can be tricky to figure out. *FYI:* That triangle is a big red flag, because it means "Do not bleach!" If there is no care label attached, avoid bleach whenever you wash silk, wool, or anything with spandex because the bleach can damage the fibers of those fabrics. And who wants saggy, baggy stretch pants?

Nix mildew smell. When it comes to getting the lingering odor out of damp towels or sweaty clothes, washing alone won't do the trick. You need extra power to get rid of the stench, so add 1/2 cup of borax to your laundry, and your clothes will come out smelling fresh as a daisy.

Grandma Putt's Magical Methods

In my Grandma Putt's day, the household cleaning schedule was such a familiar part of life that it was embroidered on hand towels and aprons—especially the all-important Wash Day! The routine made it easy to keep up with chores, and even added an element of competition to it. On Mondays, Grandma and her friends would race to see whose laundry was the whitest—or whose was out on the clothesline before anyone else's. Just in case you decide to schedule your household chores like they did in the good old days, here's the routine from way back when:

Monday: Wash Day
Tuesday: Ironing Day
Wednesday: Sewing Day
Thursday: Market Day
Friday: Cleaning Day
Saturday: Baking Day
Sunday: Day of Rest

BANISH SMOKE SMELLS

So you spent a nice evening singing around the campfire, and now everything you wore smells like wood smoke. Never fear, the Great Clean-dini is here! For woolly sweaters and other nonwashables, just hang them outside on a breezy day, and let the smell blow away. To rid your washable duds of the smoke smell, add ½ cup of baking soda to your laundry along with your regular detergent during the wash cycle, and then finish the treatment by pouring in 1 cup of white vinegar at the start of the rinse cycle. These tricks work great for cigarette smoke, too, so no one will be able to smell you coming.

Hocus Pocus

Worst offenders. Most stains are easy to remove with laundry pretreatment products, but some notorious nasties call for extra measures. Grease, ink, and red or brown foods and drinks—such as cola, wine, or spaghetti sauce—are tops on that list. So the next time you have a run-in with one of these bad apples, try any of these tricks before you launder the item:

★ Place a grease stain facedown on a paper towel. Give that spot a squirt of grease-cutting dishwashing liquid, wait a minute or two to let it work its magic, and rub it in with your fingertips. Then wash the item in cold water.

★ Blot a stain from red juice, red wine, tomato-based sauces, coffee, or colas with a wet sponge. Then sprinkle the spot with salt and pour on a splash of club soda for good measure. Wipe it clean, and launder the item as usual.

★ To make a dastardly ink stain disappear, hold the spot over the top of an empty drinking glass and grasp the garment and the glass to hold it taut. Then pour rubbing alcohol over the stain, letting it soak through into the glass. Rinse with cold water. If you still see a shadow of the stain, repeat the treatment until it's gone.

No more whining. There's many a slip twixt wineglass and lip, but if you spill a bit on your clothes, there's no need to stop the party. Don't whine about that red wine—just moisten a napkin with club soda or white wine, and blot the stain up. If you can remove the garment, pour a liberal amount of salt onto the wine mark, wait a few minutes, and then sponge it away with cold water. By golly, I think it's time for a toast—here's to emergency cleaning magic!

Wash-and-wear. If your clothes desperately need a bath when you're traveling, but you don't have extras on hand, just hop in the shower—with your clothes on! Wet yourself down thoroughly, and lather up your clothes with bar soap or shampoo. Slowly turn around in the spray, lifting the clothes away from your body so they get a thorough rinse. Then peel off your clothes, wring them out, wrap them in a bath towel to soak up more moisture, and hang them over the shower-curtain rod to dry.

Powerful Potions

Ring-Around-the-Collar Remover

Maybe we should call it "black" magic, the way the inside of a shirt collar gets so much dirtier than the rest of the shirt. What's the solution? Try this homemade "ring cleaner."

¼ cup of baking soda

2 tbsp. of white vinegar

Mix the baking soda and white vinegar to form a paste. Use an old toothbrush to scrub it into the stained collar or cuffs, let it sit for about half an hour, and then launder as usual. No more ring around the collar!

"Hand"-y help. You should always keep a tub of degreasing hand cleaner in your laundry room because it's sheer magic when it comes to getting tough, greasy dirt out of clothes. Just rub it into the stains with your fingers or an old toothbrush, let it sit for about 15 minutes, and rinse the stains away. Old stains may need two treatments before they'll ease their grip, but ease their grip they will!

Hocus Pocus

PRESERVE THAT HEIRLOOM

What a beautiful bride—oops, watch out for that chocolate fountain! With all of the accidents that are just waiting to happen at a wedding reception, it's a wonder that any bridal gown survives long enough to be handed down to the next generation. Good thing there are professional cleaning services ready, willing, and able to restore and preserve your special dress. After all, those yards of satin, lace, and beadwork need special care to stay beautiful. So go ahead and use the tricks in this book for first aid on minor stains—but take my advice and turn your precious gown over to the pros before you pack it away.

Teamwork for armpit stains. Freshen up those dingy underarm stains with a paste made of 1 tablespoon of borax and a little water. Just rub it in with an old toothbrush, and let it sit for about half an hour. Brush the crust away with a nonabrasive plastic scrubbie, and launder as usual. With a team of 20 mules working on it, that stain'll be history in no time at all!

Don't sweat it! There's no need to toss your favorite white T-shirt in the ragbag when all it needs is a little magic to get rid of those ugly armpit stains. Try one of these easy tricks, and those yellow armpits will turn bright white in a flash:

★ Sponge the stains with a generous amount of white vinegar, and let it soak in for an hour or two.

★ Pour hydrogen peroxide onto the grungy parts, let it fizz, and then launder as usual—but only with other whites because peroxide is a bleach.

★ Crush a handful of aspirins, add a few drops of water to make a paste, and rub it into those yellow stains to make 'em disappear.

Preventive medicine. After a long hot day, dab a little chlorine bleach onto the armpits of your sweaty white dress shirt (even if you don't see any stains), and throw it in the washer right away with other whites. The bleach will prevent the yellow from setting in. And to avoid sweat stains on nonwashable items, take a tip from the good old days—before antiperspirants came along—and add dress shields to your clothes.

White on black? Solid or powdery deodorants have a nasty habit of leaving telltale white stains on dark clothes, but I have a quick fix for that annoying problem. Just rub a pair of panty hose over the stains, and the gentle abrasive action will make them vanish! Or use a baby wipe to swipe the stains, and the alcohol in the wipe will dissolve the marks and evaporate, leaving you clean and dry. Pack a few wipes in your purse or pocket, and you'll be ready for emergency touch-ups anytime, anywhere.

The Great Clean-dini Speaks

Q. What can I use to pretreat stains for my big family? It seems like I'm buying stain-remover sticks every week, and the cost really adds up!

A. Stop pinching your budget, and mix up a batch of my handy all-purpose stain remover whenever it's wash day. My "1-1-1 Stain Treater" works great on any bleach-safe, washable fabric, and it'll take out food stains, bloodstains, and lots of others—including those old "mystery stains" you thought were hopeless! Mix 1 part baking soda, 1 part hydrogen peroxide, and 1 part water—1-1-1—and scrub the paste into the stain with an old toothbrush. Let it sit for about half an hour, and then scrub again until the stain is gone. Prepare this mixture just before using it, so the peroxide doesn't lose its potency. This treatment takes just minutes and, best of all, only costs pennies to make.

Collar cleaner. If you've got cruddy collars and cuffs, grab a shampoo that's made for oily hair, and use it to remove the body oils that have rubbed off on the fabric. Just squirt on a bit of shampoo, and scrub it in with an old toothbrush until the dirt disappears. You can also rub those stains away with half of a fresh lemon—it'll cut through the greasy buildup in no time flat!

Magic marinade. To remove a tough food or bloodstain from your favorite shirt, reach for a can of meat tenderizer to put the power of papain to work breaking down the proteins. Make a thick paste of about 1 tablespoon of tenderizer with a little water, rub it into the stain, and let it sit for about an hour. Toss your well-marinated clothing into the washing machine, and it'll soon be as clean as a whistle.

Solar power. Stubborn stains on white or light clothes can be a real problem, so harness the power of the sun for extra bleaching action. First, saturate the stain with lemon juice, and then hang the garment where the sun can shine full force on the stained spot. Check it in about an hour, and apply another dose of lemon juice if that pesky stain is still there. This nifty trick works great on old stains, too, so go ahead and use it on garage-sale finds, attic treasures, and family hand-me-downs.

Coffee Grinders, Coffeemakers, and Coffeepots

Once-a-day wipe. A good cup of coffee starts with fresh beans, so clean your grinder often to remove the oily residue that's left behind by the grind. Get in the habit of wiping out the grinder funnel after every use with a slightly damp paper towel, and you'll keep most of the buildup away. And remember, unplug the grinder before you clean it to protect yourself from accidental start-ups.

Stale bread solution. Coffee oils and grounds hide out not only in the funnel, but in the business end of your grinder, too. So for a thorough cleaning, run some very stale bread through the grinder about once a week or so to clean the grinding mechanism. Just drop in a couple of hard crusts, and grind away until the bread crumbs are about the size of your usual coffee grounds. Then unplug the grinder, dump out the crumbs, and wipe the funnel clean with a paper towel or dry cloth.

Rice to the rescue. Running uncooked rice through your coffee grinder will sharpen the blades as well as clean them, thanks to the slightly abrasive texture of the grain. Pour in about a quarter cup of uncooked white rice, and let the grinder run until the rice is the size of your usual coffee grounds. Unplug the grinder, dump out the rice, wipe the funnel, and take a sniff inside—still smell coffee? If you do, simply repeat the treatment.

The Great Clean-dini Speaks

Q. My coffeemaker doesn't work as well as it used to—the coffee sputters and comes out in dribs and drabs, instead of running smoothly. What's the problem?

A. It sounds like you've got a hard-water hang-up—the mineral deposits from hard water are clogging up the works. Fizz them away by using denture-cleaning tablets to do the job. Just drop a couple of tablets into the reservoir, fill it with clean water, and turn on the machine. Rinse the coffeemaker by running through two cycles with clean water. And if hard water is a problem at your house, switch to distilled water when you make your coffee, and try my marble trick at right. That way, there will be no more mineral deposits to slow down brew time or gum up the works!

Don't forget the lid. Coffee oils and dust can accumulate on the underside of your grinder's lid, so be sure to wash it every now and then with dishwashing liquid, and rinse it well so your cuppa joe doesn't taste like soapy dishes! Make sure it's thoroughly dry before you put it back in place because any moisture in the grinder can cause coffee oils to turn rancid quickly.

Snap off for quick cleanup. Spills, drips, and spatters, as well as oily residue, like to hide in the nooks and crannies of coffeemakers, so remove whatever pieces you can to make the cleaning job easier. Take a close look at how the parts fit together, so you can put them back in place after they're clean and dry. Then disassemble the pieces very carefully (don't snap off any critical components!) and wash them with a soapy sponge. It'll be time well spent.

Exterior care. To keep stains from settling in, wipe down the outside of your coffeemaker with a damp paper towel or sponge after every use. Use a sprinkling of baking soda to remove any stubborn spots from the plastic housing, wiping it off with a clean, damp cloth or sponge. If coffee drips have burned onto the heating pad, scrub it with a damp sponge and a dab of dishwashing soap, and rinse with plain water. And don't forget to unplug the appliance before you clean it, so there's no chance of having a shocking experience.

Don't lose your marbles. Those nasty mineral deposits from hard water can gunk up the inside of your coffeemaker. Nip that in the bud by putting a glass marble into the reservoir. The crud will collect on the marble, sparing the machine. And believe you me, it's a whole lot easier washing a marble than it is doing a full-scale coffee machine cleanup!

Hocus Pocus

VANQUISH COFFEE STAINS

Fresh coffee stains usually come out easily if you blot the spot with a wet cloth. But if that stain has set in, try one of these terrific tricks to get things clean again:

★ Soak stubborn coffee stains on clothes overnight in a bowl of milk, and then launder in cold water.

★ Mix one raw egg yolk, a few drops of rubbing alcohol, and about a teaspoon of water, and rub the mixture onto clothes stains with a sponge. Rinse with cold water.

★ Run cold water through the piece of clothing from the back side of the stain. Pour a bit of dishwashing liquid on the stained side, and rub it in with your fingers or a toothbrush. Wait about 30 minutes, and rinse with cold water.

★ Wet a clean cloth with club soda, 7UP®, or other clear, sparkling soda, and dab the stain off. Rinse with a clean, wet cloth or launder as usual.

★ Wipe away coffee stains on carpets or clothes with a baby wipe.

★ Mix 1/3 cup of white vinegar with 2/3 cup of cold water, and blot away the stain on carpets or clothes.

★ Mix 1 teaspoon of dishwashing liquid in 1 cup of lukewarm water, and blot the stains off your carpet. Rinse by blotting with a clean, damp sponge.

★ Blot carpet stains with a wet sponge, sprinkle on some baking soda or salt, and let it sit for about an hour. Vacuum up the residue, blot with a wet cloth to rinse, and then remove as much moisture from the carpet as you can by blotting with a clean, dry cloth.

★ Use a damp sponge sprinkled with baking soda to wipe away coffee stains on cabinets, counters, or vinyl floors.

Vinegar brew. This is a stinky solution that will keep your kitchen smelling like vinegar for a couple of hours, until the smell dissipates. So why try it? Because vinegar works wonders at removing coffee oils, stains, and hard-water deposits from your coffeemaker. So prepare yourself for the smell, and use this tried-and-true method on a day that you're not going to be entertaining. Here's how to do it:

1. Pour white vinegar into the coffeepot until it's about one-quarter full, then add water to fill the pot.

2. Run the mixture through the coffeemaker without using a paper filter. Turn the machine off at the end of the brew cycle when the pot is full, and let the pot cool down for about 15 to 20 minutes.

3. Pour the pot of vinegar water back into the reservoir, and run it through again. Turn the machine off, and wait 15 to 20 minutes for the water to cool down.

4. To rinse away the vinegar, run a full pot of clean water through the coffeemaker, turn it off, wait 15 to 20 minutes, and then repeat with a pot of fresh water. If the finished pot of water still smells like vinegar, give it another rinse.

5. When the coffeemaker is free of the vinegar smell, rinse the pot with fresh water and let it air-dry.

Coffeepot cleanup. Keep coffee from staining your glass pot by washing it daily with warm, soapy water, either by hand or in your dishwasher. If you've let the job go for too long, sprinkle baking soda on a damp sponge or nonabrasive plastic scrubbie, and have at it! Wash your filter basket, too, making sure your sponge gets into all of the little grooves.

I can see clearly now. When hard water or coffee oils leave a cloudy coating in your coffeepot, just fill the pot with vinegar and let it sit overnight to dissolve the scum. In the morning, empty the pot and wash it with warm, soapy water, using a nonabrasive plastic scrubbie to get off any stubborn spots. Rinse thoroughly until you can't smell the vinegar.

Brighten a burned pot. Scouring powders can leave a bad taste in your coffeepot, so why not let a little lemon juice and salt do the scrubbing instead? First, pour 1 teaspoon of salt into the empty pot, and add 2 cups of ice cubes or crushed ice. Then squeeze a freshly cut lemon half into the mix, and swish and shake the ice around so the salt and lemon mix can scrub those stains away. Reverse the direction every now and then, letting the swirling ice hit the stains from all sides. Voilà!—those nasty brown stains will disappear right before your very eyes.

Combs and Hairbrushes

Clean your teeth. Gels, sprays, shines—when it comes to hair care, there's more than enough stuff to gunk up a comb even without the usual lint, loose hair, and general grime. So keep those teeth sparkling clean by soaking your comb in hot, sudsy water about once a week. Begin by pulling out any loose hair, and then let your comb soak for a couple of hours to soften the buildup. You'll be able to wipe away most of the grunge with a paper towel. For any lingering crud, use an old toothbrush to scrub the last of it out of the teeth.

Got oily hair? You can remove stubborn grime from your comb by giving it a grease-cutting bath. Just dunk it in a glass filled with white vinegar to cut through the greasy residue, or squirt some shampoo for oily hair onto your comb, and soak it in a glass of warm water that's got a drop of your favorite essential oil added to it. After about an hour of soaking, rinse your comb and wipe it dry with a clean paper towel.

Perfect partners. Why clean only your comb when you can save time, money, and effort by using your comb and brush to clean each other? First, pull out any and all loose hairs and lint. Next, wet your brush and comb, squirt some shampoo onto the brush, and scrub them together, face-to-face. The teeth of the comb will clean the brush, and vice versa.

Rinse out all traces of soap under warm running water, and dab out any remaining dirt with a cotton swab. And if you have two hairbrushes, scrub them together, brush-to-brush—you'll clean both at once!

Baking soda bath. Bubble away comb dirt with good old baking soda. Here's how: Fill your sink with a couple of inches of hot water, and pour in about a cup of baking soda. Submerge your combs, letting them soak for half an hour. Then wipe off the grime, and rinse.

Clean for clean. Scrub your brush and comb before you shampoo your hair, instead of after you style it. That way, you'll be using clean tools on your clean hair—and that greasy brush won't dull your locks.

Sweeten the smell. Plastic hairbrushes and combs can soak up the perfumes from styling products, or the odor of oily hair and general dirt. So freshen them up by soaking them in a sink full of warm water with a squirt of shampoo and $1/2$ cup of borax added to it. Swish your brushes and combs in the mixture, then let them soak for an hour. Finish by rinsing them well.

Grandma Putt's Magical Methods

When natural brush bristles take in water, they swell, twist, and curl. But when wood soaks up water—well, let's just say the results aren't very pretty! So my Grandma Putt kept her high-quality hairbrushes in fine fettle by doing as much "dry cleaning" as she could on a regular basis. She pulled out loose hair by hand after every brushing, and removed lint and deep-down hair by inserting her comb at the roots of the bristles, and levering it upward. And to keep her natural bristles clean, she filled a bowl or basin with warm water, added a squirt of dishwashing liquid, and then quickly dunked the bristles a few times—while keeping that wood handle out of the water. This method won't work for a brush that's gunked up with a lot of beauty products—so save your natural-bristle brush for giving your hair an organic shine, and use synthetic bristles for styling.

Computers and Printers

Start on the outside. When you need to spiff up your computer, disconnect it from the power strip and wipe the case with a soft cloth dampened with some plain water. If your computer housing is really cruddy, try a bit of rubbing alcohol on that cloth, unless your owner's manual warns against it. Wipe the outside of the keyboard, printer, and mouse clean, and run that damp cloth over the cables, too.

Swab the small stuff. Use foam swabs to clean your keyboard and to wipe out the nooks and crannies of your mouse. You can also use cotton swabs, but they may leave some lint behind. Use the swabs dry, or moisten them slightly with rubbing alcohol or water to pick up more dirt. Just never, ever insert the swab inside the case or keyboard—there are lots of delicate parts in there!

Shake 'n' blow. Dust, hair, and crumbs from all of those snacks you're not supposed to be eating at your computer can make your keyboard act balky, causing keys to stick or fail to register. Every week or so, disconnect your keyboard, turn it upside down, and give it a good gentle shake to help loose particles fall out. Follow up with an occasional deeper cleaning by using a can of compressed air. Just tilt the keyboard, point the long, skinny nozzle between the keys, and blow that dirt out of there. After the whirlwind, give your keyboard a final upside-down shake, wipe off any loose dirt with a soft cloth, and plug it back in.

Vacuum away problems. You can also use a handheld, portable vacuum cleaner to suck dirt and debris out of your keyboard. If you have pop-off keys that the vacuum might dislodge, then secure a piece of cheesecloth over the vacuum's nozzle with a rubber band, so your ABCs don't disappear down the hatch! And don't use your regular vacuum cleaner for this job—the suction is too strong, and it can generate static electricity that will wreak havoc on that electronic brain.

Clean the screen. If your computer monitor is made of glass, as in older non-LCD models, simply wipe dust away with a dry cloth whenever necessary, and remove smears and smudges with The World's Best Window Cleaner on page 354. Always spray the cleaner on the cloth, not on the computer, so that it doesn't get inside the works. For an LCD screen, wipe with a soft cloth dampened with rubbing alcohol.

Antiglare care. If your computer screen is coated with antiglare protection, never use ammonia or other household cleaners on it because you could damage the coating. Check your owner's manual for a recommendation, and if you're not sure, stick to good old water to do the job.

The Great Clean-dini Speaks

Q. I had to replace my keyboard after accidentally spilling some soda pop into it. If there's another mishap, can I do anything to prevent fatal damage?

A. Yes indeedy, there is one surefire way to keep spills from ruining your keyboard—don't drink or eat anything while you're at the computer! Set up a TV tray table nearby, and park your soda there instead of on your desk. But since most of us are guilty of violating that rule every now and then, here's how to handle a spill: Turn the computer off immediately, and turn the keyboard upside down, so that the spill doesn't drip into the circuitry. Grab a towel or newspaper and shake the keyboard upside down over it to get out as much of the liquid as you can. While you're still holding the keyboard upside down, use a damp cloth and cotton swabs to wipe away the drips. Leave the keyboard upside down overnight to dry out, and hope for the best. Maybe you should consider switching to water—sticky soda pop and juice spills can give a keyboard a bad case of stickkkking letters!

Printer decongestant. If your ink-jet printer sits for a while in between putting out pages, the ink can dry up and clog the nozzles on the printhead, causing wavy, slanted, or poor-quality output. And that means it's time  to clean the heads—by letting the printer automatically clean itself, using the built-in maintenance software. Your owner's manual will tell you how to go about it. If the first auto cleaning doesn't work, try again—it may take a few cycles to get the nozzles flowing freely.

Hands-on nozzle cleaning. If the automatic cleaning routine doesn't work, you may want to try unclogging the heads yourself instead of taking the printer to a repair shop or replacing it. Refer to your owner's manual to find out where the printhead is located, and how to access it. Then clean the nozzles with a lint-free swab dampened with rubbing alcohol. Let the alcohol soften the gunked-up ink for several seconds, then wipe it away. Be very careful not to get alcohol on any other part of the printer because it can damage materials or circuitry. And don't try this trick on an expensive printer—let a pro handle it.

Concrete

Outdoor power. Scrubbing by hand takes forever when you're cleaning a large concrete area, so when you need to get lots of stains or general crud off your concrete sidewalk, driveway, or patio, call in the big guns—a power washer! These machines cost a couple hundred bucks, but you can rent an electric or gas-powered model at just about any local hardware store. To use it, hook up your garden hose, grab the spray wand, and turn on the power to blast that accumulated crud to bits. For stubborn stains, try my Concrete Cleaner at right to effortlessly remove old oil splotches and ground-in grime. Power washing is contagious—once your neighbors see how dingy their sidewalks look next to your sparkling clean one, I'll bet they get the cleaning bug, too!

Powerful Potions

Concrete Cleaner

Use this mixture to scrub away stains and brighten the appearance of your sidewalks, driveways, patios, or outdoor walls. You can scrub it in by hand, but it's a whole lot easier to let a power washer supply the muscle.

1 part bleach

1 part water

Mix this potion outside, so that you don't breathe in the fumes from the bleach, and wear rubber gloves, goggles, long sleeves, and old pants to guard against stray splashes when you use it. Then cover all surrounding vegetation, buildings, and materials with plastic, so they don't get damaged by any overspray. If you're working by hand, wet down the area with a garden hose, spread the solution on with a long-handled scrub brush, and apply elbow grease to get rid of those stains. Rinse the area thoroughly after you've scrubbed it. If you've got a power washer standing by, spread the solution over the wet concrete, and let the blast of water do the scrubbing for you, then rinse the area.

Soapy scrub. Remove fresh oil stains from your concrete driveway or garage floor by scrubbing them with a mix of grease-cutting dishwashing liquid and water. Just squirt the dish liquid—no water yet!—directly onto the oil, and wet down the area outside of the stain with water, so that the oil doesn't spread any farther. Use a scrub brush to vigorously work the dishwashing liquid into the stain, then add a little water to the soap and scrub again. The suds will break up the oil, so you can simply wash the stain away.

Stain attack. Get rid of brown leaf stains, purple bird droppings, or other small discolorations with a scouring powder such as Comet® or Bar Keepers Friend®. Just wet the stain, shake on a little cleanser, and scour it away with a scrub brush. Then rinse with plenty of water.

Oil stain absorber. If you've got fresh oil stains on a concrete driveway or garage floor, cover them with clay cat litter, and let it sit for at least an hour to soak up all of the grease. Next, apply a concrete degreaser or driveway cleaner, and let it soak in for about 15 minutes. Finally, rinse away the cleaner while you sweep away the litter with a broom. If your oil stains are old and dried on (not fresh spills), skip the cat litter treatment and go straight for the degreasing cleaner.

Blast 'em. If splashes and drips from your hot tub have left white stains on the concrete around it, blast them away with a power washer. The stains are mineral deposits from the chemically treated water, and a powerful blast of good ol' H_2O is all you need to make them disappear in a flash.

Rub out rust. When rust stains mar your outdoor concrete, buy a bottle of rust remover that contains oxalic acid to bleach out the stain. Apply the rust remover and let it soak in for about an hour, then rinse the area clean with a hose. Be sure to protect your eyes and skin with goggles and gloves (and all surrounding vegetation and so on with plastic) when you work with this, or any other cleaner that contains acid.

Hocus Pocus

ACID BATH

As a last resort for stubborn stains, you may want to consider using muriatic acid to clean your outdoor concrete. There's no magic here—muriatic acid is just another name for hydrochloric acid—and we all know that stuff is nothing to fool with! So wear goggles to protect your eyes and rubber gloves and long sleeves to shield your skin, don't breathe the fumes, cover all surrounding vegetation and so on with plastic, and keep your garden hose ready and waiting within arm's reach in case of spills or splashes. Read the label carefully, and follow the directions to the letter because muriatic acid can easily damage your concrete—or you!—if you mishandle it.

Send mildew marching. Clean mold and mildew off your basement walls by using a solution of 1 cup of bleach in a gallon of water. Scrub it onto the stains, let it sit for a few minutes, and then rinse it away with a wet sponge and clean water. Don't forget to open the windows and plug in a fan, so the area is well ventilated while you work. And to keep the problem from cropping up again, buy a dehumidifier to help keep your concrete basement bone dry.

The inside scoop. Decorative concrete floors are usually sealed with a special finish for indoor use. These finishes are very durable and stain-resistant, so don't haul that pressure washer into your kitchen to clean the floor! To freshen up an indoor concrete floor, run a dust mop over it to pick up dirt, and damp mop it with a squirt or two of dishwashing liquid in a bucket of warm water. Never use ammonia or vinegar to clean these floors because these liquids may damage the special finish that makes indoor concrete floors shine.

Cookware (See also Cast Iron)

Restore the shine. Get rid of the cloudy look of your aluminum pots and pans by polishing them with a soapy steel wool scouring pad. To give the surfaces a uniform shine, rub them using a back-and-forth motion instead of going around and around in circles. Or you can sprinkle some baking soda or Bar Keepers Friend® scouring powder onto the wet surface and rub—back and forth!—with a nonabrasive plastic scrubbie to polish that dulling film away.

Boil away stains. Clean stubborn cooking stains from the inside of your aluminum pan by filling it about halfway with water and adding 2 to 3 tablespoons of lemon juice to it. Bring the liquid to a rolling boil, then reduce the heat to medium-high and let the acid in the lemon juice simmer away those tough stains for about 15 minutes or so.

Plop! Plop! Fizz! Fizz! A stain can linger even after you scrub burned-on food out of an aluminum pan, but you can bring it back to brightness with this easy trick. Just fill the pan with water, drop in two Alka-Seltzer® tablets, and let it soak for an hour. What a relief it is to be rid of those lingering stains from burned-on sauces or spaghetti! And if you have no Alka-Seltzer on hand, no problem—use a couple of denture-cleaning tablets instead.

Nonstick fix. To loosen stuck-on crud from nonstick cookware, pour in 1 part baking soda to 1 part water, using just enough to cover the bottom of the pan. When the solution turns brown, lift off the food residue with a plastic spatula, and wash the pan as usual.

Handle by hand. To preserve the color and finish of your anodized aluminum cookware, wash it by hand instead of in the dishwasher. An automatic dishwasher uses extremely hot water, which may combine with the minerals in your water to discolor the finish. So do your washing up in the sink instead, using soapy water and a nonabrasive plastic scrubbie to get the gunk off that anodized finish.

Hocus Pocus

BURNED BOTTOMS

Shine away the burn marks on the bottoms of your cookware with a paste made of cream of tartar moistened with a little white vinegar. Spread the paste onto the pan, and let it sit for about 10 minutes. Then scrub that blackened bottom with a nonabrasive pad, and the black will come right off. Or you can scour the bottom with Bar Keepers Friend®, which is a gentle scouring powder recommended by many cookware manufacturers. Shake a generous amount of the powder onto the bottom of your pan, and scrub with a wet nonabrasive plastic scrubbie to remove those discolored spots. Rub the stains in small circles, and your bottoms will be shiny in no time!

Plastic for stainless. Scratches on stainless steel cookware have a nasty habit of causing food to stick, which makes cleanup a lot harder the next time. So avoid rough scouring powders and steel wool pads that may leave their mark on the surface, and when it's time to get rid of cooked-on crud, reach for a nonabrasive plastic scrubbie instead. You'll be glad that you did!

Self-cleaning solution. If your stainless steel pots and pans seem truly hopeless, here's a neat tip that'll bring 'em back to life, fast. Remove any non–stainless steel handles or knobs, and put the pots and pans in your oven while you run the self-cleaning cycle. The cooked-on grime will burn to ash, just like it does in your oven!

Easy enamel solutions. To remove burned-on food from enamel cookware, cover the blackened residue with water, add about ¼ cup of salt, and let it sit overnight. The next day, bring the salty water to a boil, let it simmer for a few minutes, and then scrub as usual when the water has cooled down. Or you can fill that cruddy enamel pan with about 1 quart of water and 3 tablespoons of baking soda, bring it to a boil, and let it simmer for about 15 minutes. After it cools down, you'll be able to get the gunk out easily with a nonabrasive plastic scrubbie.

Grandma Putt's Magical Methods

My Grandma Putt's cookie sheets got a pretty good workout, thanks to a bunch of grateful grandchildren like yours truly. And as I recall, her sheets looked mighty "disreputable" as far as today's fancy Food Network cookware goes. But my Grandma didn't waste time scouring off the baked-on grease that accumulated over the years. She treasured her "seasoned" cookie sheets because she didn't have to grease the sheets for the next batch of cookies—they simply slid right off, the same way eggs and bacon came out of her well-seasoned skillet. And that brought a smile to everyone's face!

Salt scour. Sprinkle a layer of salt onto the stuck-on food in your pan, and let it sit for about 10 minutes. Then scrub the pan, using the salt as scouring powder. You can use powdered laundry detergent or baking soda in the same way to clean it up.

Copper classic. To make stains disappear from copper or copper-clad cookware, apply a paste made of equal parts flour, salt, lemon juice, and ammonia, and let the paste sit for about 10 minutes. Then scrub the pan with a nonabrasive plastic scrubbie and apply a little more paste to scour away any lingering stains. You'll find more magic tricks for making your copper cookware gleam in the Copper entry on page 91.

Baking dish tricks. Getting the burned-on remains of a casserole or pie out of its glass dish can be a real exercise—or should I say workout? So try these prescrubbing tricks to make the job a whole lot easier:

★ Cover the gunk with ketchup, let it sit for a few hours, and scrub it off with a steel wool pad.

★ Apply a paste of 1 part vinegar and 1 part cream of tartar, let it sit for an hour or two, and scrub the problem away.

★ Loosen a burned-on crust line by filling the pan with hot water and adding a few teaspoons of baking soda to it. Let it soak for a few hours, and the crust marks will lift right off.

★ Make a paste of baking soda with a little water, and scoop it onto the burned-on spots. Let it sit for a few hours, and then—without rinsing the dish—pour a solution of 3 parts water and 1 part vinegar onto the baking soda. Let it sit overnight, and then wash as usual.

★ Use a nontoxic, biodegradable Magic Sheet®. Just wipe the wet sheet over the dish, fill the dish with water, drop in the sheet, and let it sit for about half an hour before washing as usual.

ROASTING PAN CLEANUP

It's easy to get the inside of a roasting pan clean: Just sprinkle it with either grease-cutting dishwashing liquid, baking soda, or powdered laundry detergent, then add an inch or two of very hot water, and let the pan soak for a few hours. But cleaning the sides, handles, and corners calls for tougher treatment. Here's how to handle it:

1. Set the dirty pan into a plastic trash bag, and lay paper towels on the baked-on food.

2. Pour ammonia onto the paper towels until they're saturated.

3. Close the bag tightly, and let it sit overnight. The ammonia will loosen the gunk and make it easy to scrub it off the pan.

This trick works great on stainless steel pots and pans, too. Just don't use it on aluminum or anodized cookware because the ammonia could damage it.

Dryer sheets'll do it. Here's a quick and easy way to clean crusty food residue out of your pots and pans. Hold the cookware under hot running water and wipe it out with a fabric-softener sheet. If there's still some residue left behind after the once-over, soak the pan in hot water for a while, and then give it another go.

Clean your CorningWare®. To loosen baked-on food from CorningWare, fill the dish with a solution of 1 part white vinegar to 3 parts water, and let it soak for several hours. Or you can cover the baked-on residue with a paste of baking soda and a little warm water, and let it sit overnight. Remove the residue with a nonabrasive plastic scrubbie. And to remove any gray "scratches" on your cookware, use scouring powder—the scratches are actually metal left behind when your utensils scrape against the hard CorningWare surface.

The Great Clean-dini Speaks

Q. It seems like I'm always burning something or other in my pots and pans. Even after I soak them, it still takes lots of scrubbing to get the pans clean. I'm so frustrated, I'm tempted to just throw them all away! Can you help?

A. I sure can. I have a terrific trick for getting rid of burned-on rice, potatoes, oatmeal, or what have you— by simply simmering it off! The next time it happens, fill the pot with water, add a squirt or two of dishwashing liquid, and bring the liquid to a boil. Reduce the heat, and let it simmer for about 10 minutes, uncovered. Now cover the pot, turn off the burner, and let it soak for about an hour. That's all there is to it! The burned-on stuff will come right off with a quick scrubbing. This trick works great for frying pans, too.

Sparkling sheets. Everyone loves cookies, but no one likes cleaning the baked-on grease off the cookie sheet! That's why I've rounded up a whole bunch of cleaning magic tricks to solve this problem:

★ Use a damp Mr. Clean® Magic Eraser® and a light sprinkling of baking soda to scour the baked-on grease off the sheet.

★ Spray the sheet with Greased Lightning®, which is a multipurpose cleaner and degreaser. Wait about 10 minutes, and then rinse those stains away.

★ Spritz some Dawn® Power Dissolver® onto the cookie sheet, wait about 10 minutes, and then wipe off the greasy crud.

★ To clean a cookie sheet that's got a rim all the way around it, sprinkle some powdered laundry detergent on the sheet, fill it with very hot water, and let it soak for a few hours.

Rust removal. Get rid of the rust on metal pie pans, cookie sheets, and other kitchenware by rubbing the rust spots with a freshly cut half of a raw potato dipped in lemon juice. For stubborn cases, dab a cut potato into powdered dishwasher detergent, and scour the stain away.

Last-ditch casserole cleaner. If that hard, black, baked-on crud on your casserole dish just won't budge, take the dish outside, set it on a section of newspaper, and give those bad spots a squirt of foaming oven cleaner. Let it sit overnight, and then scour the stain away with a nonabrasive plastic scrubbie. Be sure to wear rubber gloves and protect your skin from the oven cleaner, and avoid breathing the fumes when you spray it on.

Copper

Dust bath. Regular dusting may be all you need to restore the glow to decorative copper pieces. Add an occasional bath in warm, soapy water to get off any greasy residue that may have collected. Some decorative copper is lacquered, and it will stay shiny bright with this kind of cleanup. But if your objects are older pieces, you may want to consider one of my easy tricks to take off the tarnish. Of course, if that copper is an antique, keep in mind that polishing it to the color of a new penny isn't the way to go: That dull brown or green patina is part of the charm—and the value!

Anti-abrasive. Salt, scouring powders, and other abrasives can leave fine scratches in your copper, so if you prefer a nice sleek shine, try this trick instead: Put your item in a pot large enough to hold it, cover it with water, and add 1 tablespoon of salt and 1 cup of white vinegar to the mix. Bring the water to a boil, turn down the heat, and let it simmer for a few hours so the acid can go to work on that tarnish. Let it cool, wash the piece in soapy water, dry it thoroughly, and you're done.

Powerful Potions

Copper Cleaner

Clean all of your copper utensils, pots, pans, and mixing bowls with this surefire solution.

> 1 tsp. of salt
> 1 cup of white vinegar
> Flour

Dissolve the salt in the vinegar, and add enough flour to make a paste. Cover your copper piece with the paste, and let it sit for 15 minutes to an hour, depending on how heavily tarnished it is. Rinse the paste off with warm water, and if any dull spots remain, give them another treatment. You can also use the paste as a polish: Just dip in a damp cloth, and rub the grime away. Fold or flip the cloth often as you rub, so you're always using a clean area. When you've taken off all of the tarnish, wash the item in warm, soapy water, and buff it dry.

Baking soda boost. Baking soda is less abrasive than salt, so if you want to avoid scratching the copper, try this alternative. For quick touch-ups, sprinkle a little baking soda on a cut half of a fresh lemon, and rub the grime away. For heavy-duty dirt, pour 1/4 cup of bottled lemon juice into a small bowl and add enough baking soda to make a paste. Dip in a damp cloth, apply the paste to your tarnished copper, and rub. Finish up with a quick soapy bath and rinse, then buff with a soft, clean cloth.

Tartar for tarnish. Here's another low-abrasive copper cleaner: a paste made of fresh or bottled lemon juice and cream of tartar. Apply it to your copper piece with a soft, clean cloth, let it sit for 5 to 15 minutes, wash it away, and polish your piece with a soft, dry cloth.

Vinegar rinse with salt scrub. These two hardworking household helpers work magic on copper. Make a mixture for scrubbing, or try this easy technique—just wet a soft cloth with white vinegar, sprinkle salt on the dirty areas, and scrub the tarnish off. When the dirt is gone, just rinse off the piece with warm water, and dry it to a nice golden shine.

Salt and sour. Lemon juice and salt are a time-tested solution for restoring the shine to dull, discolored copper. Cut a fresh lemon in half, dip the cut side in a saucer of table salt, and rub the tarnish away.

Now, that's hot! Want to get that dull copper bright again, and whet your appetite at the same time? Just pull on a pair of rubber gloves, and use hot sauce as your polish! You can use whatever you have handy, whether it's a bottle of Uncle Jerry's Tongues of Flame (just kidding!), or that little packet of hot sauce left over from the taco joint. Pour the sauce on a soft cloth, rub it over the surface, and let it sit for about 15 minutes before you wash it away.

Ketchup cleaner. Chefs know that it's not a good idea to cook tomatoes in a copper pot because the acid in the tomatoes can react with the metal. But when it comes to cleaning (instead of cooking), that reaction is exactly what you want. So smear some ketchup onto your tarnished copper, and let it sit for 15 minutes or so to soften up the tarnish. Do a final polishing with the red stuff, wash your copper in hot, soapy water, and dry it with a soft, clean cloth.

Grandma Putt's Magical Methods

Homemade pickles were such a favorite at my Grandma Putt's house that the slices and spears disappeared from her jars in a jiffy. When that last pickle was eaten, Grandma put the leftover juice to work—cleaning her copper pots! She'd wet a rag with the brine and go to town, scrubbing the tarnish off with the sour, salty pickle juice. The same trick works great with store-bought pickles, too. So whenever you empty a jar, bring out the copper, and let the brine bring back the shine!

A really rotten polish. That's "rotten" in a good way, as in rottenstone, a very finely powdered abrasive that is used by craftsmen and woodworkers. (You'll find it in most housewares and home-improvement stores.) Pour about ¼ cup of olive oil into a small bowl, and add enough of the rottenstone powder to make a thin paste. Apply the mixture with a soft, dry cloth, rub it over the surface, and buff away any excess "rotten" polish with a soft, clean cloth. It'll give your copper a gentle gleam instead of a bright-penny shine, which is great for older pieces (like copper bookends) where the aged look is just what you're aiming for.

Corrosion cure. It's called "bronze disease," but green corrosion can also attack copper when moisture reacts with the metal. A smooth green patina is natural and desirable on weathered copper, but if you see a spotty breakout of rough, light green patches or speckles, you'll need to spring into action. Soak a soft cloth in buttermilk, lay the cloth on the affected area, and let it sit for about 15 minutes to change the chemistry that's causing the corrosion. You can also use a mixture of 1 cup of hot (heated, not spicy!) white vinegar and ¼ cup of salt for the soak. After the treatment, wash your "cured" piece of copper in soapy water, rinse it clean, and polish until it's completely dry before putting it away.

Countertops

Clean as you cook. Stains are no fun to scrub away, no matter what kind of countertops you have, which is why it's a great idea to wipe up all spills and messes as soon as they occur. This handy habit pays off big-time on some of the new countertop materials because grease, wine, and other stains can quickly ruin the look of granite and other elegant surfaces. So whether you're cooking up a fancy dinner, or merely fixing yourself a snack, remember to wipe as you go, and you'll make stains a thing of the past!

Cut the crud. Got some dried-on cookie dough, melted cheese, or other gunk on your countertop? When a simple swipe with a wet cloth isn't enough, sprinkle on some baking soda and scrub with a moist sponge or cloth until it's gone. Then rinse thoroughly, and dry with a cloth or paper towel to refresh the shine.

Grout scrubber. Clean dull, dingy grout the easy way on ceramic tile countertops or backsplashes with an old toothbrush. Just dip the brush into a solution of 1 teaspoon of bleach in 1 cup of water, and scrub your grout lines back to their pearly white condition.

Lemon stain lifter. To gently bleach stains out of a laminate countertop, rub a slice of lemon on the stain, and then let the lemon sit right on the dirty spot for about 15 minutes. Rinse the area clean with a damp cloth, and wipe it dry. If you still see a shadow of the stain, go ahead and repeat the treatment until it's gone.

Long life for laminate. Cleaning stains off laminate countertops couldn't be simpler: Just use a nonabrasive plastic scrubbie or sponge to get off the worst dried-on gunk. For stubborn stains like grape juice, make a paste of 3 parts baking soda to 1 part water, cover the stain, and let the mixture sit for about 5 to 10 minutes before you wipe it away.

Powerful Potions

Everyday Counter Cleaner

Use this mixture to remove dirt and wash away any film from countertops that are made of laminate, acrylic, ceramic tile, or cultured marble. Do not use this potion on natural marble or granite, or other natural stone, because it could be damaged by the mild acids in the mix.

1 cup of ammonia

½ cup of white vinegar

¼ cup of baking soda

1 gal. of water

Mix the ingredients in a bucket, and sponge the solution onto your countertops to wipe away grime. Rinse with fresh water, and dry with a soft cloth to renew the shine.

Fill it in. If your laminate countertop gets scratched or dinged, you can fill in those dirt-collecting gouges with a scratch-repair paste from your local hardware store. The paste comes in a variety of colors; if yours isn't available, you can blend two or more colors to match. Clean the damaged area with rubbing alcohol, fill the chip or scratch in with the repair paste, smooth it out, and scrape off any excess with a putty knife. Let the paste cure for 24 hours, and your counter will be as good as new!

Stainless steel scratch removal. You can make scratches less noticeable on your stainless steel countertops by rubbing the scratched areas with a plastic abrasive sponge. Work slowly, and rub in the direction of the grain, so the very fine scratches you leave behind blend right in with the rest of the countertop.

Stone solutions. It's easy to love the look of new countertop materials like soapstone, sandstone, and Jerusalem stone, but the ongoing care could be more than you bargained for. These materials can scratch easily, so make sure you always use a cutting board or silicone sheet to do your chopping and slicing. And since grease stains can be absorbed by these

Grandma Putt's Magical Methods

Years ago, a hefty slab of slate was the work surface of choice in country kitchens like my Grandma Putt's. Nowadays, slate is back again in a big way with lots of special products made to care for it. But you don't have to spend your hard-earned cash—just use a couple of my Grandma's oldie-but-goodie tricks! Whenever her slate looked dull, she rubbed in a dab of mineral oil to give it a natural sheen that also prevented grease and other stains from being absorbed into the stone. And when her knife slipped off the cutting board, she made the scratches vanish by rubbing them away with baking soda, wet steel wool, or fine sandpaper. A final swipe with a damp cloth, and her slate counter was ready for another week of down-home cooking!

natural stones (just as they can by granite or slate), keep a cloth handy whenever you're working with oily foods. That way, you can wipe away greasy spills and residue before they have a chance to sink in.

Fixes for faux stone. Not-quite-natural stone like Silestone®, which is a composite of crushed quartz and polymer resin, is much lower-maintenance than its natural look-alikes because it won't soak up grease or other stains. You'll find it super easy to clean, too—just give it a swipe with warm, soapy water, or spray on my Granite Countertop Cleaner (see page 99) and wipe it dry.

Speckles be gone! Sleek finishes, such as shiny granite or satiny stainless steel, can show every little water spot after you wipe up spills, unless you dry them thoroughly. So grab a paper towel or a microfiber cloth, and use long, lengthwise strokes to leave a spot-free surface behind.

HOCUS POCUS

ANTS AWAY!

Food is always a target for ants—a bit of sugar here, a greasy stove there, or an all-you-can-eat buffet everywhere! And once you see a couple of them, they seem to multiply like mad. So get on the ball as soon as you see the first scouts marching across your countertop. Here's how to make them stay away for good:

★ Wipe the countertop (sorry, ants) with a wet, squeezed-out paper towel. Then wipe it again with full-strength white vinegar, and rinse thoroughly. The vinegar will help remove the scent trails the ants laid down, so that others in the colony can't follow them to the food.

★ Store your pasta, sugar, cereal, and other food in airtight containers.

★ Keep your sink and stove clean. Don't let dirty dishes pile up in the sink, or grease spatters lie in the drip pans.

★ Empty pet food bowls, and feed your pets only as much kibble as they can eat at one sitting.

★ Set whole cloves or bay leaves behind canisters or on cabinet shelves.

★ Sprinkle cinnamon, black pepper, or red chili powder around the areas where the ants seem to be coming in.

★ Make a bait by mixing ¼ teaspoon of powdered borax with ¼ teaspoon of maple syrup or confectioners' sugar, and place it on a small square of cardboard near where the ants are entering. Some ant species eat grease, not sweets, so make another bait consisting of borax and peanut butter. The ants will carry the bait back to the colony, where the borax will kill those that eat it. *Caution:* Borax can cause health problems if it's eaten; if you have pets or children, put the bait inside a jar, and punch a few small holes in the lid so only ants can get at it.

Great-looking granite. Keep your granite looking its very best by dusting the countertop frequently with a microfiber cleaning cloth; use a blue one and you'll add a gentle shine as you wipe. To avoid stains, be careful whenever you're working with greasy or oily foods because they can soak in permanently. Blot up any greasy spills right away with a paper towel, and follow up with a swipe of a soapy sponge.

Treat marble with care. Nothing beats a marble countertop when it comes to rolling out a piecrust, but this stone is definitely high-maintenance compared to good old Formica®. Marble can absorb stains, plus it can be damaged by certain cleaners. Avoid abrasive powders and scouring pads, and never use acidic products like ammonia, lemon juice, or vinegar, which can eat into the surface. Also, use a cutting board for acidic foods, such as tomatoes, oranges, limes, and other citrus fruits, and wipe up ketchup, fruit juice, and other food spills as soon as you see them. For more cleaning tips, see the Marble entry on page 215.

Cutting edge. Bathroom countertops can be made of tile, glass, marble, and even bronze. Basic cleaning is the same, though, no matter what the material. Wipe it clean daily with a damp cloth, and dry it thoroughly. That'll keep grunge under control. When it's time for a full-scale cleaning, refer to your countertop's material by name in the index of this book, and you'll find a slew of suggestions.

Powerful Potions

Granite Countertop Cleaner

If your granite countertops are looking a little dull, try this magic mixture to wipe away the film and leave them sparkling clean.

> **¼ cup of rubbing alcohol**
> **A drop or two of dishwashing liquid**
> **3 cups of water**

Mix the ingredients in a handheld sprayer bottle, spritz the cleaner on a large area, and wipe it dry with a microfiber cleaning cloth. It'll take only a minute to restore the shine.

Crayon Marks

Wipe the walls. Removing crayon marks from a wall is as easy as 1, 2, 3: One, grab a baby wipe; two, rub the crayon away; and three, repeat with a fresh wipe if any stain remains. The alcohol and other ingredients in the wipe will loosen the crayon and lift it off in a flash.

Erase the art. A Mr. Clean® Magic Eraser® really lives up to its name when it comes to removing crayon marks, and unlike some other products, it won't leave an oily film or smell behind. So when a certain someone decides to scribble on your painted or wallpapered walls, rub the marks with a damp Magic Eraser, and they will simply vanish.

Paste the problem. A damp sponge sprinkled with a little baking soda will take care of stray crayon marks on walls, floors, and other hard surfaces. Rub the soda in small circles to remove the marks, and wipe it off with a damp sponge or cloth. Presto—problem solved!

Solve it with solvent. Some crayon makers recommend using WD-40® lubricant to remove those greasy, waxy crayon marks—but that can leave your walls or upholstery smelling like a garage. For the same results with a much better aroma, try an orange oil–based cleaner. Spray some on a clean cloth and wipe your little artist's "masterpiece" away. Solvents may leave an oily residue behind, so follow up your treatment with a soapy rinse: Just squirt a drop or two of dishwashing liquid into a cup of water, dampen a cloth with a little of the soapy stuff, and wipe the oil away.

Dryer sheet duty. Used fabric-softener sheets work wonders wiping up waxy, greasy messes—like the crayon streaks all over your wall! So recycle these sheets by putting them to work scrubbing away the marks. Rub in small circles, add a little elbow grease, and the chemicals in the dryer sheets will do the rest.

Powerful Potions

Crayon Cleaner for Clothes

It's a real "Oh, no!" moment when you find a melted crayon in the dryer along with your clothes—those smeary stains look like they'll be impossible to get rid of. That's when it's time to turn to this magic recipe:

1 cup of white vinegar

1 cup of liquid laundry detergent

1 cup of liquid OxiClean® Laundry Stain Remover

1 cup of Zout® Triple Enzyme Clean™ liquid laundry stain remover

Start filling your washing machine, using the warmest water setting your clothes can tolerate, and add the above ingredients as the water is running. When the tub is full, turn the machine off or set your "soak" cycle, add your clothes, and let them soak in the powerful solution for about 45 minutes. Finish the cycle, and take a good look at your clothes. If the stains are all gone, toss the garments in the dryer. If there's still some crayon color, repeat the treatment. (For advice on how to remove the melted crayon from your dryer walls, see The Great Clean-dini Speaks on page 102.)

Baby oil to the rescue. To remove crayon marks from vinyl floors, appliances, or other nonabsorbent surfaces, use baby oil or mineral oil. Pour a dab of oil on a dry cloth, rub off the smear, wipe off the oil with a soapy sponge, and rinse with clean water. And remember, this solution is only for surfaces that won't soak up oil—you need to try a different trick to get crayon off clothes, upholstery, wallpaper, and other stainable materials.

Hand cleaner for handiwork. Budding artists are a challenge all parents face, so when a coloring session gets out of hand and winds up on the walls or floors, reach for a jar of Goop® Hand Cleaner or other waterless hand cleaner. Dab some on a soft cloth, and it'll clean up your walls as fast as it does your hardworking hands.

Woodwork. When crayon ends up on your wood-paneled walls, doors, or floors, try the gentle abrasive action of regular toothpaste. Squeeze some non-gel paste onto a soft cloth, and rub in the direction of the grain to remove the gunk. Wipe the residue off with a damp cloth, and be sure to dry the wood afterward, so it doesn't soak up any lingering moisture. For fine wood finishes that even toothpaste might scratch, try a dry cloth dipped in mineral spirits to rub the crayon away.

Tube with a view. Did your toddler decide to decorate the TV, too? If the screen is good ol' glass instead of a high-tech material, use a paper towel

The Great Clean-dini Speaks

Q. I missed a crayon that was in my son's pocket when I did the laundry, and it melted all over the dryer. How can I get that melted mess out of there?

A. While it may look like the great crayon catastrophe, a dryer full of streaks and smears is really pretty easy to clean up. Try one of these solutions to get rid of the goo:

★ Squeeze regular toothpaste—not gel—on a clean, dry cloth, and scour the messy spots. The crayon will come off on the cloth, so keep folding it to be sure you're always working with a clean part of the cloth—there's no sense spreading the mess any further!

★ Apply Soft Scrub® gel or foam to the stuck-on remains of those crayons, and wipe the gunk away. If you have to stick your head inside the dryer to reach some of the spots, be sure to hold your breath so that you don't inhale the vapors from the cleaner.

★ Wet a Mr. Clean® Magic Eraser®, squeeze it out, and swab all of that caked-on crayon crud away.

or soft cloth dampened with rubbing alcohol to wipe the mess off. This trick works just as well on marked up windows and mirrors.

Heat treatment. When crayon marks end up on wallpaper, upholstery, or other soft surfaces, it's time to call on your trusty hair dryer to blow the marks away. Place a piece of paper towel over the stained area, hold it in place, and aim the hot air directly at the waxy mess. It'll melt into the absorbent paper towel, and you'll be able to lift it right off.

Hooray for cooking spray. For crayon control in the kitchen, give those marks a spritz with nonstick cooking spray, rub them with a dry cloth, and rinse the area with a damp sponge or cloth. The crayon will come off faster than greased lightning.

Curtains and Drapes

Down with dust. Regular vacuuming (every couple of weeks) is all you need to keep your dust-catching drapes and curtains looking good for months at a time. Use the upholstery attachment of your vacuum cleaner, and go over the fabric from top to bottom, using long up-and-down strokes. And don't forget to do the back sides, too.

A head of steam. You can clean velvet curtains on the rod by using a handheld steam cleaner, unless the care label warns against it. Start by dusting the drapes with the soft-brush attachment of your vacuum cleaner. Then fill your steamer with cold water, and when it's hissing, start at the top and run the wand down the curtains. Never touch the wand to the velvet, and be sure to use a smooth, continuous motion, so the steam doesn't condense on the fabric. If you don't own a steam cleaner, you can rent one at a local hardware store.

A sweeping statement. The next time you've got a soft-bristled broom out to sweep a floor or ceiling, use it to dust off your valances, drapes, and curtains, too. Five minutes of light sweeping will freshen them up until you have time for a deeper cleaning.

Bath time? Read the label on your window treatments to find out if you can wash them at home, or if you'll need to take a trip to the local cleaners. If your curtains or drapes are marked "hand wash only," use your bathtub to do the job instead of cramming them into your kitchen sink. You'll have plenty of room to swish them around and wash the dirt away, and you won't have to worry about splashing everything in sight. After their bath, be sure to rinse the fabric well and squeeze out the water without wringing them—there'll be fewer wrinkles and less wear and tear on the fabric that way. Roll them in a large bath towel to get out even more moisture before you toss them in the dryer or hang them on a clothesline.

Kitchen hang-ups. Grease often builds up on kitchen curtains, and the fabric can soak up cooking aromas, too. So freshen up your window treatments by presoaking them in a tub full of water with a couple of tablespoons of ammonia added to it—this'll cut the

---

Grandma Putt's Magical Methods

Finding clever shortcuts was my Grandma Putt's specialty, and she used a neat trick to make sure her drapes and curtains never ended up in her ironing basket—she hung them back up on the rod while they were still a little bit damp. She'd simply retrieve one curtain at a time from the dryer while the cycle was still going, and slip that piece onto the rod at the window. Then she'd get the next one, and the next, and so on, so the curtains never had time to stop spinning and end up in a wrinkled heap in the dryer. The weight of the slightly damp cloth helped the curtains dry straight, as did the nice cool breeze that was coming in the open window.

RINGS AND RODS

If your curtain rings are looking shabby, clean them up when you take your curtains down for washing. Wipe wooden rings with a damp cloth, dry them well, and polish them with a dab of mineral oil on a dry cloth. If your metal rings have gotten tarnished, just drop them in a saucepan filled with vinegar, and simmer them gently for about 10 minutes or so to bring back the shine.

And here's a quick trick for making your curtains easier to pull open—just rub a light coating of bar soap on a metal rod, so those curtain rings can really glide easily. To cure a balky wooden rod, grab a sheet of waxed paper and give the rod a good going-over. Your drapes will open and close as smooth as silk!

Hocus Pocus

grease and neutralize the odors. Launder as usual, and your curtains will come out smelling and looking fresh and clean.

Not chintzy at all! Preserve the glossy finish on your chintz curtains with frequent dusting, and by occasionally "washing" them right in place. After you get the dust out of all the folds and fabric, simply wipe down the curtains with a damp sponge, rinsing the sponge whenever it gets dingy. This is quick and easy, and you won't even need to iron your nice crisp curtains.

Sheer protection. Hand washing is your best bet for cleaning lace or sheer curtains, especially if the fibers are fragile or fraying. If your curtains are still in good shape, you can wash them in the delicate or hand-wash cycle of your washing machine. Just slip the curtains into a mesh lingerie bag first. Let the curtains air-dry because dryer heat can shrink them.

Increase the ecru. Machine washing can lighten the soft beige or ecru color of old lace curtains, but there's a solution to keep that aged look. Just add a cup of brewed coffee to the water at the start of the rinse cycle.

Cutting Boards

A healthy clean. Cut down on nasty, dangerous germs by keeping your cutting boards as clean as can be. Bacteria multiply like lightning, so get in the habit of washing your cutting boards in hot, soapy water immediately after you use them. And try stronger methods (like those below) to make sure those troublemaking germs are gone for good.

Powerful Potions

Cutting Board Sanitizer

This simple potion puts the power of plain old vinegar to work for you killing common food bacteria. It's the acetic acid in the vinegar that works the magic—why, it makes even big, bad germs like salmonella beg for mercy!

1 part white vinegar

2 parts water

Mix the vinegar and water in a hand-held sprayer bottle. Wash and rinse the boards as usual, and then wipe down both sides with this solution. If your cutting board is made of wood, let the solution sit for about five minutes before you dry the board, so that the germ-fighting vinegar can penetrate beyond the surface. There's no need to rinse because the vinegar smell will simply disappear as it dries.

When it rains, it pours! When the surface of your wooden cutting boards get spotted by fruit juice or other stains, you can make those marks disappear by sprinkling salt on the stain and rubbing it with a freshly cut lemon wedge. If you need stronger abrasive action than ordinary table salt, try sprinkling on some coarse kosher salt instead. And keep in mind—the sooner you wipe up a spill, the fewer stains you'll have to deal with.

How dry I am. Germs and mold can set in fast on damp surfaces, so make sure you dry cutting boards thoroughly after washing them. Use paper towels to dry the surface of the boards, then lean them upright to air-dry before you put them away.

Scrub out stains. To get deeper stains out of a wooden cutting board, try good ol' baking soda, or a mildly abrasive antibacterial cleaner like Soft Scrub® with Bleach. You can also scour the stains out with fine sandpaper. Rub in the same direction as the grain, not across it, to avoid breaking the fibers of the wood. And don't ever soak a wooden cutting board in water to try to remove stains—the wood could come unglued or crack when it dries.

Block the "bugs"! To keep your wooden cutting board clean as a whistle, rub some food-grade mineral oil into it every so often. Let it soak in for about 10 minutes, and then wipe off the excess with a paper towel. The wood will absorb the oil, and that'll help keep germs from making themselves at home in the board.

Peroxide wipe. Here's a quick and easy way to wipe out germs on your cutting boards: First, wipe down the boards—both sides!—with my Cutting Board Sanitizer at left, and then follow it up with a second swipe of hydrogen peroxide for extra insurance. Pour some peroxide onto a paper towel, and wipe it over the boards. That'll make those germs wish they'd steered clear of your work surface!

Color-coded. Bacteria are bad news, so reduce the risk of contaminating your food by using a separate plastic cutting board for meat, fish, and poultry. And try this trick I borrowed from professional cooks: Use a different-colored board for meats than the one you use for vegetables, fruits, and raw foods to make sure you don't mix 'em up. Or when it's time to slice up some meat, use a dishwasher-safe dinner plate as your cutting board.

Out with the old. Nicks and scratches give salmonella and other bacteria a great place to hide, and washing by hand isn't enough to clean all the germs out of those deep gouges in a plastic cutting board. So sanitize a battle-scarred plastic board in the dishwasher, where the heat will help kill the germs. And replace the board when it gets badly scratched.

The Great Clean-dini Speaks

Q. What's the best surface for cutting boards—wood or plastic?

A. Now that's a good question! It sure seems like non-porous plastic would be a better choice than wood, which soaks up those messy liquids. But scientists at the University of Wisconsin's Food Research Institute found out that nasty salmonella, *Listeria,* and *E. coli* bacteria survive very nicely on plastic surfaces—and die off quickly on wood. Nearly all of the bacteria died within three minutes on the wood, while the germs on the plastic lived happily ever after.

Exactly how wood manages to kill germs is still a mystery, but in the meantime, the debate over which surface is better continues. The best advice? No matter which kind of cutting board you use, don't be sloppy about safety! Wash your boards thoroughly after you cut meat, poultry, or seafood, and use a different board for other foods.

Away with odors. Try any one of this trio of tricks to keep all of your cutting boards smelling fresh and clean:

★ Rub a cut lemon half over the board after you chop onions, garlic, or other strong-smelling foods.

★ Deodorize a wooden board by rubbing the surface with baking soda and a wet sponge. Let it sit for about 10 minutes to neutralize the smell, and then wash the board as usual.

★ Fill a handheld sprayer bottle with fresh water and several drops of lavender essential oil, and spray the board to change its aroma from sour to sweet. Lavender has some antibiotic properties, so it'll help keep germs away, too.

Decks

Clean the debris. A weekly once-over will go a long way toward keeping your deck looking good because it will remove fallen leaves, bird droppings, and other debris before they can cause stains. Start by sweeping your deck with a stiff broom, and dislodge any stubborn debris in the cracks by poking it with a putty knife so it falls through the cracks. Once you have the loose dirt removed, wash the deck down with a good stiff spray from your garden hose. If bird "deposits" or other types of gunk refuse to give up their grip, swipe those tough spots with a scrub brush, and rinse the grime away.

Take the gray away. If your deck is looking rather dowdy because sunlight has faded the finish to a dull gray, try an oxalic acid deck cleaner to restore the natural beauty of the wood. Read the label before you begin, and follow the directions carefully. You'll probably need to apply the cleaner with a rag to one board at a time, scrub it in with a soft brush, and rinse thoroughly with water. And don't forget— acid is mighty powerful stuff, so dress in protective clothing, wear a pair of rubber gloves and goggles, and cover all surrounding vegetation, buildings, and materials with plastic, so they don't get damaged by any overspray.

Mighty mildew remover. Dampness can cause mildew or algae to feel right at home on your deck, so use this super solution to make it vanish. Just mix 1 part water with 2 parts bleach, pour the solution onto the slimy spots, and let it sit for a minute or two to kill the mold or algae. To avoid leaving unsightly lighter spots behind, use an oxygen bleach instead of a chlorine product. Scrub the stains with a long-handled brush or stiff broom, and rinse the entire deck with a hose to make sure all of the bleach is safely washed away.

Hocus Pocus

POWER WASH—OR NOT?

If you decide to give up on using elbow grease alone to clean your deck, keep these considerations in mind when you use a power washer:

★ Blasting your deck with a power washer will definitely remove stains and discolorations—but the force of the water can also damage the wood unless you work very carefully. If your deck is old and splintery, or if you have never worked with a power washer before, you should stick to hand scrubbing, or call in a pro.

★ Make sure the power washer has a sprayer-fan nozzle, so the stream of water doesn't hit full blast on any one spot. And aim for a spray that's got an arc of about 25 to 40 degrees.

★ Use 1,200 psi of pressure or less to blast the surface. Not all machines can be set this low, so double-check yours before you dig in.

★ Hold the nozzle at least 6 inches away from the surface of the deck and spray slowly, keeping the nozzle moving in the direction of the wood grain.

Swab the deck. Spot cleaning stains on your deck with bleach or abrasive cleaners can lighten the wood, turning that small dark spot into a big, eye-catching, lighter spot—and that's definitely not the result you're after! To avoid a patchy look, you need to clean the entire deck. Try a household floor cleaner like Spic and Span®, or mix 1 cup of bleach into a gallon of warm water. Make this potion outside, so you don't breathe in the fumes from the bleach, and wear rubber gloves, goggles, a long-sleeved shirt, and old pants to guard against splashes. Then cover all surrounding vegetation, buildings, and materials with plastic, so they don't get damaged by any overspray. Scrub the deck just as you would your kitchen floor—but use a stiff push broom instead of a mop. Rinse the deck thoroughly after you scrub it, and you're done.

Dentures

Soap and water. Wash your dentures every few days with a soft, soapy cloth, making sure you cover the entire surface, both inside and out. Place a rubber mat in the sink before you get started, so your teeth will make a soft landing if they happen to slip out of your hands. And be sure to rinse your choppers thoroughly when you're done, so they aren't flavored with soap when you slip them back in.

After-meal cleanup. Freshen up your dentures after eating by putting them into a cup filled with warm water and 1 teaspoon of vinegar. Let them soak for an hour to dissolve any residue, then scrub with an old soft-bristled toothbrush to make 'em shine.

Coffee, tea, or clean? Your favorite drinks can stain your dentures just as they do clothes and carpet. So if you regularly drink coffee, tea, cola, or red wine, give your dentures a periodic scrub with my magic stain remover—baking soda! Make a paste of the soda with a bit of water, dip in a soft toothbrush, and scrub-a-dub. To get rid of stubborn stains, let the paste sit for an hour before you scrub.

Powerful Potions

Simple Denture Soak

Baking soda works wonders polishing your pearly whites. So if you're out of denture tablets, or you want to give your budget a break, mix up a batch of this magical solution.

2 tsp. of baking soda

1 cup of warm water

Stir the baking soda into the warm water until it dissolves, add your dentures (or your kid's retainers!), and let them soak until you need them. The baking soda will loosen food particles and keep coffee and cola stains from settling in. Plus, it'll neutralize any food odors, so your dentures will taste as good as they look. Simply rinse off the solution when you're ready to wear your nice fresh teeth again.

Banish bacteria. Nasty bacteria "bugs" can stain your dentures, give them a bad odor, and even make you sick. So battle the bugs by zapping your dentures in the microwave—but only if they have no metal parts! You'll

need a microwavable container that's at least twice as high as your dentures, with a lid that's got vents in it. Put your dentures in the container, fill it with water, and drop in a couple of denture tablets. Put the lid on, and zap the container on high for about two minutes. Let it cool, rinse off your dentures, and enjoy your super-clean smile.

Dishwashers

Easy does it. Does the inside of your dishwasher look pretty grungy? Here's a quick and easy way to make greasy grime and musty odors disappear like magic. Just pour 1 cup of white vinegar into a sturdy mug or bowl, set it in the top rack of your dishwasher, and run through a dishwashing cycle on the hottest setting—with nothing else inside.

So long, stink! Food residue, moldy gunk, and greasy buildup can make your dishwasher smell downright funky, so cut the crud with a simple bleach treatment. Pour 1/2 cup of bleach into the bottom of your empty dishwasher, and run it through a full cycle to sanitize and deodorize it.

Hard-water help. To remove stubborn, built-up mineral deposits as well as general grime, try my two-step trick featuring bleach and vinegar. To make that crud disappear: First, pour 1 cup of chlorine bleach into the bottom of your empty machine, and run it through its cycle. When it's finished, pour 1 cup of white vinegar into the bottom, and run it through again. That'll be the end of any hard-water hang-ups.

Grease, begone! When your dishwasher develops a greasy coating on the racks or walls, don't get down on your hands and knees to clean it up—

Q. My dishwasher has an unpleasant odor all of the time, even right after it finishes a cycle. What can I do to get rid of it?

The Great Clean-dini Speaks

A. Start by using my "Hard-water help" trick at left to clean your machine with bleach and vinegar. Then sprinkle 3 tablespoons of baking soda in the bottom of the empty machine, let it sit overnight to neutralize the odor, and wash it away by running the dishwasher through a regular cycle.

If that doesn't do the trick, wipe the area around the drain with damp paper towels sprinkled with a little baking soda. This will remove any greasy residue that may be decaying there.

If you can still smell a problem, then you'll need to find the source of the stench. Get down on your hands and knees, and look closely at the inside of the dishwasher. Wipe out any grime you find, using a gentle abrasive like baking soda or Bar Keepers Friend®. If your dishwasher is still stinky after all of this effort, call in a plumber—the problem could be a clogged pipe.

grab a box of baking soda, and let the machine do the work itself. Pour 1 cup of baking soda into the dishwasher, and run it through the rinse cycle. It'll combine with the grease and turn it into soap, which'll go right down the drain, leaving your machine squeaky clean—and saving you wear and tear on your knees.

Crud-cutting Coke®. You can also freshen up the inside of your dishwasher by using Coca-Cola® to clean up the crud. Pour a 2-liter bottle of the real thing (use the "classic," not diet, version) into the bottom of your machine, and run it through a full cycle. And if the bottom tray is really grungy, let it soak for a few minutes before you start the cycle.

Hocus Pocus

SMART STACKING

If your dishes aren't coming out of the dishwasher perfectly clean, try stacking them the smart way, so the water spray can reach every last one of them:

★ Put plates in the bottom rack, all facing the same way.

★ Set cups and glasses in the top rack, with bottoms facing up.

★ Place bowls in either the top or bottom rack, but make sure they all face the same direction.

★ Lay spatulas and other large utensils in the top rack.

★ Put pots wherever you can fit them in, but keep their bottoms up.

★ Alternate the direction of forks and spoons: one up, one down, and so on, so that they don't nest together and block the water.

★ Point knives down, not for cleaning purposes, but so you don't get stuck when you unload the dishwasher!

Scum dissolver. Denture-cleaning tablets will dissolve dishwasher grime in no time at all. So if you have plenty of tablets on hand, drop a couple in the bottom of your empty dishwasher, and run it through a regular cycle. Soap scum and greasy buildup will disappear like magic.

A tangy tip. Use astronauts' favorite drink mix to make hard-water "scale" in your dishwasher vanish. Just pour in half of a 12.3-ounce (for 8 quarts) container of powdered orange Tang® drink mix, and run your dishwasher through its regular cycle. The citric acid in the drink mix will loosen the mineral deposits, so the water can easily wash them away. Now that's what I call far-out!

Clean out crevices. Bits of food, grease, and soap scum have a nasty habit of lurking around the dishwasher door, where they cause quite a stink as they decay. So give the gunk an extra nudge when your dishwasher door and gaskets start to look grungy. Wet an old toothbrush, dip it into some baking soda or Bar Keepers Friend®, and scrub away the residue and stains in those cracks, crevices, and corners. Wipe off the loosened crud with a damp sponge, and you're good to go.

Sparkle plenty. If your dishes or drinking glasses look cloudy after the dishwasher has done its job, then you need to try this trick: Add about ¼ cup of white vinegar to the rinse cycle. It'll cut the scum on your dishes—and in your dishwasher.

Lemony fresh. Tang® isn't the only citric acid cleaner for hard-water stains, grease, and general grubbiness in your dishwasher (see "A tangy tip" at left). Try any of these citrusy solutions to clean the machine:

★ Sprinkle one or two packages of unsweetened Kool-Aid® lemonade mix in the bottom of the dishwasher.

★ Fill the soap dispenser with ½ cup of inexpensive lemon-flavored drink mix. Any brand will do, as long as citric acid is listed as one of its ingredients.

★ Pour in ½ cup of bottled lemon juice.

★ Put ½ tablespoon of citric acid crystals or powder (available in your local pharmacy) in the detergent cup.

Run the empty dishwasher through a full cycle, so the citric acid can do its stuff. Your dishwasher will come out clean as a whistle—and as a bonus, your kitchen will smell terrific!

Give it the works. Here's another way to do hands-off dishwasher cleaning: Spray The Works® Tub & Shower Cleaner all over the inside walls and bottom of the empty machine, and run it through a full cycle.

Doors (See also Sliding Doors)

Fit to be framed. Start your door-cleaning chores by wiping the top of the frame with a soft, clean cloth—it works much better than a feather duster or synthetic mop for getting rid of caked-on grime. Then use a duster to do the frame, wiping the loose dirt off all around the door, both inside and out. Don't forget to dust the doorjamb—the side of the door frame where the door is attached—and pay particular attention to the grooves and crevices of the trim to make sure you've dusted all of the dirt away. If your door is made of wood, finish the job by spraying a little oil soap onto a soft, clean cloth, and rub it in to make that woodwork shine.

One cleaner fits all. Soap mixed with water is a good all-purpose cleaner for nearly every kind of exterior door, except for unfinished wood. Just wet a sponge in a bucket of soapy water, squeeze it out, and wipe the door with up-and-down strokes. Rinse with clean water, and wipe dry. This even works on finished wooden doors because the quick treatment doesn't allow moisture to soak in.

Doorknob know-how. To spiff up a dirty, dull doorknob or door knocker, start with an all-purpose cleaner like Formula 409®.

Grandma Putt's Magical Methods

During the height of cold and flu season, when everyone seemed to have the sniffles, my Grandma Putt wiped down her doorknobs every day to kill the germs. Her sanitizer? Plain old rubbing alcohol! Nowadays, it's usually called isopropyl alcohol, and it does such a great job of getting rid of nasty germs that surgeons use it to sterilize their hands. Just pour a bit on a clean cloth, and wipe the knob thoroughly. And there's no need to rinse because the alcohol will evaporate lickety-split, leaving a germ-free surface behind. All it takes is a couple of seconds to ward off weeks of feeling under the weather.

Spray a cloth with the cleaner, and rub the grunge away from the doorknob or door knocker and the surrounding area. If either is made of brass, chrome, or stainless steel, turn to the appropriate entry in this book, and use one of my magic tricks to make it look inviting again.

Interior eraser. When grubby hands leave their mark all over your interior doors, use a Mr. Clean® Magic Eraser® to get rid of the dirt. Simply wet the eraser, squeeze it out, and wipe away the grimy paw prints on any painted door.

Slider smarts. Most folks pay a lot of attention to cleaning the glass in their sliding doors, but the metal or wooden tracks often go neglected. Meanwhile, they're gathering quite a stash of dirt and debris (even inside the house), and the door gets harder and harder to open and close. That's when you know it's time for a deep cleaning. Here's how to get your sliding door back on track:

1. Start by using a whisk broom to dig out all of the compacted dirt from the corners, bottom track, and edges.

2. Vacuum up the dirt and any other loose debris—spiderwebs, leaves, dead bugs, and what have you.

3. Once the loose debris is gone, spray the tracks heavily with my Super Scrubber potion on page 307, and let it soak in for a few minutes.

4. Use an old toothbrush to dislodge any remaining gunk and scrub the grime out of the tracks.

5. Push a clean cloth into the tracks, and run it back and forth, allowing it to soak up the cleaning solution and gather up the grime.

6. Rinse the tracks with water, let them dry thoroughly, then spray the door rollers with a dry lubricant like Ultra Glide® (available at most hardware stores), following the directions on the label.

Down Clothes and Quilts

Find a front-loader. Always use a front-loading washing machine to clean down items because an agitator in the middle of the machine can cause the stitching (that holds the down in place) to stretch, weaken, or break. And be sure to use the gentle or hand-wash cycle to keep the down from taking too much of a beating.

Wash once, rinse twice. Soapy residue keeps feathers from drying to their fluffiest, and that cuts down on the insulating power of down—and increases drying time. What's the solution? Run the item through an extra rinse cycle to make sure the down is entirely free of soap. If you're hand washing the item, push it up and down in a tub of clean water until there are no more soap bubbles.

Stress reliever. Washing a removable duvet cover is a whole lot easier than washing an entire down quilt, so the bottom line is…cover up your coverlet! The duvet will keep your down quilt nice and clean, so you'll need to wash it only once every few years. That means less stress on the stitching and the feathers—and on you, too!

Room to move. You'll need to use an extra-large washer to clean your machine-washable down quilt, and an extra-large dryer, too, so those feathers can get their fluffiest. If your home machines aren't big enough, collect your quarters and head to the nearest Laundromat, where your quilt will have more than enough room in the supersized machines.

Fluff and fold. Even in a large dryer, only part of the down will be exposed to the heat as it tumbles around. So if you're drying a down quilt or other large item, take it out every 10 minutes or so, give it a good shake, and fold it in different ways during the process. That'll make sure all parts of it get their turn in the hot seat. Not too hot, though—drying on low heat is best for those fine feathers.

HEAVY WHEN WET

Dry down is light and fluffy, but wet down weighs a ton. So be extra careful whenever you lift a wet down item, especially if you're hand washing it, because the strain of all that weight can cause the stitching to break—which will unleash a snowstorm of feathers!

Drape a bath towel over your arms before you begin to help protect your clothes from getting wet in the process. Then support the wet item from underneath when you remove it from the washing machine or bathtub, bundling it up in your arms.

Mild-mannered soap. You need to use a very mild soap to wash down; otherwise, the natural oils in the feathers will be stripped away. Both Ivory Snow® and Woolite® do a fine job, or you can buy a special down-cleaning soap at camping-supply stores.

Wash by hand. Your bathtub is the perfect place to hand wash smaller down items. You can even use it for sleeping bags or down quilts—once the air is out of the feathers, the item will look a whole lot smaller! Fill the tub with warm water and a gentle soap, and immerse your down, swishing it around until it no longer balloons out of the water. Let it soak for a few minutes to loosen the dirt, and then gently squeeze the soapy water through it, using a lift-and-fold motion as you work— the same motion you'd use for kneading bread dough. And make sure you support the item from underneath whenever you lift it to avoid straining the stitching.

Towel dry. Blotting a freshly washed down item is a great way to shorten its drying time. So before you put it in the dryer, wrap it in a bath towel, and give it a nice big squeeze. Replace the towel with a dry one, and blot it again. You'll be surprised at how much moisture is still hiding in those feathers.

Shake, rattle, and roll. Getting the fluff back into the feathers is the biggest challenge to cleaning down items. Since wet down clumps together, you'll need to keep shaking things up so that every last bit gets thoroughly dry. Drying down can take three or more cycles in your dryer, and you'll need to keep rearranging the item throughout the process. So find a comfy seat nearby and grab a good book to read while you're tending to the dryer.

Tennis, anyone? A couple of clean tennis balls thrown into the dryer will help break up the clumps while small down items are drying. But for larger items like jackets, sleeping bags, or quilts, toss in a couple of clean canvas tennis shoes instead. Their heavier weight will bump against the down as the item spins, which will help bust up the clumps of damp feathers.

The Great Clean-dini Speaks

Q. My down quilt has a bad smell ever since I washed it. What can I do to get rid of the odor?

A. Damp feathers have an unpleasant smell, and they also make an inviting home for mold and mildew, which may have set in. Even though your quilt may have felt dry on the outside, moisture was probably lingering in the feather filling. To get rid of the smell, run your quilt through the dryer again with a couple of clean canvas tennis shoes, and hang it over an outdoor clothesline on a sunny, breezy day to air out the smell. If the odor persists, rewash your quilt, adding a cup of white vinegar to the rinse cycle to kill off any mold. Then before you put it back on the bed or fold it away, give the quilt the sniff-and-squeeze test: Totally dry down has no smell at all, and the filling won't stick together when you squeeze a handful of it.

Drains

Melt away grease. Boiling water may be all you need to give a sluggish drain a fresh start—it'll loosen greasy deposits by simply melting them away. Just heat a 2- or 3-quart saucepan of water to a full rolling boil, and then carefully pour about half of the boiling water down the drain. Wait a minute or two to let it begin working on the grease, then pour in the rest. Finish up by running very hot tap water through the drain.

Baking soda boost. Keep your drains running freely by giving them a baking soda bath about once a week. First, run the tap water until it's hot, then turn the faucet off and pour a handful of baking soda into each drain. Let the hot water run again for a few minutes, so it can wash the grease-cutting baking soda all the way down the drains.

Denture drain cleaner. Speed up a slow drain by using denture tablets to clean the pipes. Just drop three tablets down the drain, pour in a cup of white vinegar, and wait about 10 minutes. Run the hot water to flush the drain, and watch that water pick up speed.

Odor remover. Dirty drains lead to bad smells, so keep yours smelling fresh by pouring 1 cup of vinegar or bottled lemon juice in them once a week. Let it sit for 30 minutes, so the mild acid can cut through grease. Then run hot water to flush the drains.

Grandma Putt's Magical Methods

When your drains are so clogged up that water drains soooo slowly, try my Grandma Putt's quick fix, and plunge the problem away. Grab a "plumber's friend"—a hand plunger—hold it over the drain, and then give it one or two quick, hard pumps to dislodge the gunk that's causing the backup. Wear long rubber gloves for this job because you'll need to grab the hairball or other gunk before it slides back down the drain.

Clean, naturally. Instead of using caustic chemicals to clean a clogged drain, try one of these magic mixtures:

★ Pour ½ cup of baking soda into the drain, followed by ½ cup of white vinegar. The baking soda and vinegar will react with each other and fizz right through the clog. Let it work for about 10 minutes, and then flush the drain with plenty of hot water.

★ Mix 1 cup of baking soda and 1 cup of salt, and pour it into the drain. Follow it up with a quart or two of boiling water, and then run very hot tap water at full blast to flush away the scum.

Don't mix and match. Baking soda and other household products can react explosively with commercial drain cleaners, so never, ever use them before or after using a commercial product. And always play it safe by not combining any treatments.

Egg Stains

Fabric first aid. Drippy egg yolk is usually dried by the time you notice the stains on your clothes or tablecloth, so start the cleanup by scraping off the dried gunk with your fingernail or a flat knife. Then sponge away the remains with cold, soapy water. If there's still a trace, use my Prewash Spot Cleaner (see page 127), and launder the item in cold water to lift out any lingering residue.

Enzyme eaters. Protein-based stains like egg yolk and blood call for an enzyme-based detergent, which actually digests the food. So look for the word *enzyme* on the product label. And use cold water to launder the item because hot water is notorious for setting stains.

GOT EGGED? TAKE ACTION!

If the local yolk-els give you a trick instead of a treat on Halloween, get to work scrubbing off the raw eggs before they damage the paint on your car or house. Mix up a bucket of enzyme detergent, such as OxiClean® Outdoor, and wash that bad yolk away. Use a stiff brush to scrub concrete, brick, or siding, and a soft cloth on your car.

If any small discolored spots remain on your car's paint, saturate a cotton ball with a double- or triple-strength enzymatic spot cleaner, set it on the stain, and wait a few minutes before removing the mark with a soft, clean cloth.

Hocus Pocus

Grout scrub. Did you spill a little egg on your tile counter when you cracked it for breakfast this morning? Not a problem! Just wipe away most of the egg with a cold, soapy sponge, and finish the job by scrubbing the grout with an old toothbrush dabbed with a bit of dishwashing liquid. Things will soon be looking sunny-side up again.

Stone saver. To remove egg stains from a granite, sandstone, slate, or terrazzo counter or floor, use old-fashioned washing soda instead of soap. It contains sodium carbonate, which does a great job of lifting the grease that causes eggs to stain. Follow the package directions to mix up a solution in cold water, and then scrub the stain away with a soft cloth. Rinse the area with fresh water, and wipe it dry. No more egg on your face—or on your floor!

Salty solution. Before you launder an egg-stained item, give table salt a try. Simply sprinkle a layer of salt onto the wet egg spot, and let it sit for about 15 minutes to soak up the grease and gunk. Rinse the residue off with cold water, and then toss the item into the washing machine and launder using cold water for the wash and rinse cycles.

Beat leather spots. When greasy eggs leave nasty spots on your sofa, shoes, or other leather surfaces, try this two-step trick to make them disappear quickly. First, put a few squirts of grease-cutting dishwashing liquid into a small, deep bowl of cold water, and whip the soap into a froth with an eggbeater. Dip a clean, barely damp sponge into the suds, and rub gently on the stain. Dry the spot with a soft, clean cloth, and then sprinkle some cornmeal on the area to absorb any grease that remains. Wait about an hour, brush the cornmeal away, and the stain should be gone. If you can still see traces of the spot, repeat the treatment.

Stop silver stains. Eggs can discolor silver flatware and serving pieces, so be quick when you spot a drop. Wipe the wet egg off with a soft, damp cloth. If you can still see a stain, sprinkle a bit of salt on a damp cloth and gently rub the spot away. Then rinse and dry your silver as usual.

Enamel

Easy does it! Your antique claw-foot bathtub, your bright orange enamel saucepan, and that priceless Chinese cloisonné plate on your wall all have a common bond: Their surfaces are enamel, which is made by fusing powdered glass to a metal backing. And just like anything that's made of glass, they can get scratched, chipped, or even cracked. That's why, when it comes to cleaning enamel, you'll need to stay away from harsh scouring powders and steel wool, and use gentler methods like the ones you'll find here.

Suds it up. Stick to good old soap and water when you clean decorative enamelware like plates, jewelry, and picture frames, so you don't damage any paint that may be on the surface. Dust the piece first to remove loose dirt, and then give it a gentle sponge bath in the sink. It's also a great idea to pad the bottom of the sink with a rubber mat beforehand, just in case you develop a sudden attack of butterfingers!

Powerful Potions

Enamel Broiler Pan Cleaner

Tired of scrubbing away at your enameled broiler pan to get the burned-on grease off? This labor-saving potion works like magic to cut the crud on enameled pans.

1 part white vinegar

1 part cream of tartar

Mix the vinegar and cream of tartar in a small bowl; you'll need only a few teaspoons of each for most jobs. Apply it to the gunked-up spots on the edges or sides of your pans with a cloth or cotton ball. Pour the rest of the mixture into the bottom of the broiler pan or drip pan, tilting the pan so that it spreads out. Let the mixture sit for about 10 minutes, then go over the pan with a nonabrasive plastic scrubbie to lift off the crud. If any stubborn spots remain, repeat the treatment. Then wash your pans in warm, soapy water, let them air-dry, and put them back in place.

Baking soda scrub. To scrub away stains from smooth-surfaced enamel like your bathtub or cookware, make a paste of baking soda with a little water. It'll rub the spots away without scratching the surface. For more scrubbing action, use a nonabrasive plastic scrubbie instead of a cloth to apply the paste. After you rinse the baking soda off, finish the job with a vinegar rinse to leave that glossy surface gleaming.

Rinse away rust. When iron-rich water leaves rusty tracks on your enamel tub or sink, try this nifty trick to bleach them away. Soak a cloth in a solution of 1 tablespoon of oxalic acid crystals and ½ cup of warm water, and lay it on the stains. Wait a few minutes for the acid to work its magic, then rinse with fresh water. Wear rubber gloves and long sleeves to protect your skin, as you would when working with any acid. See Bathtubs and Showers on page 16 for more cleaning tricks.

Clean up cookware. When stains remain after you've eaten the last of the lasagna, brighten up your enamel bakeware by filling it with warm water and dropping in a couple of denture-cleaning tablets. Let the tablets fizz away, and when the action stops, your cookware should be clean. Need more ideas for cleaning enamel cookware? Just turn to the Cookware entry on page 85.

A refreshing fix. To brighten up dull enamel cookware or an enamel kitchen sink, try my soda pop solution. Just pour any fizzy flavor into the pan or around the drain or other stained areas of your sink, and let it sit for about 10 minutes to let it do its stuff. Rub with a non-abrasive plastic scrubbie or a soft toothbrush, and the grime'll be gone—no kidding!

Fabrics (See also Clothes; Upholstery)

Read the label. Take a minute to read the care label in your clothes and on other items before you clean them—or, better yet, before you buy them! That's the easiest way to figure out exactly what kind of TLC they'll need. Not only will you learn whether that blouse is washable, but you'll  also find out what cycle to use in the washer and dryer, how to iron it, and whether or not you can use bleach on it. With those basics in place, the only thing you'll need is advice on how to make stains disappear— and that's why I'm here—to help you keep your fabrics in tip-top shape.

Wrinkle reducer. Cotton and linen items will shrink and wrinkle unless they're specially treated—an option that's become a lot more common lately. So check the care label, or play it safe and launder them in cold water and dry them on the "cool" setting to cut down on shrinkage.

Powerful Potions

Prewash Spot Cleaner

This magic solution is just the ticket for stubborn stains on washable fabrics, including cotton, linen, polyester, and acrylics. Just spray it on to make grass stains, food stains, and other tough trouble spots disappear.

1 part dishwashing liquid

1 part ammonia

1 part water

Combine the dishwashing liquid, ammonia, and water in a handheld sprayer bottle. Shake up the bottle, and spray the solution on the stain. Wait 10 to 15 minutes, and then launder the item as usual. This cleaner works just as well, if not better, than the expensive, store-bought stuff.

And never let them sit in the dryer once they're done—unless you really love to iron! But if you do forget to take cotton or linen items out of the dryer at the end of the cycle, try this neat trick for getting rid of the worst of the wrinkles: Just wet a clean, white cloth, toss it in with the wrinkled load, and run the dryer again. The moisture will relax the wrinkles. And this time, when the clothes are dry, remove them quickly so you don't have to repeat the rescue process again.

Rayon reasoning. Rayon and viscose rayon are regular chameleons: They can look and feel like silk, wool, linen, or cotton. Cleaning methods vary depending on the finish, so pay particular attention to the care label. Don't assume that your new rayon slacks will be washable just because your last pair were—some finishes require dry cleaning, others need hand washing, and some can just be tossed in the washing machine. Just remember to keep alcohol and solvents way from these materials, and be careful when you do your makeup—nail polish remover and perfumes can damage the fabric.

Miracle acrylics. Fluffy acrylic, modacrylic, and acrylic blends are much easier to clean than the wool they are meant to resemble—you can usually toss these synthetic fabrics in the washer and dryer without worry. But check each label anyway because some items require hand washing or dry cleaning. Use low heat in the dryer, and don't forget to empty the lint trap afterward because acrylic fabrics have a tendency to shed fibers while they tumble around.

Nylon news. The original miracle fabric—nylon—is strong, lightweight, wrinkle-resistant, and easy to care for. Just pop most nylon items in the washing machine, then spin them dry on low heat—it doesn't take long! Nylon tends to shrug off stains because it's not very absorbent, but it does hoard static electricity. So add a fabric-softener sheet to the dryer to take care of that little problem, and your nylon will hang smoothly again.

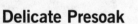

Powerful Potions

Delicate Presoak

Soak any white or light-colored delicate fabrics in this magical mix to remove stains and brighten the color. It's so gentle that you can even use it on your washable silks! Just be careful with darker-colored silks; test it on an inconspicuous part of the fabric first to make sure it doesn't alter the color.

¹/₂ cup of hydrogen peroxide

4 cups of water

Mix this solution in your kitchen or bathroom sink. Then submerge the silk, and let it soak for about 30 minutes. Rinse the item in clean water, and dry it on low heat, or as the care label directs.

Soft as silk. If your silk is washable, use my Delicate Presoak potion at left to remove any stains, and then wash the fabric with a protein-enriched shampoo. Silk strands are made of protein, just like hair, so the cleansing and nourishing shampoo will leave your fabric looking great. Just don't use a shampoo that includes conditioner because it'll leave a greasy residue behind.

Troublesome tannin. Bitter tannins protect plants from insects—and lend their flavor to red wine, tea, and coffee. But tannins can also leave their mark on fabrics when that stain sets in. So treat those drips quickly by running any washable fabric under cold water to rinse the tannin out. If you can still see a spot, spray some of my Prewash Spot Cleaner (see page 127) on the stain, and launder the fabric in cold water. And for even more super solutions to tannin troubles, turn to "Vanquish Coffee Stains" on page 76 and the Wine Stains entry on page 356.

Hocus Pocus

POPULAR POLYESTER

Polyester wears like iron, but it's a whole lot softer. We all know how easy it is to care for polyester—just throw it in the washing machine and run it through the dryer. But most of us know, too, that this fabric has its drawbacks: It snags, it pills, it holds grease stains, it collects static electricity, and it may even yellow with age. YIKES! Here's how to deal with polyester problems:

★ Turn these items inside out when you do your laundry to keep the threads from getting snagged on any hooks or zippers in the same load.

★ Use fabric softener and dryer sheets to reduce static cling.

★ To remove pills, hold the fabric tautly and use a battery-operated clothes shaver or a disposable shaver, being careful not to slice the fabric.

★ The agitation in a washing machine can make pills form on polyester or poly blends, so use a short cycle when you wash these fabrics.

★ Brighten white poly fabrics by soaking them overnight in a mixture of ½ cup of liquid dishwasher detergent and 1 gallon of water. Then add ½ cup of white vinegar to the rinse cycle to banish the yellowed polyester blues.

Hocus Pocus

Outwit Clothes Moths

The good news: These pests don't attack all fabrics. The bad news: They have expensive tastes—they love cashmere, silk, wool, angora, alpaca, felt, hair, fur, feathers, and down! Any fabric blends that include these fibers will also attract them. Plus, they'll seek out these fabrics anywhere in the house, not just in the closet, so they may attack your upholstery, your carpets, or your knitting wool, as well as your favorite sweater.

Clothes moths make themselves at home wherever fabrics are undisturbed—in the back of the closet, in the attic, or in a storage chest. They can cause serious damage, so take action as soon as you spot the first moth hole or see a moth fluttering around. Here's what to do:

★ Examine all clothes closely for eggs or larvae. The larvae live in silken webbing or tiny tubes of silk, often in hidden areas, like under the collar or pocket flaps. Brush the pests off outdoors, and then launder or dry-clean the items immediately.

★ Dry cleaning and Dryel® kill all stages of clothes moths—adults, larvae, and eggs. Hot water also does the trick, so use the hottest setting on your washing machine if the fabrics can handle it.

★ Food moths are easily confused with clothes moths, and they often leave the kitchen for other areas of the house. Clothes moths stay close to where their food is. If you're not sure which is which, put a pheromone-baited sticky trap near the clothes—if moths are stuck to it, you have the clothing kind.

★ Kill any moths you see. Only the larvae eat the fabric, but the adults will get together for a little hanky-panky and make a whole lot more.

★ Vacuum clothes closets, wool or silk carpets and upholstery, and the crevices along the floor and under heaters and furniture. Then dispose of the vacuum cleaner bag in an outdoor trash can, so the pests can't escape.

Maintenance musts. Preventing clothes moths is a lot easier than getting rid of an infestation (see Outwit Clothes Moths at left). So try these tricks to make your fabrics less tempting to these pests:

★ Cedar shavings, cedar blocks, and cedar-lined drawers all help repel clothes moths. To make sure the cedar is releasing its repellent oil, rub it down occasionally with sandpaper to bring out the scent.

★ Use airtight storage boxes or compressible storage bags for any susceptible items, squeezing out as much air as possible and sealing them tightly.

★ Mothballs are toxic, so give natural repellents a try. Oils or sachets of lavender, rosemary, cloves, mint, and thyme will discourage snacking moths.

★ These pests do their dirty work in the dark, so install a stick-on LED light and keep it on constantly in your closet.

★ Wash garage-sale or thrift-shop finds in hot water or use Dryel® right away—don't add these new items to your clothes closet or even store them in your house until you've made sure you aren't bringing in a pest problem.

Don't feed the pests. Food, formula, perspiration, and urine stains are all manna from heaven to clothes moths. They'll zero in on wool, silk, and other animal-based fabrics with these stains, and they'll even attack cotton, linen, and synthetic fabrics if the stains are edible. So the moral of the story is: Never hang up dirty clothes in a closet, or store them away for the season without getting those stains out first!

Dry-clean in the dryer. Try Dryel® to clean nonwashable fabrics at home, instead of carting them to the local dry cleaner. Pretreat stains with a dab of Dryel Stain Remover, and then bag the items as directed with a Dryel cloth. The cloth releases cleansing moisture that loosens dirt and relaxes wrinkles. It costs less than professional dry cleaning services, and it leaves fabrics smelling clean and fresh.

Hand wash? If you're willing to risk it, you may be able to hand wash certain dry-clean-only items. White or light-colored fabrics and unstructured items like sofa throws, sweaters, and lingerie hold up best to hand washing. Bright colors, dark hues, and blacks, and tailored clothes like blazers and dress slacks, usually don't.

Fabulous fakes. Warm fleece and fake fur made from synthetics are usually acrylic or modacrylic, so they're amazingly easy to care for. Most are machine washable on the gentle cycle, and will do just fine in a dryer on low heat. The only drawback to these great fakes is that they tend to build up a lot of static electricity, so they can be clingy or even...*shocking!* The solution? Just pop a fabric-softener sheet into the dryer to reduce the snap, crackle, and pop.

Save that spandex. Keep your spandex stretchy by avoiding chlorine bleach, which can damage the material; use an oxygen bleach instead. Heat can be harmful, too, so always dry garments made of spandex or spandex blends on low heat, and take them out of the dryer just as soon as they're dry.

Wool wash. If your wool clothing is washable, soak it first to loosen up the dirt before you start the wash cycle. To get dirt off felted wool, wipe it with a dry sponge; for a more thor-

Grandma Putt's Magical Methods

Instead of buying an expensive liquid soap to clean her delicate fabrics, Grandma Putt mixed up a batch of this remarkable recipe. Simply mix ½ cup of powdered laundry detergent and ½ cup of borax in a saucepan with 2 cups of water. Simmer over low heat for about 10 minutes, stirring constantly (beat with a wire whisk occasionally to break up the lumps). Remove from the stove and let it cool, then pour it into a clean plastic bottle. Use it as you would any commercial product for delicate fabrics. This gentle soap keeps practically forever, so it'll be ready whenever you need to handle your hand-washables with care.

ough cleaning, hold it over the steaming spout of a teakettle and brush it with a lint-free cloth. Handle with care to avoid stretching the damp fabric, and lay it flat to air-dry.

The sauna treatment. Washable wools are a real miracle, but frequent washing will cause the fibers to break down before their time, especially if you use a top-loading machine that's got an agitator in the middle. So instead of machine washing the wool, freshen it by hanging it up in a steamy bathroom. The moisture will lift the fibers, fluffing up the surface and easing out any wrinkles. This is a great trick to keep up your sleeve when you're traveling.

Go away, grease stains! When oily salad dressings, mayonnaise, and even makeup leave their mark on your washable fabrics, start by soaking up as much of the stain as you can by covering it with cornstarch or talcum powder. Let it sit overnight, shake off the excess powder, and then treat the stain by rubbing in some liquid dishwasher detergent or my Prewash Spot Cleaner on page 127. Let it sit for at least 10 minutes, and then wash as usual in the hottest water the fabric can stand.

Dastardly duo. Crayon, chocolate, spaghetti sauce, lipstick, and the like are combination stains—they leave both grease and a dye behind. So when you get dark, greasy gravy or a blob of pizza sauce on your fabrics, treat the grease first (you'll find a few tricks in the tip above and even more in Grease Stains on page 170). That treatment may make the dye disappear, too. But if it doesn't, dab on some ammonia or use a bleach that's safe for the fabric, and the stain will simply wash away.

Protein problems. Milk, eggs, baby food, formula, and blood are full of protein, which is why an enzyme cleaner is needed to trounce these troublemakers—it actually digests them! Use enzyme detergent in your laundry, and try an enzyme stain spray for tough spots. Always use cold water and a cool dryer to launder fabrics with protein stains because heat will only make that stain a permanent addition.

Fiberglass

Gentle on that "glass." Fiberglass is easy to scratch, so don't use harsh scouring powders or stiff-bristled brushes on it. For quick cleanup, fill a handheld sprayer bottle with white vinegar, spritz the surface, and wipe the dirt away with a damp sponge. There's no need to rinse because the vinegar smell will disappear as it dries, leaving nothing but the shine behind.

Elbow grease in a sponge. For tougher dirt on fiberglass surfaces, reach for a Mr. Clean® Magic Eraser®. Simply wet the sponge, squeeze it out, and wipe the oily dirt away. The eraser sponge won't scratch the surface, and it really does work like magic.

Soap scum removal. Fiberglass showers have a real knack for getting grungy with a buildup of soap scum, hard-water stains, and dirt. To make them sparkling clean again, try one of these easy tricks:

★ Wash away oily scum with grease-cutting dishwashing liquid. Squirt a little on a damp sponge or a nonabrasive plastic scrubbie, and rub the crud away.

★ For really stubborn spots, dampen a nonabrasive plastic scrubbie and dip it into a bowl of borax. The gentle abrasive power of the borax will cut through the crud in no time at all.

Boat hull how-to. To make a nice soapy scrub for a fiberglass boat or canoe, squirt some dishwashing liquid into a bucket and fill it with hot water. Use a long-handled brush for most of the grime and a sponge for any finish work around the nameplates or seams. Rinse the soap away with your garden hose. If the fiberglass is stained, or has a scum line from the water, mix oxalic acid crystals into a handheld sprayer bottle of water (following the directions on the package), and spritz the stains away. Wear protective clothing, rubber gloves, and safety goggles when working with

The Great Clean-dini Speaks

Q. It's tough to keep my fiberglass shower clean. Got any bright ideas for making the job a little easier?

A. You bet I do! After you scrub the shower, let it dry completely, and then go to town with car wax. Apply the wax to the shower walls according to the directions, and buff it to a grime-defying shine with a soft, clean cloth. Then the next time your shower is dirty, just use soap and water to spiff up the surface—the dirt will slide right off the waxy coating. Reapply the wax every few months, and remember—wax the shower walls only, and not the floor, because it'll make for some mighty slippery footing!

the acid, and rinse the boat thoroughly afterward. Finish up by applying a coat of spray-on wax to seal the fiberglass from the elements.

Shower floor finish. Dirt can really get ground into a fiberglass shower floor, making it look dingy no matter how frequently you scrub it. So make that grime disappear—by spraying it with a coat of fume-free oven cleaner. Wait 10 minutes or so for the foam to lift the deep-down dirt off, and then wipe it away with a Mr. Clean® Magic Eraser®. Wear rubber gloves, long sleeves, and eye protection for this job, and rinse the shower thoroughly afterward. You'll find more tricks for brightening up bathroom fiberglass in the Bathtubs and Showers entry on page 16.

Tough on textures. Textured fiberglass can be tricky to clean because a cloth or sponge slides over the surface and doesn't get down to the nitty-gritty that's in between the bumps. So scrub the textured surface with a soft-bristled brush instead. Wet the bristles, give the brush a squirt of dishwashing liquid or inexpensive shampoo, and apply a little elbow grease to make the grime disappear.

Fireplaces

Free your damper. Your fire won't burn its best if the damper has gotten all crusty with creosote, soot, and ashes that keep the air from flowing freely. So depending on how often you use your fireplace, clean the damper at least a couple times a season. When the fireplace is cool, grab a flashlight and find the damper—it's a hinged, cast-iron flap located above the fireplace in the chimney. Use a stiff, short-handled wire brush to scrub it and free up any debris that's caked on around the hinges. Open and close the damper a few times so the loose dirt drops down, vacuum it up, and check again with your flashlight to make sure all of the gunk is gone.

Glass that glows. You can wipe smoke and soot stains off glass fireplace doors with a cloth that's been dipped in white vinegar or a mixture of $\frac{1}{2}$ cup of vinegar, 1 tablespoon of ammonia, and 1 gallon of water. If the

 soot has baked onto the surface of the glass, buy a glass scraper at your local hardware store and carefully slice the stains away, then follow up with the vinegar and ammonia solution. Add a nice finishing touch by scrubbing the brass knobs with an old toothbrush—dipped in Worcestershire sauce, of course!

Finesse fireplace furnishings. Cleaning your fireplace grate and wrought-iron tools is a messy job that's best done outdoors. Scrub the soot buildup off the grate and the andirons with a wire brush. Then rub the grate, andirons, and fireplace tools with a fine (000 grade) steel wool pad dipped in mineral oil. Wipe the excess oil off with a dry cloth, and your furnishings are good to go.

Scrub the walls. To remove stubborn soot stains inside of a fireplace, use a mixture of 6 tablespoons of TSP (trisodium phosphate), 1 cup of chlorine bleach, and 1 gallon of warm water. Line the floor of the fireplace with a drop cloth and newspapers, and set the bucket inside. Dip a wire brush into the solution and scrub the blackened walls, working from the top down. Wear rubber gloves, safety glasses, and protective clothing to guard your skin from accidental spills and splashes, and be sure to use plenty of the solution—and plenty of elbow grease! To clean the brick outside the fireplace, try my Soot Scrub potion (on page 138), or check out the Brick entry on page 40.

Scrape off the soot. If the buildup of soot and creosote inside a fireplace gets too thick, it can actually catch fire. So to be safe, scrape the gunk off once or twice a season when the fireplace is cool. Remove the ashes and grate, and line the floor of the fireplace with a plastic drop cloth topped with several layers of newspaper. Then scrape the sooty walls with a wire brush that's got a metal scraper attached to it, working from the top down. As debris collects on the floor, bundle it up in the top layer of newspaper and stuff it into a sturdy trash bag for disposal.

Hide stains with paint. Some soot stains can be impossible to remove completely, no matter how hard you scrub. But don't give up—you can still freshen up the fireplace with a coat of paint. You'll find plenty of fireplace-painting kits at your local hardware store. But before you go gung ho, remember that nothing can really match the warm look of the real stuff—and painting is pretty permanent.

Grandma Putt's Magical Methods

Ashes can go flying everywhere when you sweep out your fireplace, so try my Grandma Putt's quick fix to make that chore less of a hassle. Simply sprinkle the ashes with damp coffee grounds. The flyaway ash will clump up around the moist grounds, making it a cinch to sweep them up with your fireplace brush and dustpan. And play it safe like my Grandma did—put the ashes into a metal container for extra insurance against an accidental fire.

Powerful Potions

Soot Scrub

Make black stains disappear from the brick around your fireplace with this super scrub—it gets its power from pumice, a powdered stone you can buy at your local hardware store. Before you start, cover the floors and furniture near the fireplace with plastic drop cloths to protect them from drips and splashes. And remember, soot stains are notoriously hard to remove, so even after using this potion, some blackened areas may remain.

- **1 bar of Fels-Naptha® soap**
- **3 qts. of water**
- **1 cup of ammonia**
- **1 lb. of pumice**

Slice the soap into the water in a deep saucepan, and bring it to a boil. Reduce the heat and simmer the mixture until the soap melts, then remove it from the heat and let it cool. Stir in the ammonia and pumice, mixing thoroughly. Brush the glop onto the stained brick, let it sit for about an hour, and then scrub the area with a stiff brush. Rinse off the mixture, and let the clean brick air-dry.

Stinky fireplace? Sour, smoky smells coming from a fireplace are a sure sign that moisture has seeped into the chimney and soaked into the sooty deposits inside. The first step is to clean the chimney to reduce that crud—it's not only smelly, it can be dangerous! For a permanent solution, have a chimney cap with a top damper installed to block the rain and snow, which will also keep bad smells from sinking down the chimney when the air is cold.

Gas logs. To clean gas fireplace logs, make sure they're cool, then dust them monthly with a soft brush. Be extra careful when you're cleaning around the gas vents so you don't nudge them out of position, which can cause them to malfunction.

Flatware

Sink or dishwasher? Silver and silver-plated flatware actually benefit from hand washing and drying because the gentle rubbing helps deepen the patina. Stainless steel, on the other hand, stays its shiniest when you use the dishwasher to clean it. But if you do decide to hand wash your stainless and it's looking a little dull or water-spotted, moisten a cloth with white or cider vinegar and wipe it clean.

Heat stains on stainless. The hot water in your dishwasher can cause bluish streaks or stains on stainless steel flatware. Stainless cooking utensils can also pick up a blue tinge from the heat of boiling liquids or other hot foods. To make the blue stains vanish, dip a soft cloth into club soda and rub the spots away. Then rinse the flatware off, and dry it to a shine with a soft, clean cloth.

Avoid dishwasher dulling. Stainless steel will lose its luster over the years as its shiny chromium coating wears away. Harsh soap hastens the process by dulling the finish, so always use the mildest dishwasher detergent you can find. And don't be tempted to use scouring powder or steel wool to scrub gunk off—you'll only scratch the surface.

Bad neighbors. Keep stainless steel flatware away from any silver or silver plate in the dishwasher because the combo can create some bad chemistry. The chemical reaction between the metals may leave small pits on the stainless and black marks on the silver or silver plate.

Rinse first. Get in the habit of rinsing off any flatware before you put it in the sink or dishwasher because certain foods can damage the finish if they sit for a while. Which foods are the worst culprits? Anything salty, like olives or ham, and anything with acid, including tomato sauces.

Powerful Potions

Silver Shine

Restore the gleam to tarnished or dull silver or silver-plated flatware by soaking it in this solution. The trick depends on a chemical reaction that dissolves the tarnish even in tiny crevices, leaving each piece clean and bright. A word of caution: Don't use this potion if you want to preserve the patina in the decorations on the flatware.

4 tbsp. of table salt

4 tbsp. of washing soda

1 gal. of warm water

Aluminum foil

Mix the salt, washing soda (available in your supermarket near the fabric softeners), and water in a large glass pan, and stir until the salt and washing soda are dissolved. Lay a sheet of aluminum foil in the bottom of the pan, and drop in the silver or silver-plated flatware. Let it soak for about an hour to dissolve the tarnish, then rinse thoroughly, and dry each piece with a soft, clean cloth.

Magic milk bath. To make silver or silver-plated flatware shine, try this magic milk bath to take off the tarnish. Mix about 1/3 cup of dry milk powder, 1 tablespoon of white vinegar, and 3/4 cup of water in a 9- by 13-inch glass casserole dish. Lay the flatware in the bath, let it sit overnight, rinse it thoroughly, and dry each piece by hand.

Handling hollowware. If your silver or silver-plated flatware has hollow handles, wash it by hand, not in the dishwasher. And don't let it stay submerged for more than a few minutes because soapy water can loosen the solder on the pieces. Remember—handle your hollowware with care!

Keep sulfur away. Sulfur causes silver to tarnish, so don't bundle any extra spoons with a rubber band, and avoid using latex mats in the sink because rubber contains sulfur. And when you use silver or silver-plated flatware for sulfur-rich foods, including eggs, mayonnaise, onions, and mustard, wash it right after the meal. That way, the sulfur doesn't have time to react with the metal and tarnish that nice bright finish.

Silverware polish. To clean dull silver or silver-plated flatware, make a paste of baking soda or cornstarch and a bit of water. Dab some onto a soft, clean cloth, and rub until the dullness disappears. Or you can dab a bit of non-gel toothpaste onto the piece, run it under warm water for just a second, and then work the toothpaste into a foam while you rub the flatware with a soft, damp cloth. Rinse thoroughly after either of these treatments, and dry the piece with a soft, clean cloth.

Happy holiday ware! Tie a few sticks of plain white chalk into a piece of cheesecloth, and put them in your silver chest to absorb moisture and keep flatware from tarnishing. You can also use activated charcoal or silica gel. Just pour about a tablespoon of either of these powders into a small open container, and place it in the chest. When it's time to get out the good stuff for Christmas dinner, all the pieces will be tarnish-free! For more tarnish-removal tricks, see the Silver entry on page 279.

Hocus Pocus

HOMEMADE DISHWASHER DETERGENT

Here's an inexpensive mix you can make ahead, then use every day in your automatic dishwasher: Mix 1 part baking soda and 1 part borax. Using a funnel, pour the powder into a clean, dry container with a lid (like a recycled plastic gallon jug). If you have hard water, double the amount of baking soda in the mix. Use 2 tablespoons of the detergent for each load of dishes. And for a spot-free shine, pour ½ cup of white vinegar in at the start of the dishwasher's rinse cycle.

Flowerpots

Cleaning clay. Clay or terra-cotta pots are porous, so minerals in the soil or fertilizers you use will eventually soak through them. That's what creates the white splotches on the pots—they're mostly fertilizer salts that have leached their way through the clay. Here's how to make them disappear:

★ As soon as you notice the beginnings of any white spots, pour some vinegar on a rag and wipe them away.

★ For really stubborn mineral buildup, wet the white spots with vinegar, wait about 15 minutes for it to loosen the gunk, and scrub it away with a stiff brush.

★ The best way to get clay pots super-clean is to soak them overnight in a solution of 1 part vinegar to 5 parts water. Then scrub the crud off.

The green scene. Algae and moss can make themselves right at home on clay or concrete pots that are sitting in the shade. Some gardeners like the lived-in look, but if you'd rather make the green stuff disappear, mix up a solution of 1 part bleach to 10 parts water, add a squirt of dishwashing liquid, and scrub it away. Wear old clothes, safety glasses, and rubber gloves to protect against any bleach splashes. And remember—

Hocus Pocus

WHOLESALE OPERATION

If you have several large, empty flowerpots to clean, take them to a coin-operated car wash and do them all at once. Set the dial to the soap cycle, and pressure-wash the pots. The strong blast of soapy water will cut right through a season's worth of grime. And rinsing is just as quick: Just turn the dial to "rinse," and wash the suds down the drain. This is a great trick to use at the end of the season, when you're getting ready to put the pots away until next year.

unless you move that pot to a sunnier spot, the "greenery" will eventually grow right back.

Buff up the brass. Here's a quick trick to make brass flowerpots nice and shiny—just microwave a large onion until it's soft, and rub it over the surface of the pot. The mild acid in the onion will cut through the dulling tarnish without harming the metal. Wash away the onion smell with a soapy sponge, rinse the pot, and buff it dry with a soft, clean cloth. For more classy brassy tricks, see the Brass and Bronze entry on page 36.

Easy-care pots. Plastic, fiberglass, and glazed ceramic containers are the easiest pots of all to keep clean because their nonporous surfaces don't let any staining minerals soak through. That's why keeping them clean is a snap—just wash the pot with a soapy sponge inside and out, and all traces of the previous plant will be gone. And if outdoor plastic or glazed pots get splashed with mud or dirt, wipe them down with a wet sponge and rinse with a garden hose. Now that's what I call easy-peasy!

Food Processors

Divide and conquer. You've obviously got to take your food processor apart to clean the bowl, the blades, and any other removable parts. Once that's done, wash the pieces in warm, soapy water, or stick 'em in the top rack of your dishwasher. Wipe down the rest of the machine with a soapy sponge to remove any splashes or lingering bits of food. And be careful when you handle the business end of your processor—those blades are mighty sharp!

Tomato stains. Juicy tomatoes and other fruits and vegetables can leave their mark on a food processor. So when spills or splashes leave ugly stains behind, make a paste of baking soda and a little warm water, and rub them away in a flash.

The Great Clean-dini Speaks

Q. Sometimes I use my food processor like a blender and don't use the feeder tube. But the cleanup is still a chore. Do you know any shortcuts?

A. Sure do! Here's a neat trick that'll keep your food processor lid squeaky clean when you use the machine without the feeder tube. Before you put the lid on, cover the filled bowl with a sheet of plastic wrap, making sure it hangs over the sides a bit. Then screw the lid on right over the wrap. After you've finished processing, unscrew the lid and set it aside, gather up the dirty plastic wrap, and toss it in the trash. This is a time-saver you can wrap your mind around!

Spray the shaft. Sticky dough and other gooey foods can make a mess of the main part of a food processor—the center shaft that keeps the blades whirling. So keep your cleanup to a minimum by giving the shaft a spritz of nonstick cooking spray before you start mixing, and those sticky foods will slide right off. A quick swipe with a soapy sponge is a whole lot easier than scrubbing off gunked-on food.

Solve the smell problem. Does your food processor bowl still smell like the garlic or onions you chopped last week? If so, then use baking soda to make those pungent odors disappear. Here's the simple solution: Fill the food processor bowl with a mix of 1 part baking soda to 1 part water, and let it sit for at least half an hour. Or do this just before you go to bed, and let it sit overnight. Give it a good rinse with hot water in the morning, and you'll find that those lingering odors have vanished into thin air.

Furniture (See also Antique Furniture; Upholstery)

Cleaning upholstered furniture. Dust accumulates on your upholstered furniture as fast as it does on that coffee table you dusted—was that just yesterday?! If you vacuum the dirt away about once a week, your upholstery will live a longer, happier, and cleaner life. The allergy sufferers in your household will be sniffling less, too. Use the upholstery-brush attachment to clean the big surfaces, and switch to the crevice tool to clean around the seams and armrests. And don't forget to collect the spare change before you vacuum underneath the cushions!

Down dilemma. A vacuum cleaner can suck fine particles of feathers right out of the fabric of down cushions, so use a soft brush if your seats are stuffed with down. Stroke the fabric first in one direction and then in the other, and don't forget to give dust the brush-off from the bottom of the cushions, too.

Doggone it! If your dog loves lying on the couch, your upholstered furniture will eventually smell just like he does. Deodorizing sprays don't work for long, so use this nifty trick to soak up that funky smell. Simply sprinkle the couch with baking soda and let it sit overnight (Fido will have to snooze elsewhere in the meantime!). It'll absorb the doggy aroma like magic, and your sofa will smell fresh and clean when you vacuum the baking soda away.

HOCUS POCUS

HANDLE WITH CARE!

Mineral spirits (see Waxy buildup on page 146) are poisonous and flammable, and the vapor can be harmful if inhaled. So read the label and follow all the cautions *to the letter*. Wear protective clothing and gloves, and work in a well-ventilated area. And never put the mineral spirits or your cleaning cloth near a flame—not even a pilot light!

Stop oily soil. Skin and hair are full of body oils that rub off on upholstered furniture, leaving a greasy residue that attracts dirt like a magnet. So if this is a problem in your house, dig out those old doilies or other removable covers and use them, especially on the armrests. And toss a throw over the back of the sofa to keep hair and grease away from your upholstery.

Easy dusting does it. Don't be tempted to polish your wood furniture frequently because waxes or sprays can leave a cloudy buildup. Instead, stick to frequent dusting to keep that wood looking good. Use a dry microfiber cleaning cloth or a chamois, which will glide over the surface without leaving lint or scratches behind. If the wood piece has carved or raised decorations, use a synthetic or lamb's wool duster to really get in the groove.

Poly polish. A lot of today's wood furniture is coated with a clear polyurethane finish, which protects the wood and provides a long-lasting finish—so you may not need to polish it at all. Regular dusting will usually do the trick. For stubborn dirt, just wipe the piece off with a damp cloth or sponge, and then dry it with a soft, clean cloth. And don't worry—the moisture won't sink in past the poly finish as it would on an unlacquered table.

Waxy buildup. When wood furniture looks dull, give it a vigorous buffing to remove the waxy buildup. If that doesn't do the trick, strip the wax by rubbing the wood with a bit of mineral spirits on a dry cloth (see Handle with Care! on page 145). Once the old buildup is stripped away, let the piece dry for several hours before you apply a new coat of wax. On older furniture, test the finish first—this trick could damage the lacquer. Simply dip a cotton swab into some mineral spirits, apply to an inconspicuous place, and wait a few minutes to see if the finish gets sticky or softens. If it does, don't go any further!

Wax or oil? If your wood furniture isn't coated with a clear protective finish, you'll need to polish it about once a month to maintain the gentle shine—or wax it about twice a year. Oil-based sprays are quick and easy and require less buffing than waxes, but waxes do a better job of protecting the wood. Whichever kind you use, wipe it on the wood in the direction of the grain, and then buff the polish off with a soft, clean cloth to leave a gleaming finish. And be sparing with furniture polish because a little goes a long way.

Greasy kid stuff. Furniture polish sprays are so easy to use and smell so good that it's mighty tempting to use them often. But they'll eventually build up until the wood feels greasy to the touch and every fingerprint will show quite clearly. To get rid of the extra oil, sprinkle a little cornstarch over the surface, let it sit for at least an hour, and then wipe it away with a soft, clean cloth.

Powerful Potions

Teak Oil Finish

Help teak furniture keep shedding water and bring out its natural, gentle sheen by wiping it down with my homemade potion, which works just as well as the store-bought stuff, and it costs a whole lot less, too! Be sure to wear rubber gloves and work in a well-ventilated area; the noxious turpentine fumes can irritate your nose. And don't mix the stuff or work with it near a fire or a burning cigarette because these oils are highly flammable.

1 part turpentine
1 part linseed oil

Pour both ingredients into a glass jar with a screw-on lid, and shake it well to blend. Put some of the potion on a dry cloth, and wipe the wood in the direction of the grain. Let it sit for at least an hour or more, so the wood can absorb the oil before you use the furniture.

Stained wood. When a stain soaks into wood furniture, dampen a cloth with mineral spirits (see Handle with Care! on page 145) and rub the area gently with the grain. If that doesn't help, switch to a dry steel wool soap pad or extra-fine steel wool (0000 grade), and rub until the stain disappears. Wipe the area clean with a dry cloth, and wax or polish the wood to make it blend into the rest of the surface.

Alcohol anonymous. Keep alcohol-based products away from all wood furniture because they can soften or dissolve the finish. And it's not just that evening cocktail that can cause problems—cough medicine, cologne, and perfume can damage the shine, too. So if alcohol spills on a wooden piece, rub the spot with a cloth dampened with ammonia to counteract the effect. If the spill has already soaked in, make a paste of baking soda and mineral oil, and rub it in with the grain. Wipe away any residue, and buff the piece with linseed or lemon oil to make the mark blend in.

Grandma Putt's Magical Methods

Whenever a scratch showed up on my Grandma Putt's favorite wooden sewing table, she mixed up a little "salad dressing" to make it vanish. All it takes is about 1 teaspoon of fresh lemon juice mixed with 1 teaspoon of vegetable oil to get rid of unsightly scratches. Dip a soft cloth into the mixture, rub the scratch, and it'll simply disappear! For deeper scratches, my Grandma had another great trick—she rubbed the nut meat of a black walnut or pecan into the scratch and let the "juice" sit for about half an hour to darken the wood. When she polished the table, the scratch was darn near invisible.

Grease stains. Wood furniture that's not coated with polyurethane or another tough top coat can absorb grease, leaving a nasty stain behind. It's not easy to remove the mark because the oil penetrates the wood fibers. So try this: Place a folded paper towel over the spot and iron it gently to draw out

Q. There's an ugly white ring on my end table where I had a vase of flowers. How can I make it disappear?

A. When water soaks into wood, first try removing the white marks by letting oil soak in. What kind of oil? Mayonnaise! Just spread some mayo over the stain, let it sit for about an hour, and then wipe it off with a soft, clean cloth. If the white spot reappears, try one of these quick fixes to rub out that stain:

★ Rub the spot with a bit of non-gel toothpaste on a damp cloth.

★ Dab a moist cloth into a mixture of 1 tablespoon of baking soda and 1 tablespoon of white non-gel toothpaste, and rub the stain in circles for about five minutes.

★ Mix table salt and olive oil, and rub until the stain is gone.

★ Sprinkle some wood ash from your fireplace on the stain, add a few drops of vegetable oil, and rub the white spot away.

After trying any of these treatments, wipe off the residue, and polish the table as usual.

the grease. Then dust the piece with talcum powder or cornstarch, and let it sit overnight to soak up still more. If you can still see a spot, use extra-fine sandpaper (0000 grade) to get down to fresh wood, and then rub in some furniture wax or polish to make the area match the rest of the surface and give the piece a nice shine.

Scratch hiders. To camouflage a scratch that exposes lighter wood, simply color it in with a brown crayon. You can also buy scratch sticks in all shades of wood finishes for a more exact color match, or reach for the iodine. That's right, dab it on—it's a great match for reddish mahogany.

Garbage Disposals

No shortcuts, please! Bad smells are the bane of garbage disposals, but it only takes a few seconds to keep the odors from building up. Instead of switching the disposal off as soon as you hear that high-pitched whine, let the water and disposal run for an additional 30 seconds. This trick will wash away the food residue that's splashed on the insides of the disposal and drainpipe, so it doesn't build up and start to decompose.

Cold water only. Always use cold water to wash garbage down a disposal. Hot water will melt the fats in the food, leaving a layer of grease in the pipes that can soon turn rancid and start to smell. If you chill out, you'll keep your garbage disposal from smelling bad.

Citrus clean. You can freshen up your kitchen by grinding a handful of citrus peels in your garbage disposal. Use whatever you happen to have on hand—lemons, oranges, grapefruits, limes, or what have you. They all have citrus oil in their skins that will cut any grease in the disposal, while lending a nice clean scent to the surrounding area.

Hocus Pocus

KITCHEN VOLCANO

You can keep your drain running freely by fizzing away any old food residue with this magic trick. Pour ½ cup of baking soda down the drain, and follow it up with 1 cup of white vinegar (don't run the disposal). You'll hear a lot of action as the chemicals react with each other, fizzing the crud away. Follow it up by carefully pouring about 2 quarts of boiling water down the drain, and finish the job by letting the hot water run for at least 30 seconds. Getting out the grunge about once a week is all you need to keep odors from erupting into a full-blown mess.

Powerful Potions

Garbage Disposal Scrub

Hard items like peach pits and bones are obviously big no-no's in the disposal, but ice cubes are just the ticket for scrubbing down a sour one. With this potion, the blades fling the chunks against the drainpipe, where they help free up the gunk in the disposal, while the vinegar washes the stinky bacteria down the drain.

2 cups of ice cubes

1 cup of white or cider vinegar

With the garbage disposal turned off, put the ice cubes in the drain and pour in the vinegar. Turn on the cold water, and run the disposal. Keep it going for at least 30 seconds after the clunking, thunking, and growling noise changes to a steady, high-pitched whine. Just don't try this trick when company's coming because it'll take an hour or two for the sharp smell of vinegar to disappear.

Fend off fibers. Don't use your disposal to grind up any garbage that's full of stringy fibers. Toss those corn husks, pea pods, string beans, celery, and artichoke leaves onto your compost pile instead, so that the fibers don't tangle up the blades. If you've already sent the stuff down the drain and the blades have ground to a halt, turn off the circuit breaker to make sure you stay safe, and pull out as much of the stuff as you can with a pair of pliers (not your hands!). Then try my "Soapy flush" tip below to unclog the rest of that stringy mess.

Soapy flush. If foul odors have started to seep out of your disposal, then send a sink full of soapy water down there to flush out any rotting slurry that's lingering in the pipes. Simply fill your sink about two-thirds of the way up with hot, soapy water, unplug the stopper, and switch on the disposal. The whirlpool of water will drive those smells right down the drain. Follow up by rinsing everything with cold water.

Lemon soda. For a fast and easy drain deodorizer and degreaser, drop half of a fresh-cut lemon in your disposal, followed by $1/2$ cup of baking soda. Run it through, and your whole kitchen will smell fresh and clean. Or you can fill your sink with a few inches of warm water and add 1 cup of baking soda to it, flushing it through while the garbage disposal is turned on. Run plenty of cold water through afterward to flood the crud out of there.

Under cover. The rubber cover that keeps food from splattering all over when the disposal is working can get mighty slimy. So get rid of the goo in a hurry by scrubbing with an old toothbrush dipped in hot, soapy water. The job is easy if you remove the cover, but if yours is permanently attached, lift the flaps to scrub the undersides. And make sure no one is anywhere near the switch while you're doing the job!

Garden Fountains and Ponds

Pump primer. Debris can keep a garden fountain pump from putting forth its best effort, so be sure to clean it in the spring—and every now and then throughout the season. Lift the pump out of the water and wipe the grime off the outside casing with a clean cloth. Then open the lid or back of the pump and wipe out the inside, too. If need be, use an old toothbrush to reach into the tight spaces. Finish by rinsing the filter screen, and you'll have a leg up on keeping the water clean.

Pure water. Water from a garden hose can be full of minerals that'll leave nasty deposits in a fountain. Hard-water buildup can even clog the pump, just like it does an indoor showerhead. So whenever you fill a fountain, use distilled water. And keep a couple of jugs handy to replenish the water supply whenever the fountain needs topping off.

Put fish on a diet. Overfeeding fish will leave lots of troublemaking nutri-ents in the water, and that'll mean more algae to deal with. So keep fish food to a minimum, and let any finny friends fend for themselves—they'll find plenty to munch on in the bottom of the pond.

Anti-algae clay. If you have fish in your pond, try adding a natural clay to the water to nourish the good bacteria that help keep the water clean. It's called calcium bentonite/montmorillonite clay, and you'll find it at stores that sell pond supplies. The clay produces cleaner water and makes for happier fish—it's loaded with minerals they need for good digestion.

The Great Clean-dini Speaks

Q. My big fountain looks great—except when it gets all scummy. It seems that no matter how often I scrub it, the algae keeps coming back. What can I do to make the slimy stuff vanish forever?

A. Unfortunately, even a thorough scrubbing won't hold algae at bay forever. If your fountain keeps getting slimed up, try one of these nifty tricks to prevent the crud from making itself at home:

★ Add a nontoxic product like all-natural CareFree Enzymes™ to the water. It won't harm birds, kids, or fish, and it'll keep the water clean for a long time.

★ Add ¼ cup of lemon juice or white vinegar to the water to inhibit the growth of the green slime. Or use ¼ cup of Listerine® instead—in whatever flavor tickles your fancy! They're all totally safe for birds and people.

★ Copper stops algae from growing, so empty your jar of copper pennies into the bottom of your fountain. And don't forget to make a wish—for no more algae—FOREVER!

Fountain scrub. Sometimes there's just no avoiding a full-scale scrubbing when algae or hard-water buildup gets out of hand. Luckily, the same trick works great for solving both problems at once. First, check your owner's manual to make sure my magic ingredient—white vinegar—won't harm the fountain. Then follow these easy steps to make it sparkling clean again:

1. Drain the water by either pulling the plug or using a wet/dry vac to empty it out.

2. Remove any stones that are in the basin, and soak them in a bucket filled with ½ cup of chlorine bleach and water.

3. Tackle tough mineral buildup in the basin by covering the spots with a rag saturated with white vinegar. Let it sit for about half an hour on each problem area.

4. After soaking the stones, scrub them with a stiff brush (don't forget to wear protective clothing to guard against bleach splashes!). Then rinse them with a garden hose and set them aside.

5. Dip an old scrub brush into white vinegar, and rub away any mineral deposits and algae in the basin. Use an old toothbrush to get into the cracks and crevices.

6. Rinse the basin thoroughly with a garden hose, refill it, replace the clean stones, plug the pump back in, and enjoy!

Pool tool. A long-handled skimmer is your best bet for regular pond-cleaning chores. Use a swimming pool skimmer, or buy one that's specially made for ponds, and scoop all of the leaves and debris out at least once a month before they decay or clog  up the pump and filter. If you get tired of hand labor, check out a pond vacuum cleaner, which does a great job of sucking up that smelly sludge from the bottom.

Glasses and Sunglasses

Breathe deeply. Even dust particles can scratch your glasses, so never wipe them when the lenses are dry. Just breathe deeply and "huff" on each lens to add some moisture before you wipe it with a cleaning cloth. This trick works great on glass lenses, but you'll need more than mere water to remove smudges from many of today's modern materials. So give them a spritz of my Lens Cleaner (below).

In a fog. Use a dab of shaving cream to keep your glasses from fogging up in cold weather. Just squirt a bit on the clean lenses, rub it over the surface on both sides, and wipe the lenses dry. It'll work like magic to keep your glasses from steaming up when you come in from the cold.

Soften up. No matter how soft they feel, facial tissues and paper towels can scratch your lenses—and your shirttail is even worse! Even a soft cotton T-shirt can turn your precious lenses into Scratch City. So don't take any chances with your glasses: Get in the habit of carrying a microfiber lens cloth with you at all times. You can buy the cloths at a discount store or pharmacy, or ask your optician for some extras—you may even get them for free!

Lens Cleaner

Modern lenses need more than water to leave them crystal clear and smudge-free. So skip the old-fashioned spit polish, and use my magic potion instead. It works just as well as commercial lens cleaners, and it costs a lot less, too. Plus, you can use it on sunglasses!

1 part rubbing alcohol
1 part water

Combine the alcohol and water in a small sprayer bottle, spritz a little on both sides of the lenses, and wipe them dry with a lens-cleaning cloth. That's all there is to it.

Q. My metal glass frames are greenish around the bottoms, where they touch my skin. I clean the frames regularly, but the green keeps coming back. Help!

A. Your skin's natural oils and perspiration can discolor metal frames, so if your glasses are resting against your face, stop in at your optician and have them adjusted. It's simple to move the nose pads, and a pro has the tools and know-how to do it without damaging the frames.

Clean the cloth. Using a dirty cleaning cloth is just as bad for your glasses as using your shirtsleeve to polish them. So keep a supply of cloths on hand, and replace your current one at least once a week. Toss the dirty cloths into the laundry to get the dirt out, but don't use fabric softener or a dryer sheet because each can leave an oily residue behind.

No more nasty nose pads. When greasy dirt builds up in those nooks and crannies around the nose pads of your glasses, start the cleanup by dunking them in warm, soapy water to soften the crud. Then scrub the gunk out from around the pads with a very soft toothbrush. If your lenses are made out of plastic or have special coatings, use a cotton swab instead because even a soft brush can leave scratches. And if there's any stubborn gunk left in the tight corners, carefully remove it with a toothpick.

Sink solution. You can bring a shine back to your mirrored sunglasses by cleaning them under running water with a drop or two of dishwashing liquid. Just swish it around on the lenses with your fingers, rinse it off, and dry your sunglasses with a microfiber cloth. Now that's what I call made for the shades!

Glassware

Rinse with shine. Want your glass to really sparkle? Then add white vinegar to the rinse! If you're washing by hand, add a capful to a sink full of clean water; for dishwashers, pour 1/4 cup into the rinse cycle. White vinegar counteracts the film that hard water can leave behind, and your glassware will be squeaky clean with no streaks or spots.

Hand wash your good glass. Dishwashers are quick and easy, but they can etch and even dull your lead crystal or gold- and silver-rimmed glass. So when you need to clean the good stuff, do it by hand—unless you're a real butterfingers. Start by padding the sink with a rubber mat, and lay a bath towel over the front edge. Move the faucet out of the way, too, so you don't accidentally whack the Waterford. Then wash each piece in warm, soapy water and rinse with the sink sprayer.

Take off the jewelry. How do you tell if a diamond is real or not? You guessed it—that rock'll cut glass! So always remember to slip your fancy ring off before you wash your glassware. And remove your other rings and bracelets, and your watch, too, because even if they're not diamond encrusted, they can still scratch the glass.

Grandma Putt's Magical Methods

Hard water takes a toll on glassware because the minerals leave dull spots or streaks on the surface. When my Grandma Putt's good glassware got dull, she brought it back to life by soaking the pieces overnight in a bowl of vinegar. If that wasn't enough to restore the shine, she polished them—with toothpaste! That's right; simply squeeze some white non-gel toothpaste onto a moist cloth, and rub the glass inside and out. Cheap toothpaste from one of those stores where everything costs just a dollar works wonders!

CRYSTAL CHANDELIERS

Hocus Pocus

When dust and greasy grime dull a crystal chandelier, use this trick to make it sparkle—without taking it down. First, mix 1 part rubbing alcohol and 3 parts water in a handheld sprayer bottle. Lay a couple of towels under the chandelier in case any crystal falls during the job. Then put your ladder in place and pull on a pair of clean white cotton gloves.

Spray one glove with the solution, and wipe that gloved hand over every piece of crystal until the whole thing is bright and clean. If you've neglected the job for a while, detach the crystals, hand wash them in warm, soapy water, and dry each one with a soft cloth. And wear cotton gloves when you rehang the crystals, so your fingerprints don't leave smudges.

Stemware safety. What will they think of next? Now there are special dishwasher racks that'll hold delicate stemware in place so that it doesn't get bumped and broken. If you're tired of washing your wineglasses by hand, pick up one of these handy helpers at a cooking-supply store. They cost about $15, but the amount of time they save is priceless!

De-stain decanters. With that wide base and narrow neck, decanters are doggone hard to clean. You can buy bendable foam brushes to reach down in there and swab out the bottle, or you can try one of my easy hands-off tricks instead:

★ Pour 1 cup of white vinegar or ammonia into the decanter, fill it with water, and let it soak overnight.

★ Pour 1 cup of rice into the bottle, add just enough water to cover it, and shake and swirl the decanter until the residue falls off.

★ Fill the decanter with enough hot water to cover the stained areas, and drop in two denture-cleaning tablets. Let it soak overnight, and you'll be good to go.

Speedy stemware. Bartenders have plenty of tricks up their sleeves, and here's one that will make cleaning up after a dinner party go a lot faster. Start by filling your sink with hot, soapy water. If you have a double sink, fill the other side with hot, clear water; if not, then fill a large bowl with hot water. Grasp each wineglass by the stem, hold it upside down, and quickly pump it up and down several times in the soapy water. Rinse the glass by dunking it in the clear water, and set it aside to dry on a dish towel. Pump, rinse, and you'll be done in a flash!

Down with dull. Dishwashing detergent or old age can cause the surface of lead crystal to look dull, but here's how to get rid of that cloudy look. Fill your sink with warm water, a squirt of dishwashing liquid, and about 1 tablespoon of ammonia. Let the crystal soak for about 30 minutes, wash with a soft cloth, and rinse thoroughly. Or you can drop three or four denture-cleaning tablets into a sink full of warm water, and soak the cloudy crystal overnight. That'll clear things up for sure.

Gloves

Washing gloves. Just like other items of clothing, gloves have a care label inside of them, so check it first to see if yours need special treatment. If they are machine washable, then launder them in a mesh lingerie bag so they don't get stretched out of shape—or lose their mate in the washing process.

Dry scrub for suede. Suede doesn't take too kindly to water, so start with a bath towel rub—it'll remove a lot of the surface dirt. Rub any stains with an art gum eraser or a bit of white vinegar on a damp cloth (don't worry, the smell will fade). Pay extra attention to the fingertips and seams because that's where grime tends to collect. Finally, use a small soft brush or a special suede brush to whisk away any remaining dirt and restore the velvety nap.

Spot-clean stains. Spot removal may be all your fine leather gloves need to spiff them up. So before you subject them to a full-scale cleaning, use a spray-on commercial leather cleaner to spot-clean them. Or try one of these nifty tricks:

★ Rub any dirty spots on light-colored leather gloves with a pencil eraser—the crud will come right off.

★ For most grease stains, spray the spots with hair spray, blot the area, then wipe the mess away.

★ Stubborn grease spots need special treatment: Apply a little rubber cement (no kidding!) to the stains, let it dry, and rub the stuff until the spots are gone.

Soap up dressy leather. If the general grime on your leather gloves has gone beyond the spot-cleaning stage, rub in some saddle soap while you're wearing the gloves, following the directions on the package. Then sponge the suds off and work in a dab of neat's-foot oil to restore the leather's suppleness and gloss. Finally, remove the gloves by holding the finger-tips while you pull out your hands, and let the gloves air-dry flat. Slip your hand inside each one periodically while it's drying to gently stretch the damp leather, which will shrink as it dries.

GRIME BUSTER

Foam car seat cleaner works wonders to remove stubborn grime from tough leather work gloves. The next time you're at the auto parts store, pick up a can of cleaner that's made for leather seats (not vinyl or cloth), and follow the directions on the label.

Wear-and-wash garden gloves. Now here's a neat trick—clean your garden gloves while you are still wearing them. Just lather them up with soap and water after you finish working, and scrub 'em together to get rid of the grime. Rinse them under running water, strip them off, roll them in a towel, and give them a squeeze to soak up the water. If the gloves are leather or suede, lay them flat to dry; if they're cloth, just clip them to your clothesline. They'll be stiff as a board when they're dry, but don't worry—they'll soften up as soon as you start digging in to the next round of garden work!

Q. My daughter is a soccer goalie, and her gloves get filthy—they're full of mud and dirt inside and out, plus, they just plain stink! How can I get them clean?

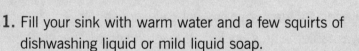

The Great Clean-dini Speaks

A. If you could read the care label through all of the crud, you'd discover that most goalkeepers' gloves aren't machine washable. But it's easy enough to wash them by hand. Here's how to do it:

1. Fill your sink with warm water and a few squirts of dishwashing liquid or mild liquid soap.

2. Soak the gloves in the soapy water for about 30 minutes.

3. Turn the gloves inside out and let them soak in the same water for another 30 minutes.

4. Empty the grungy water and refill the sink with clean water and another couple squirts of soap. Add 1 cup of baking soda to the soapy water to help reduce any lingering smell.

5. Scrub the inside of the gloves with an old toothbrush. Then turn them right side out and scrub some more.

6. Rinse each glove thoroughly, inside and out, and hang the pair up to dry.

Glue Stains

Which glue is which? Glues are obviously made to stick, but some stick better than others. So treating glue stains promptly is vital. Your first step is to determine what kind of glue you've got. Check the label, find the right trick below, and above all else—work fast!

Don't mess with epoxy. Whether you use the two-step or ready-mix kind, this incredibly strong glue forms a permanent bond that even magic can't break. So be extra careful whenever you use epoxy. Always wear old clothes, cover nearby surfaces to guard against drips, and wipe up spills *immediately* before the glue has a chance to set.

Powerful Potions

Wet Spotter

Keep this mixture on hand for whenever you get clear household glue on finicky, but washable, fabrics, including rayon, acetate, triacetate, fiberglass, wool, and silk. And if the label says "dry-clean only," let a pro deal with the stain.

- 1 part glycerin
- 1 part dishwashing liquid
- 1 tsp. of white vinegar
- 8 parts water

Mix the ingredients in a plastic squeeze bottle, and shake it well before you use this cleaner. To remove glue stains from those special fabrics, squeeze the potion onto a cloth and sponge the fabric, working outward from the center of the spot. If any glue remains, cover the stain with a paper towel that's saturated with the potion, let it sit for about 15 minutes, and sponge the remains away. Then rinse with clean water, and launder the item with an enzyme detergent.

The Great Clean-dini Speaks

Q. I managed to "decorate" my jeans with the hot glue I was using for a project. Is there an easy way to get it off?

A. When hot glue ends up on your clothes instead of on crafts, there's no need to come unglued. Just pull this magic trick out of your hat:

1. Cut a piece of aluminum foil about the size of a paper towel and set it on your ironing board.

2. Cover the foil with a paper towel.

3. Set the glue stain over the paper towel with the right side of the fabric—where the glue is—against the paper and the wrong side facing up.

4. Run a hot iron back and forth over the stain, so the glue will leave the fabric and transfer onto the paper towel.

5. Quickly lift off the once-gluey clothing before the glue has a chance to reset. That's all there's to it!

Remove residue. To get rid of the gunk that's left behind after you peel off adhesive tape, start by gently scraping away as much of it as you can. Then moisten a paper towel with my Extra-Strength Dry Spotter potion on page 164, and wipe the rest of the adhesive away. Or you can rub the residue with an orange oil–based cleaner or dry hand cleaner.

Superglues be gone! When you accidentally glue your fingers together with Super Glue®, Krazy Glue®, or something similar, pour acetone-based nail polish remover onto your skin to unstick it. If the glue is on fabric, soak a cotton swab in nail polish remover, set it against the glue for 30 seconds, and then wipe off. You may need to repeat the trick, so use a fresh swab for each swipe. And always test the fabric first.

Powerful Potions

Extra-Strength Dry Spotter

Use this potion to remove really tough stains like household cement, cooking grease, and motor oil. *Note:* You can buy coconut oil at pharmacies and scientific-supply stores.

3 tbsp. of a liquid dry-cleaning solvent, like AFTA® Cleaning Solvent

1 tsp. of coconut oil

Wait until you're ready to use this potion before making it because the solvent evaporates quickly. And be careful—dry-cleaning solvents are poisonous and flammable, so make sure you have good ventilation well away from fire and flame. Mix the solvent with the coconut oil in a clean glass jar, dip in a dry cloth, and wipe the stain away. Use a small glass jar with an airtight lid to store any leftovers for future use.

Hold the (household) cement. This clear, water-resistant glue is sold under lots of brand names, including Loctite® and Elmer's ProBond®. Clean up spills on fabrics by scraping off the excess glue, and sponging the spot with my Extra-Strength Dry Spotter potion (above). But don't try this trick on rayon, silk, fiberglass, or wool—it'll damage the fabric. Instead, use my Wet Spotter potion on page 162.

Smooth moves. You may be able to scrape glue drips off vinyl, linoleum, glass, tile, or other hard surfaces with your fingernail or an old credit card. If that doesn't do the trick, scrub the spot with warm, soapy water, or use an old toothbrush and a little Bar Keepers Friend®. Still no luck? Then you'll need some amyl acetate, which is a solvent that's sometimes called banana oil because it smells just like a ripe bunch of you-know-what. Ask your pharmacist for it, or try a scientific-supply house. Mix a few drops of the amyl acetate into a bowl of warm, sudsy water, dip in a soft cloth, and wipe the glue away.

Gold

Soap-and-water soak. Twenty-four-carat gold is all gold and nothing but gold. Lesser carat numbers like 10K, 14K, and 18K have other metals mixed in, and that's why they react with hair spray, body oils, perfume, and even the air itself. So if your gold starts looking a little dull, give it a bath in warm, soapy water, and use an old toothbrush to gently scrub the film away and bring back the shine. Don't use abrasive cleaners because gold scratches easily.

Salt shaker solution. You can scrub the dull film off gold by shaking it in a mixture of salt and vinegar or lemon juice. Start by filling a small bottle about three-quarters of the way with table salt, and then slowly pour in white vinegar or lemon juice almost to the top. Drop in your gold pieces, and set the bottle aside. Give it a shake several times a day, so the salt can gently scrub off any discoloration. After a week of shaking things up, empty the bottle, and thoroughly rinse your nice clean family jewels.

Keep away from chlorine. Chlorine discolors gold, eventually turning it black. So always wear rubber gloves when you're working with chlorine bleach, powdered cleansers, or other products that contain chlorine. And don't forget to take off your gold jewelry before you jump into the pool!

Grandma Putt's Magical Methods

My Grandma Putt taught me this really simple way to clean precious gold pieces—it takes just a minute to make, and a minute to work its magic. Mix 1 part ammonia with 6 parts warm water in a small bowl that's deep enough to cover the gold. Set the gold in the solution and let it soak for 1 minute. Then remove the items, rinse them under cold running water, and dry them with a soft, clean cloth.

Joy in the morning. Bring a little joy to your gold-cleaning process by combining 1 part Joy® dishwashing liquid with 1 part ammonia and setting your jewelry in the mixture for a few minutes. It'll remove the dirt from the crevices as well as from the surface in a flash. When they're done soaking, rinse the pieces until there's not a soap bubble to be found.

24-carat smile. White toothpaste (not the gel kind) is a gentle gold cleaner. Just squeeze a bit onto a soft cloth or an old toothbrush, and gently rub the pieces until they shine. Rinse thoroughly, using the toothbrush to coax paste out of the crevices. And check for loose stones before you begin because you don't want any baubles going down the drain.

Grass Stains

Bad news, good news. Grass stains are one of the hardest stains to remove—just ask any mom! They're actually a dye that's left behind by the chlorophyll, which makes grass green. And unless you're careful, you can make them permanent with common cleaning products. Now for the good news—you're about to discover so many cleaning tricks that there's no way those green stains can hang around for long.

Thou shalt not. Mordants are materials that fix a dye so it doesn't wash out. That's great when you don't want the colors to run, but not so great for unwanted green on the knees. So keep ammonia and alkaline detergents and degreasers away from grass-stained clothes until every trace of the spot is gone—they'll act as mordants on the stain. Instead, use the acidic detergents and degreasers that follow.

Wash after treating. No matter which grass stain removal trick you try, always wash the item as soon as the treatment is done. Don't let it dry, or the stain could set back in. And don't wash a grass-stained item before you treat it, or that green may not disappear.

Sweet on vinegar. Acidic vinegar works great to remove dye stains, including those grass skid marks on jeans. So give one of these vinegar-based solutions a try:

★ If the stain is still fresh, sponge it off with undiluted white vinegar. This simple solution may be enough to make a surface stain vanish.

★ For a deeper grass stain, soak the spot in vinegar for up to two hours. If the item isn't colorfast, dilute the vinegar with an equal amount of water.

★ Is the stain still being stubborn? Then make a paste of baking soda and water and rub it into the stain. Slowly pour on some white vinegar and watch it bubble the stain into oblivion. Sponge off the residue, and repeat the treatment until the stain is gone.

Repeat if necessary. Because grass stains are so doggone ornery, you may need to repeat a trick to completely remove them. Check your garment after you wash it and before you dry it—if you can still see green, then treat the stains again. Whatever you do, don't put the clothing in the dryer until you're sure all of the green is gone.

Hocus Pocus

DIGESTION AID

Enzyme cleaners and bleaches work like magic on grass stains by digesting the proteins that keep the stain bonded to the clothes. To make your own DIY enzyme pretreater, buy some digestive enzyme capsules (like D-Enzymes™), and break two or three of them into a small bowl. Mix the powder with a bit of water until it's the consistency of toothpaste, spread it on the stains, and rub it in with an old toothbrush. Let the item sit for about an hour, and then launder as usual—using an enzyme detergent, of course!

Grandma Putt's Magical Methods

My Grandma Putt shaved a piece of Fels-Naptha® soap into every load of her laundry, but when she needed extra power to eliminate stains, she'd rub the bar right on the cloth like a stain stick. Fels-Naptha worked like magic on grass stains, chocolate stains, and all kinds of other spots—we even scrubbed it onto our skin to prevent poison ivy! To put this old-fashioned helper to work on your grass stains, wet the stained fabric and vigorously rub the soap into the spot before you launder the item as usual. Look for Fels-Naptha in the laundry section of your supermarket.

Rub in alcohol. Pour some rubbing alcohol onto the grass stain, and let it soak for about an hour. Then rub the wet spot with a sponge that's been dampened with more rubbing alcohol, using a circular motion to lift the dye out of the fibers. Next, rub in some liquid detergent with color-safe bleach, and wash the item as you usually would. Just don't use this trick on silk, rayon, or wool garments because they might be damaged by the alcohol.

Sugar rush. Here's a really sweet trick for getting rid of grass stains—pour a dollop of molasses or Karo® syrup directly on the stains, rub it in with your fingers, and let it sit for about 15 minutes. Then wash the item as usual. This trick is tailor-made only for darker clothes because the sweet syrup might discolor whites.

Say "goo-goo." Here's another way to mow down grass stains—rub a glob of Goop® or a spritz of Goo Gone® into the stains, and wait 15 minutes. If the fabric is sturdy (like denim), scratch the stains with your fingernail or a nickel to help pull out the dye. Then launder the item as usual.

Yes, we have no bananas! Banana oil gets its name from its aroma, not because it comes from bananas. Its proper name is amyl acetate, and you can find it at most pharmacies. Apply a liberal amount to a grass stain and rub it in with an old toothbrush until the stain disappears.

Look, Ma, no grass stains! Get good news at checkup time by using non-gel toothpaste to scrub away stubborn grass stains. Simply wet the fabric, squeeze some paste onto an old toothbrush, and scrub it into the stains. Wait about half an hour, make sure the stains are gone, and then launder as usual. This is one checkup that you'll look forward to!

Milk soak. Before you wash a pair of grass-stained jeans for the first time, soak the spots in a small bowl of whole milk for about 15 minutes. Scrub it with an old toothbrush, and let it soak for another 15 minutes. Launder as usual and you're all set (but the stains won't be).

Dry spotter. To remove grass stains from water-sensitive fabrics like rayon, silk, acetate, triacetate, and wool, use my Extra-Strength Dry Spotter potion on page 164. Sponge it on the stains and cover the wet spots with a cloth that's been dampened with more of the potion. Blot the cloth against the stains, and fold it to a clean side as it picks up the green. When no more green comes off, wash the item in cold water, and you're done.

The Great Clean-dini Speaks

Q. I've tried stain-treater sprays and sticks to get grass stains out of my son's blue jeans, but there's still a visible spot of green. I don't want to use bleach because I'm afraid it'll take the color out and make it look even worse. Is there any hope?

A. If you've tried everything else and those stains still won't budge, sprinkle them with powdered Cascade® dishwasher detergent and rub it in vigorously. Let it sit for 30 minutes and then scrub the spots—with an ice cube! When the ice cube has melted down to nothing, wash the item in cold water, and the stains should melt away, too.

Grease Stains

Dish soap prewash. Before you put any grease-stained clothes into your washing machine, squirt some grease-cutting dishwashing liquid on the stains as a pretreatment. Rub it in with your fingers, and let it sit for at least 10 minutes. Then it's into the washer and out with the stain!

Soapy soda. Most grease stains on washable fabrics will come right out if you scrub them with a paste made of dishwashing liquid and baking soda. Use an old toothbrush to work the mixture into the fabric, wait about 10 minutes, and then wash the item as you usually do.

Slice through with shampoo. Shampoo for oily hair cuts grease on fabric just as it does on your tresses. To make oil or butter stains disappear, rub a dab of shampoo into the spot before you wash the item. There's no need to let it set for a while—the shampoo will do its stuff during the wash cycle. Just use a shampoo that doesn't contain a conditioner, which can leave oily residue behind.

Grandma Putt's Magical Methods

How'd those grease spots end up on your wallpaper? Who cares, when you can make them vanish with this easy fix, courtesy of my Grandma Putt? Whenever she wanted to clean up wallpaper, she'd make a paste of cornstarch and a little water, spread it over the stain, and let it dry. Then she'd brush off the powder and check the spot—if she could still see it, she'd repeat the treatment until it was gone, baby, gone!

Gee whiz, Cheez Whiz®? Strange as it may sound, a squeeze of that orange stuff works wonders at lifting out tough grease stains like the black marks your bicycle chain left on your pants cuff. Just smear the cheese generously on the grease mark, and then throw the item into the washing machine.

Q. My family has a lot of allergies to cleaning products, so I'm trying to go "green." Do you have any all-natural tricks for getting rid of tough grease stains?

A. Check this out: There's nothing greener than an aloe vera plant—the one that's sitting on your kitchen windowsill to soothe accidental burns. And it works great as a grease remover, too! Just wet the fabric, break off a piece of aloe vera, and rub the broken end against the grease stain. Rub the juice in with your fingertips, rinse, and the stain will be history. If you don't happen to have a plant on your kitchen windowsill, a bottle of aloe vera gel will work just as well.

The Great Clean-dini Speaks

Soda pop solution. Here's another unusual grease cutter from the fridge—Coca-Cola®. Saturate oily stains with the soda pop, let the item sit for about 10 minutes, and then wash it as usual. For extra power, you can even add a 2-liter bottle of Coke to the wash cycle. And best of all, this trick works wonders on those old set-in stains that have already gone through the laundry several times.

Spray it away. Try a spritz of hair spray to make your next grease stain vanish. Just spray the spot until it's thoroughly soaked and wash the item as usual. Hair spray works on ballpoint pen and marker stains, too, so keep an extra can handy in your laundry room.

The power to dissolve. If you've already sent that grease stain through the washer and dryer a few times, turn to Dawn® Power Dissolver® to treat a stubborn set-in stain. This mighty foam is made for breaking up greasy crud from cooking, but it works like magic on grease-stained (or greasy) work clothes, too. Just spray the spot with the cleaner, wait about 10 minutes, and launder the item as usual.

Grandma Putt's Magical Methods

Whether it was cleaning a cruddy kitchen floor or scrubbing greasy work clothes, my Grandma Putt relied on the same hardworking helper for all of her toughest jobs—Lestoil®. To take out grease stains, she simply poured some heavy-duty, full-strength Lestoil directly onto the spots and rubbed the fabric vigorously to work it in. And as an extra precaution, she'd rinse the spots under running water and pour on another dose of Lestoil before the stained item went into her washing machine. You'll find this old standby in the floor-cleaning products aisle (not the laundry aisle) of your local supermarket.

Grease be-gone. To remove a really old grease stain, give it a spritz of WD-40®, and let it sit for about 20 minutes. Then squirt some grease-cutting dishwashing liquid onto the spot, and rub it in well to dissolve the grease and the WD-40. Rinse the spot thoroughly, and give it another squirt of dishwashing liquid before you launder the item as usual. But be prepared: WD-40 is pretty strong-smelling stuff, so use it outside or in a well-ventilated room.

Lighter fluid. Solvents dissolve grease stains, and lighter fluid is an easy way to put that power to use—but use it on whites only, since it can take the color out of fabrics. Sprinkle a little fluid on the grease spot, let it sit for a few minutes, and then rub the fabric together to work it in deeper before you launder the item as usual. And always, always, always work in a well-ventilated area, and never around a fire or flame!

The power of powder. Talcum powder and cornstarch are great grease soaker uppers, so when you get a stain on your carpet or upholstery, give either one a try. Liberally sprinkle the powder onto the stain, rub it in, and let it sit overnight. The following morning, brush the talc or cornstarch off with a dry washcloth, and the grease spot will be gone. This nifty trick works like magic on silk and wool, too.

Nonwashable remedy. To remove a grease stain from nonwashable rayon, silk, or wool, or from carpet or upholstery, start by sprinkling the spot with a generous amount of cornmeal. Let it sit overnight to absorb the grease, and then brush it out of the fabric or vacuum it away. If you can still see a spot, moisten a cloth with my Extra-Strength Dry Spotter potion on page 164, press it against the stain, and let it sit for about 10 minutes to finish the job.

Brown bag it. To remove oil or grease stains from carpet or upholstery, place a brown bag over the spot and gently run a warm—not hot—iron over the area. The heat will cause the grease to soak into the absorbent paper. Keep turning the bag to a clean area, and repeat the treatment until the stain is gone. This trick also works just as well on wallpaper.

Hocus Pocus

OUTDOOR GREASE CUTTER

When grease from that nice juicy steak drips onto your patio, or a car leaves an oily mark on your driveway, use this trick to make those stubborn stains disappear:

1. Make a solution of ½ cup of washing soda and 1 gallon of boiling water. *Note:* Wear rubber gloves when you're working with washing soda—it can irritate your skin.

2. Pour the mixture on the stained area.

3. Make a thick paste of fuller's earth (a powdered clay that's available at most hardware stores) mixed with hot water, spread it onto the stain, and let it sit overnight.

4. The next day, wash the whole shebang away with a strong blast from your garden hose.

5. If you can still see spots, repeat the treatment until the stains disappear.

There's the rub. Rubbing alcohol works as a solvent to dissolve grease stains, so it's just the ticket to use on upholstery or carpet that doesn't take kindly to being soaking wet. Simply sponge the alcohol onto the stains and blot it away with a clean, dry cloth. If the stain persists, dip an old toothbrush into a mixture of 1 part dishwashing liquid to 10 parts water, and scrub the spots. Sponge the soap off, and blot dry.

Handy hand cleaner. A bottle of waterless hand cleaner (like Purell®) makes a great laundry aid for treating stubborn grease stains. Just rub a small amount into the stains before you wash the item, and it'll magically remove the oily spots just as quickly as it cleans grubby hands.

Handbags and Luggage

Quick cloth cleanup. You can take a cloth purse to the dry cleaner, but if you'd rather clean it at home, use a gentle liquid detergent (like Woolite®) to spot-clean any stains and get the grime out of the grungy seams. Use a clean white cloth dipped in soap and water, and blot, don't rub, the dirtiest parts first. Then gently go over the whole surface, and sponge all of the soap off with a damp cloth.

Renew vinyl and plastic. To clean vinyl or plastic handbags and luggage, use an all-purpose household cleaner. Rub the cleaner over the surface with a nonabrasive plastic scrubbie, and rinse it off with a damp cloth. And if you like your vinyl shiny, wipe down the clean bag with an ArmorAll® Original Protectant Wipe.

Lather the leather. Saddle soap is a tried-and-true performer for getting deep-down dirt out of leather handbags and luggage. Just lather it onto the surface (following the directions on the package), and sponge it away. Then follow up with a coat of neat's-foot oil or commercial leather conditioner to restore the gloss.

Alcohol rub. You can clean ink marks off light-colored leather bags by dabbing them with a cotton ball soaked in rubbing alcohol. Don't rub the spots—simply dab the cotton ball to wet the stains with the alcohol, let everything sit for about 15 minutes, and renew the shine with leather moisturizer. For more tips on how to clean leather, see Leather and Suede on page 200.

Baby those stains. When makeup or ink stains the cloth lining of your best handbag, wipe the smears and smudges away with a baby wipe. The alcohol and soap in the wipe will remove the dirt with a few quick swipes. Baby wipes also work great for general cleaning of cloth bags; just lightly rub the fabric with a wipe, and the dirt will lift right off.

Grandma Putt's Magical Methods

My Grandma Putt got plenty of use out of her light-colored handbag in summer—but that meant the bottom got dirty from sitting on the floor. So she came up with a simple solution that works great—she added "feet" to it. She cut small circles out of a piece of felt that closely matched the color of her bag, and glued them to the bottom four corners with white craft glue. Snip a few extra circles while you're at it, so you can change the bag's "feet" whenever they get grungy. If you prefer, double-sided Glue Dots® (available in the scrapbooking aisle) make it easy to stick the circles onto the bottom of your bag. Those felt "feet" will keep your bag off the dirty floor—and no one will ever know your secret!

Soap and water for soft sides. Soft-sided luggage is usually made from durable polyester because it's highly resistant to abrasions. But that doesn't mean it won't get dirty! Luckily, it's easy to clean. Just rub the surface with a cloth or nylon brush that's been dipped in soapy water. Clean the entire side (not just the spots that are visibly dirty), so you don't end up with a blotchy effect. And avoid saturating the fabric by squeezing the excess water out of the cloth before you start to rub.

Nylon niceties. You can spiff up your nylon backpack, handbag, or soft-sided luggage with spray-on carpet or upholstery cleaner. Just sponge the cleaner on lightly and work from the middle toward the edges. If the bag has oily stains on it, use my Extra-Strength Dry Spotter potion on page 164 to remove them before you clean the entire surface.

After-travel cleanup. Whenever you come home after a trip, don't just empty your luggage—clean it up before you put it away. That means wiping down the surface and interior, and doing a little detail work around the handle and wheels. A damp cloth will get rid of the grime; dab it in white vinegar if you need some extra cleaning power. A little effort now means the next time you pack your bags, they'll be ready to go.

Wild 'n' woolly. If your luggage is made from a fuzzy fabric like easy-care acrylic or tweed, sponge on an upholstery cleaner that's specially made for wool-nylon blends. Spray some of the foamy stuff onto a cloth, and

THE NOSE KNOWS

So your dirty socks or damp bathing suit left a lingering odor in your luggage? Musty smells are no problem when you have a bit of cleaning magic on your side. Try one of these quick fixes to leave your luggage smelling as fresh as a daisy:

★ Sprinkle some baking soda in the bag, close it up, and let it sit overnight to soak up the smells. Then vacuum up the baking soda before you store the bag away.

★ Drop a handful of cedar balls or a couple of cedar blocks into your suitcase before you put it away. They'll keep musty smells (and pests) at bay.

★ Put a piece of charcoal (not pretreated with lighter fluid) in the case. Tie it in a piece of cheesecloth first to keep it from smudging the lining.

wipe down the entire surface. After you've gotten the dirt off, spritz the bags with fabric protector to help repel water and grime. Just keep the cleaner away from any leather trim or handles on the bags; use leather cleaner to spiff those parts to a shine.

Hardware helpers. If the hardware on your handbag or luggage becomes tarnished or scratched, make it shine again by rubbing it with fine steel wool (000 or 0000 grade). Then paint the metal with clear nail polish to protect it from future tarnish. And if the lock is sticky, apply a small amount of powdered graphite to it, following the directions on the container, and vacuum away any stray bits of lubricant. Never oil the lock or hinges because the oil may leak inside the lining and stain your clothes the next time you use the bag.

Houseplants

Dust the jungle. Those lush, beautiful houseplants sure do look nice—but they're real dust catchers. So when it's time to dust your furniture, take a minute to dust your foliage, too. If the leaf stems break easily, hold them underneath for support before you send the dust flying. You can use a feather duster, a synthetic duster, or an old T-shirt to do the job. For houseplants with fuzzy or hairy leaves (like African violets), use a soft brush to flick the dust off.

Blushing beauty. The chubby brush that comes with blusher makeup works great for cleaning fuzzy-leaved African violets, spiny cacti, or sharp-edged pineapple plants. It has just the right amount of stiffness to coax the dust out of the crevices, and it'll keep your fingers out of harm's way, too! You can also use it on the clustered leaves of bromeliads and on other houseplants that have lots of nooks and crannies.

Leaf wipe. Greasy grime can build up on plant leaves, especially if your houseplants live in the kitchen, where oily molecules go airborne. If a simple dusting doesn't make your foliage shine, wipe each leaf with a damp sponge dipped in a gallon of water with a few drops of grease-cutting dishwashing liquid added to it. Dab off the soapy residue with a clean, damp cloth so the pores on the surface of the leaves can breathe.

Two-handed trick. You can cut your houseplant cleaning time in half by wiping the top and bottom of each leaf at the same time. Just drape a damp paper towel or cloth over each hand, and slide your hands gently down the leaf from the stem end to the tip. This nifty trick works great on peace lily, dracaena, and other plants with smooth, sturdy leaves.

Rain bath. If you want to clean a bunch of houseplants at the same time and you have a handheld sprayer in your shower, then give 'em a gentle wash. Place the plants in your shower stall, pull the curtain or door almost closed, reach in, and use the handheld sprayer to wash away the grime. Set the water temperature to lukewarm, and aim the spray side-

Powerful Potions

Houseplant Wipe

Use this simple solution to shine the leaves of any ivy, philodendron, or other smooth-leaved houseplants. It'll wipe away the dust and leave the leaves gleaming.

½ cup of nonfat dry milk

1 qt. of warm water

Mix the milk and water in a bucket, dip in a cellulose sponge, and wipe the top and bottom of each leaf. Wipe gently and don't rub, so you avoid damaging the natural coating on the leaves. When you're done, there's no need to rinse; just let the milky mixture dry to a shine.

ways to get both the tops and bottoms of the leaves. Keep the sprayer head moving so that the force of the water doesn't damage the foliage. Leave the plants to sit in the moist air for an hour afterward, and let the extra water drain. Then dry the pots and put them back in place. If you have only a small collection, use your kitchen sink sprayer instead.

Sock it to me! Give palm trees and other smooth-leaved houseplants the white-glove treatment by putting a pair of soft, white cotton socks on your hands when you clean them. Wet the socks under lukewarm water, make a fist to squeeze out the extra moisture, and then slide each leaf between your, ahem, palms. Use only very gentle pressure so you don't wipe off the natural waxy coating on the leaves.

Grandma Putt's Magical Methods

Whenever I finished eating a banana at my Grandma Putt's house, I knew better than to throw away the peel. Why? Because using a banana peel was Grandma's favorite way to polish her big philodendron leaves. To use her secret method on any houseplant with large, smooth leaves, simply hold each leaf of the houseplant and wipe the surface with the inside of the peel. The natural oil in the banana skin gives the leaves a nice shine.

Make it shine. If you like a high-gloss look on your houseplants, try my Houseplant Wipe at left, or use one of these simple tricks. They work just as well as any commercial spray, but cost a whole lot less:

★ Wipe the leaves gently with a bit of mayonnaise on a soft, clean cloth.

★ Sprinkle a few drops of glycerin on a soft, clean cloth and wipe it over the leaves.

★ Beat an egg white to a froth and wipe the foam on the leaves.

Ink and Marker Stains

Into the wash. When your kids go wild with washable markers, do exactly what the name says: Wash those stains away! Rub in some liquid laundry detergent before you throw the clothes in the washing machine, and then wash them in the hottest water the fabric can stand. If the marks are on your upholstery or carpet, blot up some of the ink with a wet cloth, and follow up with a soapy one. Don't rub, or you'll set the stain in deeper. And be sparing with the water—rinse the soap away by blotting it with a clean, wet cloth.

Rub-a-dub. Permanent ink is a tough stain to remove, but I've got a whole bag of tricks for you to try. Start by laying the item on top of a clean, old white towel or T-shirt because the ink will bleed. Dab rubbing alcohol directly onto the stain, folding the cloth underneath to a fresh part as it absorbs the ink. Keep dabbing and refolding until that nasty blot has vanished, then rinse and wash the item as usual. Keep in mind that your towel or T-shirt will get stained, so use one that's ready for the ragbag.

Manicurist's makeover. Try acetone-based nail polish remover to make those stubborn ink stains disappear. Just dab it on until the fabric is saturated, and wait a minute or two for the solvent to break the stain up. Continue blotting until the stain is gone, and launder as usual. To avoid spreading the problem, work on top of a towel or T-shirt, as you did with the alcohol trick (see "Rub-a-dub" above).

Dairy delight. For a fresh ink stain, dip the fabric into a small bowl of milk, and let it sit for about 15 minutes. Pour more milk through the fabric to rinse away the ink. Repeat, using a fresh bowl of milk, until all of the ink has disappeared, then rinse the milk out with cold water and laun-

LET'S GET PERSONAL

The next time you get ink on your clothes, try a trick using one of these three personal care products—shampoo, acne cream, and insect repellent. Here's how to put them to work:

★ Lay a paper towel over the spot, pour on the shampoo, and let it sit for about 15 minutes. Blot the stain with the soapy paper towel, and finish up by blotting it with fresh water. Once the ink is gone, launder the item as usual.

★ Most acne creams contain 10% benzoyl peroxide, which is an ingredient that goes to town on ink stains. Apply the cream to the stain with a cotton swab, let it sit for an hour, wipe it off, and wash the item as usual. This trick works like magic on permanent marker stains.

★ Use insect repellent as you would hair spray on ink marks, spritzing it directly onto the stain and then blotting it up with a soft cloth. Repeat the treatment until the ink is gone.

der as usual. And if the ink is on your carpet, apply a paste of milk and cornstarch to the stain and let it dry, which will take a few hours. When the paste is dry, brush away the residue with a dry washcloth and run your vacuum cleaner over the area to remove any last bits of the ink-absorbing paste.

Hair spray help. Today's hair sprays have a much lower alcohol content than they once did because too much alcohol can dry hair out. Still, there's more than enough stain-removal action left in that spray to clean up ink stains, particularly on polyester and poly blends. So give it a shot when you've got an ink stain on polyester upholstery or clothes. Spray the stain liberally, blot the ink up, and repeat until it's completely gone. *FYI:* Cheap hair sprays often have a higher alcohol content than more expensive brands.

The Great Clean-dini Speaks

Q. How do I know which trick I should try to get rid of an ink stain?

A. Ink stains are notoriously stubborn, so you may have to try a few methods before you find one that works. Feel free to experiment with anything the fabric can tolerate. As long as you rinse the cloth out in between, you can even try a few methods all at once. Just wait until the ink is gone before you launder the item because hot water or dryer heat can set the stain, making it darn near impossible to remove. Or try this combo trick, which works like magic even on old stains:

1. If the ink is from a ballpoint pen, pour glycerin onto the stain, let it sit for about 30 minutes, and skip to Step 4.

2. Not a ballpoint stain? Then mix 1 teaspoon of dishwashing liquid with 1 cup of water and ¼ cup of white vinegar, rub it into the stain, wait at least 30 minutes, and rinse. If you still see a mark, proceed to Step 3.

3. Saturate the stain with rubbing alcohol and blot the ink up with a clean, dry cloth. When no more ink comes off onto the cloth, rinse out the alcohol, let the fabric air-dry, and move on to Step 4.

4. Wet the stain and rub in a dab of dishwashing liquid and about 1 teaspoon of ammonia. Let it sit for 30 minutes or so, blotting the ink now and then. Rinse the fabric with white vinegar and then with water. That pesky stain should be gone. If it isn't, your last resort is to use a bleach pen if your clothes can tolerate it; but never use bleach on wool, silk, or spandex.

Banish the ballpoint. When a ballpoint pen slips and leaves a streak down the front of a nice white shirt, reach for the nearest bottle of white vinegar to get rid of the evidence. Saturate the stain with the vinegar, let it sit for about 15 minutes, and rinse it away. If you can still see the mark, repeat the treatment until it's gone.

Off the wall. Got an ink stain on a wall? Here's a neat trick that'll clean it right up: Squeeze white non-gel toothpaste onto the stain and spread it out to cover the marks. Wait about 15 minutes, and wipe it clean with a damp sponge. Repeat the treatment if necessary, or wait until the wall is dry, then give it a good squirt of hair spray. Wait a few minutes to let the alcohol in the spray break up the ink, and then blot it off the wall.

Grandma Putt's Magical Methods

When a leaky pen makes a mess all over your fingers, use my Grandma Putt's trick to clean your hands in a flash: Put a dollop of solid shortening in your palm, and rub your hands together to take off the ink. My Grandma also used this trick on her vinyl floors. And when your kids decide to scribble on poor old Dolly's vinyl face, you can try it there, too! After you smear the grease on, wipe it away, then wash the vinyl with a warm, soapy cloth to remove the oily residue.

WD for wood. When marker stains mar your wood furniture, use good old WD-40® to get rid of them. Spray the spot with the solvent and cover it with a piece of plastic wrap to hold the moisture in—and to keep the smell from spreading. Let it sit for about five minutes while you mix up a bowl of soapy water made with grease-cutting dishwashing liquid. Wipe the area with a sponge dipped in the soapy solution to remove the solvent and the last of the ink, blot up the moisture with a paper towel, and finish the job by polishing the wood after it's completely dry. WD-40 is stinky and flammable, so remember to work in a well-ventilated area away from any fire or flame.

Irons

Vinegar inside and out. White vinegar makes a great cleaner for every part of an iron. To clean the outside casing, just pour some vinegar onto a soft cloth and wipe the grime away. Use the same cloth to wipe the residue and any brown stains off the bottom. And as you'll see below, you can even use vinegar to clean out clogged steam vents.

Get steamed. To loosen old starch or mineral deposits lurking in an iron's steam reservoir and vents, fill the reservoir with white vinegar, set the iron on a wire baking rack over an old towel, and let it steam for about five minutes. Turn the iron off, let it cool, and refill it with clean water. Let it steam for another five minutes. Finally, run the iron back and forth over an old washcloth to remove any sediment that could stain your clothes. To prevent the problem in the future, use distilled (instead of tap) water to fill the reservoir.

In the pokey. When white, crusty buildup clogs your iron's steam vents, open those holes up by poking them with a pipe cleaner dipped in vinegar. Push the pipe cleaner in and out of each vent, being careful not to scratch the bottom of your iron with the wire. Then fill the reservoir with distilled water, and let your iron steam away at full force for about five minutes to blow out the rest of the gunk.

Not nonstick? Most modern irons are made with nonstick bottoms that don't take kindly to harsh abrasives. But if yours is made of plain, uncoated metal, you don't have to worry about scratches wrecking the finish. Just dampen a nonsoapy steel wool pad, and rub it vigorously over the grungy brown stuff until the bottom of your iron is shiny clean. Then use toothpicks to poke any built-up residue out of the steam holes. When your iron looks like new again, run it across a sheet of wax paper to give it a homemade nonstick finish.

Hocus Pocus

SCORCH STAINS

As soon as your iron scorches an item, rub some liquid laundry detergent into the fabric and launder it in cold water with more detergent and an oxygen bleach. If the mark is only a faint one, and you act fast, you may be able to sponge it away with white vinegar. But once the stain has had time to set in, or if it's severe, you'll need stronger cleaning magic. That's when it's time to give one of these tricks a try:

★ Lay a white cloth saturated with hydrogen peroxide on the stain and run a moderately hot iron over it a few times. Repeat until the stain is gone.

★ Rub the stain vigorously with a freshly cut lemon half, then set the item in the sun for several hours. Rinse the lemon juice out and repeat if necessary.

★ Sponge the scorch mark with a mixture of 1 tablespoon of borax and 1 cup of warm water, then launder the item as usual.

★ If your iron leaves a light scorch stain on linen, rub a freshly cut onion over it, then soak it in cold water overnight.

★ Wet the stained area thoroughly and spread dry whiting or pipe clay over it. Let it sit for a few hours, then rub the fabric against itself under warm water to rinse the whiting or clay out. If a mark remains, repeat the treatment.

★ Dip the scorched spot into hydrogen peroxide mixed with a few drops of ammonia, and rub it into the stain with your fingers. Rinse thoroughly, then wash the item in cold water.

★ Cover scorch stains on washable silk or wool with equal parts of glycerin and borax. Let sit for about an hour, then hand wash the item in cold water.

★ Scorch marks are nearly impossible to remove from fuzzy wool fabrics. But if you rub the spots with very fine–grade sandpaper, you may remove enough of the burned fibers to disguise them.

Oily bottom. If fabric softeners or greasy work clothes leave an oily film on the bottom of your iron, use ammonia to cut the crud. Dampen a cloth with ammonia and rub the bottom of a cool iron over it to cut through the sticky stuff in no time flat. Wipe the ammonia off with a clean, wet cloth, and your iron will be ready to roll.

Melted mess. When plastic or polyester fabric melts on your iron, it can sure seem like a hopeless situation, but you can remove that major mess with this easy trick. First, heat your iron to warm and scrape off as much of the residue as you can with a wooden spatula. Next, let the iron cool down and tackle the remaining mess with a nonabrasive plastic scrubbie that's been dipped in a paste made of baking soda and water. To remove melted polyester, wipe the iron with an acetone-based nail polish remover. Finish by wiping the bottom of your freshly scrubbed iron with a wet cloth, and running it over an old towel.

Bottoms up! If those brown starch and scorch stains on the bottom of your iron are really stubborn, add a gentle abrasive to your arsenal when you scrub.

Grandma Putt's Magical Methods

I sometimes wonder if my Grandma Putt didn't invent the first nonstick iron. Whenever hers got a little balky, she'd wax the bottom to make it glide over the sheets and shirts. Her trick took just a few seconds: She'd simply run the hot iron over a block of paraffin wrapped in a cotton cloth, which she kept within easy reach at the end of her ironing board. At the touch of the hot iron, the paraffin melted through the cloth, leaving a thin, smooth coat of wax on her iron. After a while, the cloth became stiff with wax, which made the job even easier. And when her iron got full of brown gunk from starch, she would sprinkle some salt onto a sheet of wax paper, and iron the paper with the iron set on warm. The salt scrubbed off the brown residue, and the wax on the paper melted onto the iron. Yes, sir, now that's a first-class finish!

Try any of these simple recipes to make the bottom of your iron smooth and clean again:

★ Sprinkle table salt onto a piece of aluminum foil, lay the foil on your ironing board, and run your cool iron across it several times.

★ Heat ½ cup of white vinegar and ½ cup of table salt in a saucepan until it's moderately warm. Then rub the solution on the cool bottom of your iron, and watch those stains disappear.

★ Squeeze some toothpaste onto a soft, clean cloth, and rub the residue away. Use non-gel toothpaste; the cheaper the brand, the better.

★ Make a paste of baking soda and water, and use it to scrub off the gunk. Wipe off the paste with a damp cloth.

★ Make a foamy mix of vinegar and baking soda, apply it to the bottom of your iron, and let it fizz away the baked-on stuff.

After you're done, run the iron over an old washcloth to make sure all traces of the abrasive are gone before you start pressing any clothes.

Jewelry (See also Gold; Silver)

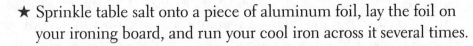

Finishing touches. Makeup, hair spray, and other lotions and potions will dull your jewelry, so always do your "beautifying" before you put on your fancy doodads. And make sure you wipe your jewelry with a soft, clean cloth after you take it off to remove any traces of perspiration, perfume, or other dulling substances.

Strain your gems. A loose setting can mean a lost stone, but not if you put your jewels in a strainer that's set on top of a bowl before you clean them. If the settings are loose, the gunk that builds up around the gems may be the only "glue" that's holding your stones in place, and the strainer and bowl will prevent you from washing your jewels down the drain.

Diamond details. To get the crud out of the setting of your diamond ring, use your Waterpik® to blast that dirt away. Or you can soak the ring in a mixture of warm water and mild soap for about 10 minutes, using a soft brush to clean out the nooks and crannies. Remember to plug the drain before you start, so your diamond doesn't make a clean getaway.

Sterling silver spuds. The next time you boil a pot of potatoes, pour the water into a heat-proof bowl and drop your tarnished silver jewelry into it. Let the jewelry soak for about half an hour to dissolve the tarnish, then wash it under water with a soft cloth and/or old toothbrush to get the gunk out of the crevices. Rinse and buff it dry.

Ammonia is good as gold. To brighten dull gold jewelry, mix up a solution of 1 cup of warm water, 1 teaspoon of ammonia, and 1 teaspoon of dishwashing liquid. Soak your pieces in the solution for about five min-

The Great Clean-dini Speaks

Q. I bought some rhinestone jewelry at a garage sale and when I soaked the pieces to clean them, they turned dark and blotchy. What did I do wrong, and how can I do it right next time?

A. I'm afraid it was that soaking that killed the shine. Rhinestones get their glitter from a foil backing that can tarnish or peel if it gets wet, so you can't let any liquids penetrate them. The next time, instead of submerging them, spray an artist's brush—sparingly!—with The World's Best Window Cleaner potion on page 354, and then dab it into the tight spaces between the rhinestones to get the dirt out. Finish by wiping the surface with a soft, clean cloth that's been moistened with a little rubbing alcohol. There's no need to rinse because the alcohol will dry right up, leaving your rhinestones sparkling clean.

utes, and then use a very soft brush to clean the crevices. Rinse your jewelry in clean water, and dry it with a soft cloth. But don't try this trick if your gold pieces include any stones, because they might be damaged by the ammonia.

Not for chores. Steam irons, hot dishwater, and household cleaners can damage opals, pearls, and other jewelry, so save your good stuff for special occasions instead of everyday wear around the house. Even something simple like doing the laundry (with chlorine bleach) can blacken silver beyond all recognition. Play it safe, and you'll keep your jewelry out of harm's way whenever you're working around the house.

Pamper your pearls. The softly gleaming, iridescent layer on the outside of your pearls is sensitive to chemicals, including sweat, perfume, lotions, and makeup. And once that outer surface is damaged, all you'll have left is a dull string of beads! So wipe your pearls with a damp microfiber cloth after you take them off, let them air-dry, and then put them back in their case or soft pouch so they don't get scratched by other jewelry. You should also use the same procedure to clean any pieces that contain mabe pearls, mother-of-pearl, or abalone.

Grandma Putt's Magical Methods

When your silver jewelry starts looking a little dull, bring back its good-as-new glow with this little trick from Grandma Putt. Sprinkle baking soda over the bottom of an aluminum foil baking pan, place your jewelry in the pan, and then pour enough boiling water over it to completely cover the pieces. Let them soak for two or three minutes, and the tarnish will simply disappear. Take your jewelry out with plastic tongs (so you don't burn your fingers or scratch the metal), rinse it under cold water, and buff it dry with a soft, clean cloth. Boiling water is safe for silver, but not for stones (real or fake), so use this trick on all-silver pieces only.

Tickle the ivory. Erase dirt from your ivory jewelry like magic by rubbing it with an artist's pencil-tip vinyl eraser. The skinny tip makes it a cinch to get into dirt-collecting nooks and crannies, and it's easy to blow the residue away. You'll find the erasers at art-supply or craft stores.

Fizz dirt away. Here's a quick homemade jewelry cleaner that works great on just about anything other than pearls, amber, opals, and rhinestones. Drop two Alka-Seltzer® tablets into a glass of warm water, add your dirty jewelry to it, and let the tablets fizz the dirt away for two minutes or so. Rinse the pieces under cool water, and dry them with a soft, clean cloth. What a relief it is—to clean your jewelry just like magic!

Damp cloth for delicate stones. You should clean the surface of amber, lapis, turquoise, pearls, and other natural stones with nothing more than a damp cloth. Don't soak these soft stones or expose them to hot water, chemical cleaners, or an ultrasonic jewelry-cleaning machine. Once you're done cleaning, let the pieces air-dry for at least an hour before you put them away, so there's no moisture lingering in the settings. A simple swipe works wonders for hard gemstones, too.

Juicers

Rinse it real quick. You'll save yourself a lot of scrubbing if you jump on that juicer right away, before the pulp gets a chance to dry and harden. So as soon as you empty out the juice, give the screen, pitcher, and other parts a quick rinse with warm water.

Pipe down! Nasty bacteria can get a toehold in the pouring spout of a juice cover, so don't overlook that little opening when you're cleaning the machine. Use a pipe cleaner to get any stray bits of pulp or residue out of the spout, or buy a small bottlebrush that's just the right size at a kitchen-supply shop.

Screen scrubbers. To clean all of the gunk out of a juicing screen, you'll need a brush with bristles that are stiff enough to scrub those tiny holes. A nailbrush, veggie brush, or old toothbrush will do the job. Hold the strainer under running water and brush the underside of the screen first. Then flip it over and brush the pulp out of the top side. Plain water is all you need unless you've been juicing oily foods; if the screen feels greasy, add a little dishwashing liquid when you scrub. Rinse thoroughly.

Citrus soak. Pulp on a filter basket—and on the blades inside—can be hard to remove once it gets a chance to dry and harden. Soften it up by soaking the basket in a solution of 1 part lemon juice to 9 parts warm water; bottled lemon juice works just fine. Let the basket soak for 30 minutes, then clean the blades and basket with a nylon brush. Use an old toothbrush to reach into the blades—and watch your fingers!

HOCUS POCUS

CARROTTOP?

Peter Rabbit's favorite food is notorious for staining the plastic parts of juicers. Since it's only the dye that lingers, and not the flavor, you can simply ignore the stain. But if you don't want to be reminded of that last batch of carrots, try one of these tricks:

★ Run a grapefruit or a couple of oranges or lemons through the machine. The citric acid will eliminate that "carrottop"!

★ Wipe the stains away with a little olive oil or vegetable oil.

★ Apply a paste of baking soda and water to the discolored plastic, let it sit for about half an hour, and then scrub the stains with a nonabrasive plastic scrubbie. Rinse and repeat if needed.

★ Soak the plastic parts in white vinegar for 15 minutes, rinse, and repeat, soaking for 30 minutes the second time.

Ketchup Stains

Sponge 'n' done. A glob of ketchup on your shirt or carpet may look pretty ghastly, but it's actually one of the easiest stains to remove. Just wet a sponge or paper towel with lukewarm water, add a dab of dishwashing liquid, squeeze the extra moisture out, and blot the spot. Whatever you do, rein in your urge to rub the stain—too much elbow grease may mat the carpet fibers, or drive the stain in deeper. To rinse the area, blot with fresh water until the suds are gone.

Join the club. Fresh ketchup on your carpet? Start by blotting it up with paper towels. Then pour a little club soda directly onto the spot, and immediately blot it again with a clean, dry cloth. Repeat the trick a few times until the spot is gone.

Grandma Putt's Magical Methods

Here's a neat trick I learned from my Grandma Putt: The back of a spoon makes the perfect tool for blotting up ketchup stains on carpet. Just lay a moist cloth over the stained spot and press the spoon against the cloth to soak up the remains of the stain. Then work in a bit of dishwashing liquid and water, using the same technique. Finally, sponge the soap away with fresh water, and blot it up by pressing the spoon against a clean, dry cloth.

Dry disaster. Oops! A splash of ketchup went AWOL on your armchair, but you didn't notice it until the next day. Gently scrape the residue off with a butter knife, and loosen the stain by wetting it with lukewarm water. Remove it by following the simple steps in "Sponge 'n' done" above.

Ammonia soak. If you didn't treat a ketchup stain when it was fresh, soak the stained area in a mixture of 1 part ammonia to 1 part water for 15 to 20 minutes. Rinse the fabric, and if the stain has disappeared, launder the item in cold water. If a spot is still visible, repeat the treatment. Don't try this trick on silk, rayon, or other fabrics that may be damaged by ammonia, and always test it in an inconspicuous area first to make sure it won't take the color out along with the stain.

Set-in stains. Dryer heat can set a ketchup stain—which is why you should always pretreat stains before you do the laundry. But if you've already sent a shirt through the washer and dryer and the stain remains, try one of these tricks to make it vanish:

★ Rub glycerin into the stain with your fingers, on both sides of the fabric. Wait about 15 minutes, and launder the item in cold water.

★ Mix 1 teaspoon of a mild, nonalkaline, nonbleaching detergent (like Woolite®) into 1 cup of lukewarm water, and pour it on the stain. Let it sit for 15 minutes, then launder the item in cold water.

Knives

Carbon or stainless steel? Carbon steel knives are harder than stainless steel, so they stay sharp longer. But there's a trade-off for that fine edge: Carbon or high-carbon knives rust when they're exposed to moisture or acidic foods because the steel contains more iron than stainless does. So always dry carbon steel knives immediately after you wash them, especially if they've been exposed to any kind of juice.

Bye-bye, bacteria. You should always wash your knives in hot, soapy water immediately after cutting meat, poultry, or fish. Bacteria can multiply like lightning, but a quick cleanup will nip that problem in the bud. In fact, cleaning knives right after you use them is a good habit to get into, even if you haven't been cutting bacteria-laden foods. A quick rubdown will keep the blades from tarnishing or rusting, and you won't have to deal with dried-on food later.

High quality = hand washing. Good knives cost a pretty penny, so don't put these costly cutters in the dishwasher where they can be jostled, nicked, and bent out of shape. The high heat and steam can also damage wooden handles. So wash them by hand, and you'll save yourself a lot of aggravation. Set the knives on the side of your sink and wash them one by one; then if you drop one in with the rest of the dishes,

The Great Clean-dini Speaks

Q. My multitool knife sure comes in handy, what with all of those screwdrivers and blades in my pocket, but the tools are getting really hard to open and close. What can I do to make it work smoothly again?

A. Utility knives can get balky when gunk builds up in the slots and hinges of the attachments, but I've got just the trick to get rid of it—boil the gunk away. Here's how to do it:

1. Open all of the tools. Find a pan that's big enough to hold your knife, and add water until the pan is about two-thirds full. Bring the water to a boil.

2. Put the opened knife in the boiling water for no more than 60 seconds. Keep a close eye on the time because a longer session could crack any plastic on the knife.

3. Carefully pour off the boiling water, refill the pan with warm tap water, and let it sit on a cool stove burner for another minute.

4. Use a pair of tongs to remove the hot knife. Let it cool, then scrub the gunk out of the crevices with an old toothbrush.

5. Allow your knife to completely air-dry, and then rub a tiny bit of vegetable oil onto the blades for smooth sailing.

the sharp edge won't take you by surprise. Dry the knives with a cloth instead of letting them air-dry, and you'll keep them on the cutting edge.

Rust removal. Rust can set in fast, even if you keep your knives in a knife block or drawer. So check frequently for signs of trouble. As soon as you notice any telltale reddish brown spots, scrub the blade with warm water and baking soda. For harder cases of rust, use a nonsoapy steel wool pad that's been dipped in rubbing alcohol to scrub the spots away. Rinse the knife, and dry it thoroughly before you put it away.

Happy hunting. Most hunting knives are made with carbon steel blades, so wipe these blades dry with a chamois after each use to remove fingerprints and soak up moisture. Then let the knives air out every now and then when you store them, instead of always keeping them in their sheaths, where moisture can collect.

Lamps and Lamp Shades

Damp wipe. When a lamp needs more than just a simple dusting, use a damp cloth with a drop of dishwashing liquid to remove the grime. Unplug the lamp before you work on it, and don't forget to dust the lightbulb, too!

Hit the spot. Remove dirty fingerprints from lamp shades by rubbing them gently with a baby or hand wipe. A few quick strokes are all it takes to get rid of most grungy fingerprints. Then make sure you wipe down the rest of the shade after you make the smudges disappear, so the clean spots don't stick out like a sore thumb.

Quick dry. After you clean a lamp shade with soapsuds or a damp wipe, put it back on the lamp and turn on the light. The heat from the bulb will help the shade dry quickly.

Grandma Putt's Magical Methods

My Grandma Putt knew that washing a lamp shade could make the metal frame rust, so she used this "dry cleaning" trick: She'd put the shade into a large plastic trash bag, pour in about 1 cup of table salt, and close the top securely. Then she'd enlist one of us young 'uns to shake the bag energetically for a few minutes. The salt gently scrubbed the dirt off, so when we opened the bag, all we had to do was shake off the salt and the lamp shade was ready to shine!

Breathe in, breathe out. You can use the upholstery brush attachment on your vacuum cleaner to suck the dust off lamp shades. Or take the opposite tack, and try a blast of compressed air to blow the dust out of those pleats and folds. And while you're at it, use that high-pressure air to get the dust out of the fancy nooks and crannies in the lamp bases.

Dust brush. To whisk dust out of the folds and seams of fabric or pleated lamp shades, use a clean, dry paintbrush. The bristles are stiff enough to swish the dust away without damaging the fabric, and they'll reach into all the hidden spaces, too. And here's another trick: Take the shades outside to do the job, so that dust doesn't end up on other surfaces in the room.

Dry rub. To clean a fabric lamp shade without getting it wet, try a baking soda rub. Remove the shade from the lamp and sprinkle baking soda over the surface. Rub it gently over the fabric, let it sit for about 10 minutes, and brush it off with a dry washcloth. The baking soda will absorb the grime and odors, so the tired old lamp shade will look (and smell) fresh and clean.

Pet hair pickup. Tidy up the lamp shades in your pet-friendly home by using a baby wipe or a sticky lint roller to do the job—either one picks up stray hair in a hurry.

Fabric facts. Silk, linen, and other fabric lamp shades can be tricky to clean because water can shrink the cloth, rust the metal framework, or loosen glued seams or trim. So don't saturate these shades unless you've tried every other trick in the book. Then as a last resort, try this method:

1. Fill your bathtub with lukewarm soapy water, using Woolite® per the directions on the label, or mild dishwashing liquid.

2. Dip the lamp shade into the tub, and plunge it up and down a few times to lift out the dirt.

3. Treat stubborn dirty spots by rubbing them gently with a soft brush or washcloth.

4. Drain the tub, refill it with fresh water, and dunk the shade a few more times to rinse out the soapy residue.

5. Blot the shade with a bath towel to remove as much water as you can, and hang it from your shower curtain rod to air-dry. You can speed up the drying process with a fan or hair dryer set on the cool setting. The saggy fabric will tighten up as it dries.

Hocus Pocus

DON'T COME UNGLUED!

Shades made of paper or parchment are usually glued together, so don't go dunking them underwater. Instead, give them a special suds-only shampoo. First, use an electric mixer to whip ¼ cup of dishwashing liquid and 1 cup of warm water into a thick foam (the consistency of whipped cream). Sponge just the suds over the inside and outside of the shade, and rub gently. Wipe the soap off with a clean, damp cloth and dry the shade with a soft, clean cloth. This trick works great on fabric shades, too, and on shades that have glued-on fancy trim. And always handle lamp shades with care, so you don't make dents or creases in them.

Fiberglass shades. Older lamps sometimes have a shade that's made of textured fiberglass, which can be nearly impossible to clean with the usual methods. But here's a trick that works great, especially if the shade has become discolored from cigarette smoke. Set it in your bathtub and spray it down, inside and out, with a foaming bathroom cleaner like Scrubbing Bubbles®. An amazing amount of dirt will start to run off. Repeat the treatment two or three times, and then rinse the shade with hot water. After the rinse, press any dents out with your fingers, and ta-da! You've given an old lamp shade a new lease on life.

Erase the evidence. When someone leaves his or her dirty paw print on a paper or fabric lamp shade, use an art gum eraser to rub the mark away. Rub gently, and support the shade behind the spot so you don't bend or crease it. Another alternative is to use a damp Mr. Clean® Magic Eraser® to make that smear disappear.

Lawn Mowers

Cover the vents. If your lawn mower has a vented gas cap, you'll need to protect it from moisture before you clean it. Remove the cap, cover the opening with a couple of layers of plastic wrap, and screw the cap down over the wrap. When you're done cleaning the machine, remove the wrap and you're good to go.

Hose it off. Lawn mowers are built to withstand moisture, at least when it comes from the top down. So use a garden hose to rinse any grass and other debris off the top of the mower after you finish cutting your lawn. Be careful; don't aim the nozzle at the side of the engine, where the water could enter the air filter or other parts. And if you need extra cleaning power, swab the deck and engine cover with a bit of car shampoo. Then let the mower air-dry before you put it away.

Under the deck. Grass clippings can clog your mower's blades or block the discharge chute, so clean the bottom of it several times a season, preferably while the grass is still fresh. All it takes is a good strong stream of water from your garden hose to rinse the loose debris away.

A mighty wind. Here's a neat idea: Use a leaf blower to make quick work of cleaning away grass clippings that are on and under your mower deck. Just move the mower to the middle of the lawn, and have at it. If the clippings are wet and clumped together around the blades, use a small broom or stiff brush to loosen things up before you blow 'em away.

Stuck like glue? If you've neglected the built-up clippings on the underside of your mower, they aren't going to give up their grip without a fight. First, scrub the underside with a stiff brush that's been dipped in hot, soapy water. Then use a putty knife to dislodge the gunk that has hardened in place, including the buildup on the discharge chute. Finish by washing the clippings and debris away with a blast from your garden hose. That should do the trick!

Screen the clippings. Here's a handy hint to keep grass clippings from washing onto your lawn when you're cleaning your mower: Lay an old window screen underneath the mower before you tilt it up to hose it down. The clippings will wash down onto the screen, while the water drains through it. When you're done, just carry the screen and the clippings to your compost pile for recycling.

Safety first! You'll need to tilt your mower to clean the underside, so always take these precautions to guard against accidents. Pull the spark plug wire off before you start, so the engine doesn't accidentally kick in. Make sure the gas and oil caps are screwed on tightly, and then tilt the mower so that the gas cap is angled upward to prevent any accidental spills. Now you're good to go.

Leather and Suede

Lather your leather. Remove the surface dirt from leather furniture, handbags, or clothes by rubbing it with just the lather from a bar of gentle, moisturizing hand soap. Dab the suds onto a soft, damp cloth, and rub the dirty spots on the leather. Wipe the lather away with a clean, damp cloth and buff the area with a dry towel. And remember, use as little water as possible, so you don't make water spots while you work.

Take a powder. To make grease stains disappear from leather or suede, blot the area with a dry cloth, then sprinkle cornstarch or talcum powder on the spots. Let the powder sit for several hours to absorb the oil, and then brush it away with a clean, dry cloth or a clean, dry nailbrush.

Mildew removal. Handbags and leather clothes can pick up mildew when they're stored in a closet, and pesky mold can even get into your leather furniture if it's up against a damp wall. To remove mildew, wipe the affected areas with a mixture of 1 cup of rubbing alcohol and 1 cup of

Powerful Potions

Heavy-Duty Leather Cleaner

Use this paste to treat extra-dirty areas on any leather item.
It works great on heavily soiled spots like the front edge of a
couch, or the "head prints" left by oily hair.

> 1 part fresh lemon juice
> 1 part cream of tartar

Mix the ingredients into a paste in a small bowl, and work it into the soiled areas
with a soft, dry cloth. Wipe it off with a damp cloth. If you still see dirt, reapply
the paste and let it sit for a few hours to soak up the stain before you wipe it
away. This potion won't keep, so make only enough to do the job at hand.

water. Don't soak the stain—a few good swipes are all you need to
wipe the problem away. Dry the area with a soft, clean cloth, and aim a
fan or hair dryer (set on cool) at it to make sure every bit of moisture is
gone with the wind.

Soaked stiff? Wet leather stiffens and shrinks as it dries, so it makes lovely
leather items as hard as boards—and a size or two smaller! You can
stop the shrinkage by putting the wet footgear on shoe trees to dry, or
by pulling on wet gloves a few times as they dry out. When the leather
is dry, it's easy to restore its softness: Just use my Leather Softener and
Restorer potion on page 204.

Cure for water spots. When water soaks into leather items (and leaves a
distinct spot behind), cure the problem by giving it more water. That's
right—moisten the spot and the area around it with a damp cloth, and
blow it dry with your hair dryer turned to the cool setting. Then rub
leather conditioner over the area and the spot will blend right in with
the rest of the finish.

Ink out. When smooth leather gets spotted with ink stains, dip a cotton swab into some rubbing alcohol or nonoily cuticle remover, and rub it into the stains. You can also spritz the spots with an inexpensive aerosol hair spray. Wipe away whichever cleaner you use with a soft, clean cloth, and finish the job with my Leather Softener and Restorer potion on page 204 until the spots blend in with the rest of the surface.

Sticky situation. When your favorite leather handbag gets all gummed up with Dubble Bubble®, rub a ziplock plastic bag full of ice cubes over the gum to harden it up until you can lift the mess off. Then heat the residue with a hair dryer and rub any remaining bits off with a soft, dry cloth.

Old salt. When leather winter boots or shoes show white stains from snow-melting salt, blot the spots away with a solution of 1 part white vinegar and 1 part water. Repeat the treatment until the stains are gone, and then polish the footwear as usual. And while you're at it, add a waterproof spray to make sure salt stains don't set in the next time you or your loved ones are out walking in a winter wonderland.

Banana split. You can shine smooth leather shoes by rubbing them down with the inside of a banana peel. Buff the leather with a soft cotton cloth to work in the banana oil and bring out the shine. And as an added bonus, the shoes will smell great!

The power of paste. To make ground-in dirt disappear from leather shoes or couches, scrub the spots with toothpaste. Work in a dab of white non-gel paste and wipe off the residue with a clean, damp cloth. Let the leather air-dry completely, and you're good to go.

Kitchen conditioner. Use a dab of olive oil or walnut oil to help hide scratches and restore suppleness to smooth leather items. Rub a small amount of either oil in with a soft, clean cloth, wait an hour or so to let it soak in, then buff the surface to remove any excess. Try this in an inconspicuous spot first to make sure it doesn't discolor the leather.

Light a candle. Sturdy work boots can be made waterproof by rubbing them with melted beeswax. For easy application, melt a beeswax candle in the microwave oven, starting with about 10 seconds. Adjust the time, depending on the candle size and microwave power. Beeswax will leave a visible film on work boots, but it's cheap, tough, and usually lasts longer than expensive weatherproofing sprays.

Hocus Pocus

SPIT SHINE

Leather contains natural oils, so all it usually needs to make it shine is some good old-fashioned elbow grease. But to get that deep-down gleam that military folks call a "spit shine" takes some special know-how. Here's how to do it:

1. Start with spit, and yes, I do mean spit! Rub the shoes or belt with a dab of saliva, working in small, vigorous circles to remove surface dirt and get the shine started.

2. Polish the leather with a leather polish paste. Some older vets swear that adding cigar ash to the polish is the secret to their success. And don't skimp on the elbow grease!

3. Apply more polish, using small circular motions until you build up a thin, dull layer. But don't buff it yet; let it dry to a dull film.

4. Now it's time to really shine: Rub that polish until you can see your face in it. A hank of cotton wool, once common in first-aid kits, was the traditional buffing cloth, but you can also use a cotton cloth or a chamois to get that really deep-down shine.

Powerful Potions

Leather Softener and Restorer

This simple solution will clean leather and keep it smooth and supple, adding a gentle shine that also repels water and stains.

2 parts linseed oil (available at hardware stores)

1 part white vinegar

Short, wide glass jar with tight-fitting lid

Pour the linseed oil and vinegar into the jar, screw on the lid, and shake well before using. To apply, wipe the softener lightly over shoes, sofas, or other leather items, and let it soak in for about an hour. Buff the leather with a soft, dry cloth to remove any excess softener and bring out the shine. Leftovers will keep indefinitely, so store the jar in a cool, dark cabinet.

White glove treatment. Clean the dirt out of the nooks and crannies of leather purses, glasses case, or other small places by using your fingers. Just pull on a pair of white cotton gloves, dip your index finger into a bottle of hair conditioner, and rub the seams and other dirt-collecting crevices. The hair conditioner does double duty by softening the leather while wiping away the dirt.

Belt it out. Belts are usually made of hard finished leather, but even they can pick up dirt and stains. If yours get dirty, clean them with a little white vinegar, followed by some nut oil, olive oil, or melted beeswax to restore the shine. Let the polish sit for about an hour, then vigorously rub with a soft, clean cloth or chamois.

White leather wow. Freshen up white leather shoes by rubbing them with a well-beaten egg white. Rub in the egg white with cotton balls, using a circular motion, then let it dry. Buff the shoes with a soft, clean cloth and the summer whites will be ready for steppin' out in style!

Patent pending. Make patent leather shoes dazzle again by cleaning them with white vinegar and then rubbing on some petroleum jelly, baby oil, or mineral oil. Buff the entire surface with a soft cloth and the shoes will look better than new. And if the black patent leather gets scuffed so badly that the natural leather color shows through, dab a black permanent marker onto the spot before you rub on the gloss.

Steam out smoke smells. When fancy leather duds smell like stale smoke after a night out on the town, freshen them up with a citrus-scented steam bath. Pour about 2 cups of boiling water over the sliced peel of a grapefruit or a couple of oranges to release the oil, and strain the liquid into your bathtub. Fill the tub with a few inches of very hot water, and let the leather clothes hang in the steamy bathroom with the door closed for a couple of hours. Presto—no more smell!

Water-stained leather tabletops. To remove a white water spot from your best leather-topped end table, rub a bit of mayonnaise into it. Let the mayo sit for an hour or so, then wipe the area clean with a soft, dry cloth.

Erase dirty suede. To get rid of water spots, dirt, or other marks on suede, rub the area with an art gum eraser. Brush off the eraser shreds with a dry washcloth as you work, and when the spot is gone, use an emery board to fluff up the nap. A Mr. Clean® Magic Eraser® also works; wet the eraser, squeeze it out, and stroke that stain away.

HOCUS POCUS

TIME FOR A NAP

If the nap on suede shoes, clothes, or furniture looks smooth and shiny instead of soft and velvety, you may be able to improve the texture with a suede brush or nailbrush. If that isn't enough to do the trick, rub the flattened part with a scrap of sandpaper or a nonsoapy steel wool pad. Rub very gently in small circles, and be careful not to overdo it—you're trying to rough up the texture of the surface, not sand a hole through it!

Degreasing suede. Suede soaks up grease like nobody's business. Once you've got a grease stain, a commercial suede-degreasing product or professional cleaner is probably your best bet. You might be able to lessen the stain by sprinkling it with an absorbent powder (see "Take a powder" on page 200). You can also try blotting the spot with a tiny bit of white vinegar on a soft, clean cloth. Test the vinegar in an inconspicuous area first to make sure it won't damage the color, and never pour it directly on the suede—pour it on the cloth instead.

Lunch Boxes and Thermoses

Daily wipe. To keep unpleasant odors from building up inside of a lunch box, wet a paper towel with white vinegar and give everything a good going-over. It's smart to do the job as soon as you can, so the box doesn't remain closed up for any longer than necessary.

Odor absorber. To soak up nasty smells inside of a soft-sided lunch box, sprinkle some baking soda in it, making sure you get it into the folds in the lining, where odors may be hiding. Zip it closed and let it sit overnight. After the baking soda has had a chance to absorb the odors, wash and dry the container, and it'll be ready to be put to good use.

Vinegar sandwich. If a lunch box is pretty stinky, a simple wipe often won't be enough to get rid of the odor. So try this trick: Put a slice of bread inside the box and pour white vinegar on it until it's moist, but not soggy. Then close the box and let it sit overnight. The next morning, remove the vinegar "sandwich," rinse the box, and let it air-dry with the lid open. The vinegar scent will evaporate as the box dries.

Stop bacteria buildup. To get rid of bacteria that may be contributing to the smell inside of a lunch box, spray it with a solution made of 1 tablespoon of bleach and 1 quart of water. The chlorine will kill germs instantly. Wash the solution away with a warm, soapy cloth after you spray it on, and the box will be food-safe for next time.

A silver lining. If a stiff plastic lunch box has a removable lining, you can throw the lining into your washing machine (along with a few towels) to make it smell fresh again. Or you can soak it in warm water with a couple of tablespoons of bleach added to destroy the odor-causing bacteria. Rinse it thoroughly and let it air-dry completely before reusing.

Q. My daughter's soft-sided lunch box just plain stinks! What can I do to remove the sour milk smell?

A. Luckily, I have a neat trick that'll get rid of bad smells lickety-split: Simply add that stinky lunch container to your next load of towels in the washing machine. Be sure to open the box before you put it in, so the inside gets a good scrubbing. Dry it with a paper towel, or let it air-dry, and it'll be odor-free, at least for a while. This method works like magic on any soft-sided box, but don't try it on a stiff plastic box—you'll need to try one of my other solutions to get rid of smells in there.

The Great Clean-dini Speaks

Scrub-a-dub-bubbly. To remove coffee or tomato soup stains from inside of a thermos, fill it with warm water, drop in three or four Alka-Seltzer® tablets, and let it soak for about an hour. That fizzing action will make the stains vanish like magic!

Thermos shake. If the inside of a thermos is looking kind of grungy, follow this routine: Fill it about halfway with hot, soapy water, screw on the cap, and shake it vigorously. Rinse it out and pour in 2 tablespoons of baking soda. Then fill the thermos with boiling water, put the cap back on, and let it sit for about an hour before rinsing it thoroughly. This trick will go a long way toward keeping the thermos nice and clean.

Freshen up. If a thermos smells a little sour, pour 1 cup of bottled lemon juice into it and shake it up. Then fill the thermos—don't empty the lemon juice—with warm water, put the cap on, and let it sit for a while to give the juice time to soak the bad smell away.

There's the rub! When a thermos is all crusty with dried-on food that simple washing won't remove, put the power of eggshells to work. First, put a few eggshells on a cookie sheet and dry them in your oven on low heat for 5 to 10 minutes. Let them cool, coarsely crush them, and drop them into the thermos. Add 1 teaspoon of salt and a few ice cubes and then shake, rattle, and roll the crud away.

Vinegar soak. Coffee can make even the cleanest thermos mighty dirty. The tannins in the coffee stain the liner and an oily residue can build up on the walls. To make that gunk disappear, pour 1 cup of white vinegar in the thermos, fill it with warm water, and let it soak overnight. In the morning, empty out the vinegar water and wash the thermos with hot, soapy water. Rinse it thoroughly and your next cuppa joe will taste better than ever!

The bottom line. To clean the walls and bottom of a thermos, wrap a long-handled wooden spoon with a hot, soapy dishcloth and rub the residue off. Do this every time you use the thermos and it'll smell fresh as a daisy. And don't forget to wash the area around the cap thoroughly to get out any grime that's settled in the grooves.

Hocus Pocus

CARRYING A COLLECTIBLE?

Old-style lunch boxes are hot as collectibles, and they're fun to carry, too! So when you find one of these treasures, spruce it up with these five easy steps:

1. If the hardware or metal handle is tarnished or rusty, clean it with a combination chrome polish/rust remover (available at local hardware or auto-supply stores). Be careful not to get any polish on the box.

2. Scrub off any rust spots inside or outside the box with a dab of white non-gel toothpaste and an old toothbrush.

3. Dip a sponge into warm, soapy water, squeeze it out until it's moist, and wash the rest of the box. Wipe with a damp sponge and dry the box immediately with paper towels. Pay attention to the hinges, latch, and handle, where rust can get started if moisture lingers. You can also use rubbing alcohol to clean the box, but test it first—it may damage the colored pictures.

4. After the box is completely dry, apply a light coat of car wax to the outside to give it a protective shine.

5. If the lunch box has a matching thermos, use the same tricks to make it look good again. If the lid is stuck, give it a squirt of WD-40® to loosen the threads. Wipe off any solvent that runs down the bottle so it doesn't damage the finish, and then wash the thermos again with warm, soapy water. Dry it completely, and screw the cap back on—not too tightly, now!

Makeup Stains

Clean as a baby's bottom. Baby wipes provide a quick and easy way to remove many makeup stains (including eye shadow, eyeliner, face powder, and the dreaded red lipstick), especially when the marks are still fresh. The next time you smear or spill your makeup, grab a baby wipe and swipe those marks away. So carry a small packet of wipes in your purse, and you'll have an instant solution for mishaps away from home.

All-purpose stain remover. If eye shadow, blush, or face powder has stained any of your washable items, reach for my favorite all-purpose cleaner—the bottle of grease-cutting dishwashing liquid under the kitchen sink! Squirt some on the stain, work it in with your fingers, and let it sit for about 15 minutes. Then launder the clothes as usual, and the stain will wash right out.

Start with the A's. Alcohol or ammonia can make a lipstick stain on clothes, upholstery, or carpet disappear. Blot the stain with a clean cloth dipped in either solution (but not both), and keep folding the cloth as

HOCUS POCUS

BRUSH AWAY BACTERIA

Makeup brushes are breeding grounds for bacteria, so keeping them clean will help stop the spread of germs and maybe even prevent nasty breakouts on your skin. You can kill the bugs and remove the makeup residue in just a few seconds by simply swiping the brush back and forth over an antibacterial wet wipe. When you need to do a more thorough cleaning, wash the brush under running water with a bit of shampoo. Blot up excess moisture with a bath towel, and always let the brush air-dry before you put it away.

Grandma Putt's Magical Methods

Although red was my Grandma Putt's favorite color of lipstick, it's one of the hardest shades to get out when it's smeared on a collar or shirt. Why? Because a lipstick stain is part grease and part dye. So my Grandma came up with a great three-step trick for handling this tough customer. Here's how to do it:

1. Gently rub a bit of vegetable or mineral oil into the stain, letting it soak in for about 15 minutes. Then blot the spot with paper towels to remove as much oil and lipstick as possible.

2. Sponge the stain with rubbing alcohol to lift the dye and cut the grease.

3. Wait about five minutes for the alcohol to work its magic, and then toss the item into the washing machine, using the cold water setting. If any stain remains after washing, don't put the garment in the dryer—apply more alcohol, wait about five minutes, and wash it again.

it picks up the color. If the item is washable, rub in a bit of dishwashing liquid and let it sit for a few minutes before you launder it as usual. And remember, don't use ammonia on silk, wool, or rayon fabrics because it can damage the fibers or change the color.

The eyes have it. When mascara or eyeliner leaves unsightly black tracks on nonwashable items, use my Extra-Strength Dry Spotter potion on page 164 to remove it. Apply the Spotter, blot up the black, and the stains will be gone before you can bat an eyelash. And to get those streaks of mascara or eyeliner off washable items, pretreat the stains by rubbing some grease-cutting dishwashing liquid into the gunk before you launder the articles as usual.

Use your head. Try a spritz of hair spray to take a lipstick stain out of clothes. Hair spray contains alcohol, which works great at breaking down an oily stain. Simply spray the stain, wait a few minutes, and blot the lipstick away. Cheap hair spray often has a higher alcohol content than the fancy brands, so keep a can in your cabinet for handy stain removal.

Shave off stains. Next time you drip a bit of liquid foundation onto a clean shirt, squirt some foam shaving cream directly onto the stain. Work it in with your fingers, then rinse in cool water, and the dirty spot will be gone in a flash.

A dab'll do it. To remove a face powder stain from clothes or upholstery, dampen a cloth with my Extra-Strength Dry Spotter potion on page 164 and dab it quickly against the stain a few times. Don't rub the spot because you'll only drive the stain deeper into the fabric. This may be all you need to make the stain vanish, but if any traces remain, repeat the treatment. Just be certain to test the potion first in an inconspicuous area to make sure the fabric is colorfast.

Shake the foundation. Liquid makeup is an oily product, so you need to treat it with a powerful grease cutter. Squeeze a little dishwashing liquid directly onto the stain, and work it in with your fingers. Let it sit for about 10 minutes, and then launder the item as usual. If foundation spilled on an item you can't toss in the washing machine, use my Extra-Strength Dry Spotter potion on page 164 to make that smear vanish into thin air.

Wave bye-bye! When oily hand lotion stains your clothes, reach for the grease-cutting dishwashing liquid and follow the steps in "Shake the foundation" above. And if hand lotion winds up on your upholstery, whip up a sudsy froth of dishwashing liquid with a little water, and blot the grease away with the foam (see The Great Clean-dini Speaks at right for the how-to).

Q. My makeup keeps rubbing off inside the collar of my suede jacket, and it's a real mess. But professional cleaning is so expensive! Is there anything I can try at home to get the stains out?

The Great Clean-dini Speaks

A. Of course there is—and all you need is a little cornstarch and some dishwashing liquid. Follow these steps to spiff up that soiled collar with some of my cleaning magic:

1. First, rough up the stained part of the collar with a dry washcloth. This will help the cleaning solutions penetrate the stain more easily.

2. Powder the stain with a liberal coating of cornstarch, and let it sit overnight to soak up the oil. Brush off the residue the next morning with a dry washcloth.

3. Get out a hand mixer and whip up a batch of soapsuds in a small, deep bowl. Use a few good squirts of dishwashing liquid in about 1 cup of water, and beat the solution until it forms a billow of thick, frothy suds.

4. Next, dip a sponge into just the suds—not the water—and sponge the foam onto the stain. Rub it in gently, making sure to completely cover the stained area. Let it sit for a few minutes, and then wipe it away with a clean, damp cloth.

5. Dry the suede with a blow dryer (set on cool), and brush the nap up with a small stiff brush. Now that the stain is gone, don't forget to tuck a scarf inside your collar the next time you wear the jacket, so you won't have to deal with messy makeup stains ever again!

Toothpaste scrub. When lipstick, mascara, or other oily makeup ends up on your walls or floor instead of on your face, first try wiping it away with a warm, soapy cloth. If you need more scrubbing power, squeeze a dab of white non-gel toothpaste onto an old toothbrush, and scrub the wayward marks away.

Handbag help. Remove makeup stains from the inside of a handbag by scrubbing the spots with a dab of grease-cutting dishwashing liquid on an old toothbrush. Rub in one direction, not in circles, and wipe off the soap with a clean, damp cloth. Use a blow dryer (set on cool) to dry the lining, and you'll be good to go!

Good-bye to dye. Dyeing your hair at home can be quite messy, but you can easily remove any smudges and drips with rubbing alcohol. You may need to repeat the treatment a few times, especially if you're using a dark permanent dye. If the alcohol isn't enough to take out all the color, blot the spots with a cloth that's been moistened with mineral spirits to dissolve any colorful residue.

Fizz away carpet stains. If you've got a makeup stain on your light-colored synthetic carpet, mix ¼ cup of hydrogen peroxide and 1 tablespoon of ammonia, and blot the stain with a cloth that's moistened with the solution. Let the cloth sit on the area for about 10 minutes, so the peroxide can bleach the stain away. Then spray the area lightly with water, and blot it with a clean, dry cloth. Use a fan or blow dryer (set on cool) to dry up any remaining moisture.

Clean your drawers. No need to blush—I'm talking about the drawer in your bathroom vanity! To clean up the streaks and spills on the wooden bottom and sides of a makeup drawer, pour about 1 teaspoon of Avon Skin So Soft Original Replenishing Body Lotion onto a cotton ball, and wipe the marks away. You'll get rid of other dirt at the same time, and the drawer will smell great, too! You can also use this trick to wipe off smudges on the outside of a wooden vanity.

Marble

Acid is the enemy. Marble is a porous stone, which means it can absorb spills and stains quite easily. But what's even worse is that marble can actually be dissolved by acid. That's why it's important to wipe up spills as soon as they happen. Why, even something as harmless as fruit juice or cola can contain enough acid to eat into your marble. So keep the paper towels handy, and always use coasters on marble surfaces.

Wet wipe. The best way to keep marble looking good is to avoid cleaning products altogether, and use only plain water to wipe it down. If there's greasy residue on the surface, use a mild solution of dishwashing liquid in a bucket of warm water to wash off the oily film, and rinse it with clean water right away. Then dry the marble with a soft chamois, so the water doesn't spot the stone.

Soda for stains. To remove mild stains from marble surfaces, sprinkle some baking soda onto a damp cloth and rub the spots away. For more stubborn stains, make a paste of baking soda and water, apply it to the stains, and let it sit for about an hour before rinsing it away. And don't worry—baking soda is alkaline, not acidic, so it won't eat into the marble.

Bleach bonus. To remove coffee, tea, wine, and other dark liquid stains from marble, you'll need to bleach them out. First, lay a paper towel saturated with hydrogen peroxide on the stains. Then cover them with plastic wrap, and hold it in place with masking tape around the edges so the peroxide doesn't dry out. Check the stains after an hour or so, and if they're still there, wait a while longer. It may take as long as 48 hours to completely bleach out the spots, so be patient.

Powerful Potions

Marble Poultice

Whiting is calcium carbonate that's been ground to a fine powder. What's calcium carbonate, you ask? Nothing but plain old white chalk. When it's mixed with a stain-removing chemical to make a paste, it's called a marble poultice, which can make stains vanish without harming the marble. You'll find the banana oil (amyl acetate) for the paste at the drugstore; it's not made from bananas, but it smells just like them!

3–4 tbsp. of whiting

2 tbsp. of banana oil

Stir the whiting into the banana oil, adding 1 tablespoon at a time until it becomes a creamy paste. Spread the poultice onto the stain, and cover it with plastic wrap. Use masking tape to hold the plastic wrap in place. Remove the poultice after about 30 minutes, and wipe the residue off with a moist cloth. Be careful when you work with the banana oil because it's highly flammable: Don't use it near a flame or spark! Also avoid breathing the fumes, no matter how good they smell, and keep a window open to ventilate the area.

Grease begone. When butter, hand lotion, or any other oily product soaks into marble, sprinkle the spots with cornstarch, letting it soak up the grease overnight. Wipe the powder off the next morning, and scrub the spots with a sponge dipped in hot water and grease-cutting dishwashing liquid. Rinse, dry, and hope for the best. If you can still see a spot where the grease soaked in, try my Marble Poultice above.

Salty grapefruit. Citric acid is normally a no-no on marble, but when it comes to taking out surface stains, it may be worth a try. Pour some table salt on a dinner plate, and push a freshly cut grapefruit half into the salt. Then rub the salty grapefruit over the stains. Immediately rinse the residue off, and dry with a soft, clean cloth or chamois.

Microwave Ovens

Spray and zap. Here's a quick and easy way to clean a dirty microwave oven. Spray the inside lightly with plain water, being careful not to direct the spray into the vents, close the door, and zap it on high for 60 seconds. Then open the door, and wipe away the crud. It doesn't get any easier than this!

Tray time. You'll find it a lot easier to clean your microwave tray and/or turntable if you take them out of the oven to do the job. Soak them in warm, soapy water to loosen any baked-on grime, and then wash them with the rest of your dishes. Dry the pieces before you put them back in the microwave.

Dishcloth bake. You can soften the crud in a microwave by zapping a wet dishcloth on high for about one minute. Let it cool off for three or four minutes with the door closed, so the steam can loosen the grunge inside the oven. Then wipe down the inside with the same cloth.

Hocus
Pocus

EXPLODING WATER

Heating water in a microwave can be dangerous because the water won't boil with bubbles, unless there's something else in the dish. The hot water isn't able to let off steam, so it gets superheated, just waiting to explode in a rush as soon as you move the container.

To avoid a nasty burn, always drop something into the container when you zap water in a microwave oven. Put a lemon wedge or a toothpick in the dish of water, and it'll solve the problem and keep you safe. Just remember, though, that microwave-heated water will still be mighty hot, so always handle it with care.

Powerful Potions

Soot and Smell Dissolver

When you burn food in a microwave, white vinegar does a great job of eliminating the black soot, but quite often, yellow stains are left behind on the oven walls. To make the final traces of the cooking accident disappear, wipe the walls down with acetone nail polish remover. Rinse them thoroughly, then finish up the job with this mix:

> ¼ cup of bottled lemon juice
>
> 2–3 cut-up chunks of fresh lemon
>
> ½ cup of water

Put all the ingredients in a microwave-safe bowl and zap it on high for one to two minutes. The citrus will make the oven smell as clean as it looks.

Vinegar power. Vinegar is a great grease cutter, so put its power to work inside your microwave—not with elbow grease, but with steam. Fill a Pyrex® measuring cup halfway with white vinegar, and zap it on high for two minutes. Keep the door closed for five minutes, so the steam can get to work. Carefully remove the cup, dip a sponge into the hot vinegar, and wipe the residue away.

Something's fishy. When smelly foods leave their aroma behind after you microwave them, use lemon water to get rid of the stink. Fill a microwave-safe bowl halfway with water, drop in a wedge or two of fresh lemon, and zap it on high for two minutes. Keep the door closed for five minutes while the water steams and cools down a bit. Remove the bowl, dip a cloth into the water, and wipe down the interior. The lemony moisture will leave a nice fresh scent behind.

Burnt to a crisp. Uh-oh—burnt popcorn! Whenever your food gets zapped and ends up black, use this quick trick to neutralize the odor and make your oven (and kitchen) smell good again. Put a used coffee filter (including grounds) into a microwave-safe dish. Pour in just enough water to cover the grounds, and zap it on high for a couple of minutes. No more stinky burnt smell—just the great aroma of fresh-brewed coffee!

Musical Instruments

Be precise. Fiddling around with the delicate parts of a precision instrument can lead to real problems because it takes special know-how to clean them. Your local music store has the products and tools you'll need and the experts who can advise you. In this section, you'll find some handy hints to keep *other* parts of the instruments in fine fettle.

An old softie. Fingerprints can be real troublemakers on musical instruments, but cleaners can cause even worse problems by stripping the lacquer finish or damaging the intricate works. So use a soft, dry, lint-free cloth to polish paw prints off the surface of trumpets, guitars, flutes, or other music makers. Microfiber cloths work best because they won't leave a trail of lint, or you can use an old soft cotton handkerchief or piece of flannel.

Q. The keys on my old piano have really yellowed over the years. Is there anything I can do to make them white again?

A. Ivory naturally turns yellow as it ages, and some people consider it part of the charm. But if that yellow tinge is bugging you, you can improve the color by wiping the keys with mayonnaise. Simply dab some mayo on a soft, clean cloth, rub it into the keys, and wipe it off with a soft, dry cloth. They won't turn snow-white, but they will be whiter, and they'll feel silky to the touch, too. And here's another trick to help those yellow keys see the light: Keep your keyboard open on sunny days and let the keys enjoy a nice gentle bleaching from the sun.

The Great Clean-dini Speaks

Tickle the ivories. Genuine ivory is a treasure, so if your piano keys are the real deal, treat them with extra care. Wipe the keys with a soft, clean cloth to remove fingerprint oils and dust. For stubborn dirt or stained areas, try something you use on your own ivories—a dab of toothpaste. Rub it gently onto the spots with a damp cloth, wipe it away with a clean, damp cloth, and buff the keys dry.

Plastic is the key. Most pianos are made with plastic keys nowadays, so keep them clean by occasionally rubbing them down with a solution made of 1 part warm water and 1 part vinegar. Simply dampen a clean, dry cloth with the mixture and wipe each key from back to front. That'll keep the sides of the keys from getting wet, which can warp the wood they're made of. Dry and buff the keys after you clean them, using a microfiber cloth or chamois.

Dry-clean your piano. Keep the wood case of a piano looking its very best with a simple dusting. Use a soft, clean cloth for large surfaces, and hook up the soft-brush attachment of your vacuum cleaner to make any cobwebs disappear. Pay special attention to the foot pedals, where dirt tends to build up.

Sticky pads. If the pads on a flute start to make a little noise when they lift up, there's probably some moisture inside that keeps them from working smoothly. So slide a piece of clean cigarette paper under the sticky key and close it with a little more pressure than you would if you were playing. That'll squeeze the moisture out, so the absorbent paper can quickly soak it up. Release the key, remove the paper, and the flute will be a real smooth operator again.

Minerals in the mouthpiece. Calcium often builds up inside the mouthpiece of a flute, but it's easy to soak it away. Just dip a cotton ball in white vinegar and wipe things down in there. Let the vinegar soak into the mineral deposits for a few minutes, then wipe it away with a damp cotton ball. Be sure to keep the vinegar only on the metal and away from the cork, which it could damage.

Nix the polish. Have you ever wondered why that priceless old Martin D-18 guitar under your bed sounds so great? Over the years, the wood gradually dries out—and that's a good thing when it comes to acoustic guitars because it makes the sound more resonant. Furniture wax, polish, and lubricants all slow down the process, but there's another reason to avoid them: They can lead to a muddy tone when they build up. So keep the polish away from the wood, and use only a soft, dry cloth to clean it.

Hocus Pocus

PLAYING CLEAN

Whether you play a cheap harmonica or a fine flute, your instrument will stay cleaner if you keep your hands and mouth clean. So wash your hands, brush your teeth, and wipe your lipstick or lip balm off before you start jammin'. And don't sip on a soft drink or juice during breaks—the sugar in your saliva can make the keys mighty sticky.

Swipe your strings. Cleaning guitar strings helps them last longer, and it'll make them sound better, too. Here's how to do the job in just a few seconds: Take an inexpensive alcohol hand wipe, wrap it around each individual string, and run it along the length. It'll take the sweat and grime off faster than you can say "Cheap Trick"!

Don't fret about it. A well-used guitar gathers a lot of dirt along the fret board, especially if your hands tend to sweat when you're playing. Clean the board whenever you change the strings by wiping it down with a soft, dry cloth. And to get the grunge out from around the metal frets, use a stiff piece of cardboard or a guitar pick. Just be sure to work around them carefully, so you don't gouge the wood while you're digging the gunk out.

Mustard Stains

Fresh fix. All stains are easiest to remove when they're fresh, and that's especially true for mustard. So put down that hot dog and jump into action when a blob of the yellow stuff goes astray. Blot away as much as you can with a paper towel, and immediately apply a commercial laundry stain treater to the area. Wash the item in cold water and then check the spot. If a stain remains, try one of my other stain-busting tricks in this section.

Scrape 'n' shake. Once a dried glob of mustard gets wet, the stain can spread. So before you apply a liquid cleaner, scrape off as much of the dry residue as you can. Use the edge of a credit card or a spoon to scrape away the crust, and shake the stained item vigorously to make sure that all of the specks you scraped off are no longer on the fabric. Take the item outside to scrape and shake it, so those specks don't end up on a rug or furniture—or the clothes you're wearing!

Hair of the dog. It may seem like backwards logic, but applying more mustard to an old stain can actually make it easier to remove. The fresh stuff will help lift the dye out of the fibers, so the cleaner you use for the next step won't have such a tough task. Use the same kind of mustard as in the original stain, and squeeze a dab right onto the spot. Let it sit for about a minute, and then rinse the spot with warm water. Rub some liquid laundry detergent into the stain, wait about 10 minutes, and launder the item as usual.

Sink soak. A long soak might be just the trick you need to remove a stubborn mustard stain. Wet the stained area, rub some liquid or powdered laundry detergent into the stain, and soak it in a sink full of warm, soapy water for about 12 hours. The next day, rinse the item and check the stain—if it's still there, rub some more detergent into the spot, wait about 10 minutes, and launder the item as usual.

The Great Clean-dini Speaks

Ready to cut a rug? When mustard drips onto the carpet, you could always cut out the spot and patch it with a fresh piece of rug. But before you reach for the scissors, try this treatment to remove the stain:

1. Start by blotting up as much of the wet mustard as you can with a paper towel, and then apply my Extra-Strength Dry Spotter potion on page 164 to the spot.

2. If the stain remains, sponge the area with fresh water to rinse out the Dry Spotter potion, then apply my Wet Spotter potion on page 162.

3. Still have a spot? Rinse the Wet Spotter potion, blot up the extra water, and moisten the area with hydrogen peroxide. Drizzle a few drops of white vinegar on top. Let the solution fizz for about 15 minutes, rinse the carpet, blot up the excess moisture, and use a fan or blow dryer (set on cool) to dry the area thoroughly. *Caution:* Peroxide is a bleach that can affect the color of your carpet, so always test it in an inconspicuous area first.

That's fantastic! Here's an easy trick that will lighten up a mustard stain. After you scrape off any extra mustard, spray the spot with fantastik® All-Purpose Cleaner. Let it sit for a few minutes, then rub the stained fabric against itself and rinse it with cold water. Repeat the treatment several times, and the mustard spot should become practically invisible.

Sour soap. To encourage an old mustard stain to give up the ghost, make a mixture of 1 teaspoon of dishwashing liquid, 1 teaspoon of white vinegar, and ½ cup of water. Lay the stained area on top of an old absorbent towel, pour the solution onto the stain, and let it soak for about 10 minutes. Rinse the area with hot water, then launder the item as usual. Repeat the treatment if you can still see the spot.

Grandma Putt's Magical Methods

When my hot dog went haywire, my Grandma Putt made a mixture of 1 part rubbing alcohol and 3 parts dishwashing liquid, laid an old towel underneath the item, and poured the solution right on the spot. She let it soak for about 10 minutes while the stain darkened—a sure sign that her trick was working. After that, she rinsed the stain with hot water, rubbed some laundry detergent into the spot, and washed the item as usual. More often than not, by the time the wash cycle had finished, the mustard stain had vanished!

Sunshine stain fighter. If a mustard stain remains even after trying my tricks, let the sun finish the job. Set the wet, freshly washed garment outside in full sun for a few hours. This works best in summer, when the sun is at its strongest. Sunlight can fade the colors in clothing, so save this trick for white or light-colored items only.

Get the yellow out. Chlorine bleach will make old mustard stains vanish from white garments. Use the presoak cycle of your washing machine, adding ½ cup of bleach to the water. Then wash the item as usual with more bleach according to the directions on the label.

Nail Polish Stains

Blot it away. When nail polish goes astray, reach for the nail polish remover. Dab the stain with an acetone-based remover to pick up the polish, but don't rub because it will only drive the stain in deeper. When the polish has disappeared, blot the spot with a warm, soapy cloth and rinse with clean water. This trick works on most fabrics, but don't try it on silk, wool, or rayon, which acetone can damage. And remember, it's always a good idea to test a stain-removal trick in an inconspicuous area first, especially if you're working on expensive furniture, carpet, or designer duds.

Acetone flush. If nail polish remover isn't strong enough to handle an old, dried-out nail polish stain on clothes, pick up some pure acetone at a beauty products shop. Place the stained area over an old bath towel, and pour the acetone onto the stain. It'll soak through the fabric into the towel. Repeat until the stain is gone, then launder the item as usual.

Suede scrub. Remove hardened nail polish from soft suede by rubbing it with an art gum eraser. If the spot is extra stubborn, try an emery board or a piece of very fine sandpaper (6/0 or 8/0 grade). Rub carefully, so you take off only the polish and not the leather. Finish the job by using a short, stiff brush to fluff up the nap.

Hocus Pocus

YES, WE HAVE NO BANANAS

Nail polish can really do a number on vinyl, acrylic, and other plastics, so you need to act fast. Wipe up the spill with a wet cloth, and then sponge the rest of the stain with amyl acetate, which is sometimes called banana oil. Thoroughly rinse the plastic surface with warm water after you use the banana oil, and the stain will simply slip away.

Powerful Potions

Old Salt

There's no need to cry over spilled nail polish when you can use this easy trick to treat a fresh stain on carpet or upholstery.

1 part dishwashing liquid

1 part coarse kosher salt

2 parts water

First, blot up the excess polish. Then combine the ingredients to make a syrupy mixture. Pour the syrup directly onto the stain and work it into a lather with a stiff brush. Blot and wipe the area, rinse the syrup off with a clean, damp cloth, and let the spot air-dry.

Dry-spot the stain. To eliminate a nail polish stain from fabrics like rayon, silk, or wool that can't take the acetone treatment, start by scraping the blob of polish with a dull knife to remove as much of it as you can. Then apply my Extra-Strength Dry Spotter potion on page 164 to an absorbent pad of paper towels, and lay them on the stain to soak up the rest. Apply more Dry Spotter whenever the paper towels begin to dry out, and keep folding them to a fresh section as they soak up the polish. There's no need to rinse—just let the item air-dry.

Metal makeover. If you find a few drips of nail polish on an object made of aluminum, stainless steel, iron, or tin, scrub them off with a steel wool soap pad. Rinse, and dry thoroughly with a soft cloth so rust doesn't set in.

Marble paste. When the dye from a nail polish spill seeps into a white marble surface, your best bet is to spread a cleaning paste over the stain to draw out the dye. Mix 1 tablespoon of hydrogen peroxide and 1 tablespoon of water with enough powdered laundry detergent to make a paste, and smear it onto the stain. Cover the paste with a damp cloth, and let it sit until the stain has been bleached away. Then wipe the paste off with a moist cloth, and polish the marble with a soft, dry cloth.

Make mine a double! If a nail polish disaster hits your carpet, you need a double dose of alcohol. Saturate the stain with rubbing alcohol, and blot with a clean cloth to take the gunk off that's near the surface. Then soak the stain with cheap hair spray—which has a high alcohol content—and rub the deeper dye out. Keep folding the cloth so you don't spread the stain, and be sure to test the trick on an inconspicuous area first.

Shaving solutions. Both shaving cream and aftershave contain a good deal of alcohol, so keep them in mind the next time you need a fast fix for a nail polish spill on carpet or upholstery. Apply either of the products to the stain, wait a few minutes for them to work on the dye, and blot the color up with a dry cloth. Repeat the treatment until the stain is gone. And remember, always wipe up as much of the fresh nail polish as you can before you raid the bathroom cabinet.

Bubbly scrub. To lift a nail polish stain off carpets or upholstery, try the foaming action of hydrogen peroxide. Pour some peroxide on the spot, let it fizz for a few minutes, and then scrub the area vigorously with a stiff brush. Blot the peroxide and nail polish up with an old washcloth, and then use paper towels to sponge out as much moisture as possible. Peroxide is a bleach, so this trick is best for light-colored fabrics.

Grandma Putt's Magical Methods

When nail polish landed on my Grandma Putt's painted walls, linoleum floor, or other hard surface, she harnessed the power of the 20-mule team. A single teaspoon of borax mixed in 1 cup of water did the trick, along with a big helping of elbow grease. Of course, Grandma always wiped up as much as she could while the spill was still fresh, before she called in the mighty mules.

Needlework

Shake it off. To remove dust from needlework pillows or wall hangings, give them a good shaking. Do the job outside on a breezy day, and keep your back to the wind so the dirt blows away from you. The fresh air will make the needlework smell fresh and clean, but don't leave it outside for long because sunlight can fade the fibers.

Screen the stitches. Using a vacuum cleaner to suck the dust off needlework may work just fine, but the suction can sometimes pull threads loose, especially if it's an older piece. If you'd rather not take any chances with those delicate stitches, cover the artwork with a clean window screen, then vacuum the dust up through the screen. Just make sure the screen has no sharp edges that could snag the threads or fabric.

Banish bloodstains. Did you prick your finger while you were counting your cross-stitch? A little dab of blood is a common problem when you're working with needles, but you can use one of these simple solutions to make the stains disappear:

- ★ Saliva will lift off a spot of blood, so go ahead and spit on it. Then blot up the saliva and the blood.

- ★ Rinse the piece with plenty of cold water. Don't soak it, though, or the dye in the thread might run.

- ★ If you don't want to get your artwork wet, rub the spot with an ice cube until it lifts out the blood, then dab off the stain.

- ★ Mix 2 tablespoons of salt with enough cold water to make a paste, apply it to the stain, and let it sit for about 15 minutes. Rinse with a wet cloth, then repeat if necessary.

- ★ Wet the stained area with cold water and rub some meat tenderizer into both sides of the fabric. Let it sit for about 30 minutes, then rinse the stain away.

DON'T BE CREWEL

Wool thread can shrink or bleed when it gets soaking wet, so be sure to use very little water when it's time to clean your crewelwork or other wool-embroidered pieces. Here's how to clean wool—crewelty-free:

Hocus Pocus

1. Use a hand mixer to whip up a combo of Woolite® and cool water until you have plenty of nice fluffy suds.

2. Dip a white washcloth into the suds, not the water, and dab the canvas firmly over the entire surface. You'll be able to see the white cloth pick up the dirt, so keep switching it around to a clean part.

3. "Rinse" the clean piece by moistening a clean cloth and dabbing the soapy residue away. Let it air-dry, and the woolly work will be "shear" perfection!

Cookie sheet soak. Here's a trick that can make an old stained piece of needlework look like new again. Pull out a clean cookie sheet that's got a rim, and fill it almost to the top with a solution of cold water and OxiClean® Versatile Stain Remover powder according to the directions on the package. Lay the needlework piece in the tray and submerge it in the cleaning solution. Let it soak for about 10 minutes, then rinse it in a sink full of cool water and roll it in a bath towel to blot it dry.

Say "neigh"! What do savvy stitchers swear by when it's time to wash their needlework? Believe it or not, it's a horse shampoo called Orvus® that works like magic on needlework. This shampoo is sold in tack shops, farm stores, stitchery shops, and discount stores. The paste makes lots of suds, so only use about ¼ teaspoon to a quart of cool water. Fill your sink with enough soapy water to cover the needlework, submerge the piece, and let it soak for about 30 minutes. Rinse the needlework, blot it dry, and the piece will be as clean as a whistle.

Antimildew measures. If speckles or blotches of mildew or other mold appear on needlework, wet the spots and rub a mixture of salt and lemon juice into them to gently bleach away the discoloration. Rinse the areas with white vinegar, and let them air-dry. Just don't try this trick on any piece that's got metallic threads—the acid in the lemon juice and vinegar may tarnish them.

A matter of size. Needlepoint canvas—not the kind sold for cross-stitch—is treated with sizing to keep it stiff. The sizing dissolves in water, so if you wash or wet the piece, it'll turn limp and floppy. For needlework that needs more than a simple dusting, ask your favorite stitchery shop to recommend a local dry cleaner.

Cleaning cross-stitch. Cross-stitch cloth is made from cotton, polyester, and other washable fabrics, so cleaning these pieces is a cinch. Hand washing works great, but some cross-stitch fabrics are machine washable. Check the label, and use the delicate cycle and cold water setting if you decide to let your washing machine do the cleaning.

Iron it dry. After a cross-stitch piece has had its bath, spread a dry bath towel on an ironing board and lay the damp piece of needlework facedown on top of it. Iron it on a low or medium setting with no steam, and keep the iron moving as you work. When the piece is nice and flat, turn it right side up and let it air-dry.

Grandma Putt's Magical Methods

The dyes used in older embroidery floss aren't usually colorfast, so the colors may run when they get wet. That's why my Grandma Putt "dry-cleaned" her needlework—by dusting it with potato flour. She'd sprinkle some flour onto the surface and let it sit overnight to absorb the greasy dirt, and then shake or vacuum it off the next day. If you don't have any potato flour on hand, cornmeal works well, too.

Ovens

Vinegar wipe. A regular wipe-down with white vinegar will go a long way toward keeping an oven spic-and-span. Vinegar cuts through greasy crud quick as a wink, so just pour some on a sponge, wipe down the oven, rinse it with a moist sponge, and you're good to go!

Salt those spills. When a sticky pie bubbles over onto the bottom of an oven, sprinkle the goo with a layer of salt while the oven is still hot. The salt will soak up the mess and keep the oven from smoking. As soon as the oven is cool, scrape off the hardened residue with a nonscratch spatula.

Self-cleaning safety. If your oven is the self-cleaning type, open a window before you start the cycle so the sooty smoke can escape instead of stinking up your kitchen. (This also will help prevent triggering your smoke alarms.) Take hot pads or other items off the stovetop, remove any dish towels hanging on the oven door, and pull off any plastic stove knobs because it's gonna get mighty hot in there—900°F to be exact! After the oven has cooled, wipe up the gray ash with a damp cloth and clean the door, window, and oven seal with my Super Scrubber potion on page 307.

Baking soda scrape. Use baking soda for a simple, safe oven cleaner that works while you sleep—with no stinky fumes! Before you go to bed, sprinkle a thick layer of baking soda on the bottom of the cool oven. Spray the soda with water to wet it down, close the oven door, and say good night. By morning, all of the grunge will have loosened up, and you can wipe it out with a wet sponge. This works well to spot-clean messy oven spills, too.

Powerful Potions

Easy Oven Cleaner

Use this powerful paste to wipe up spills or to give your oven a good, thorough cleaning. Just be sure the oven is cool before you start to work.

1 part ammonia

1 part white vinegar

2 parts water

Enough baking soda to make a paste

Combine the ammonia, vinegar, and water in a large glass or ceramic bowl, then stir in the baking soda until it makes a creamy paste. Rub the paste all over the bottom and sides of the oven, as well as the door and the inside of the window. Let the paste sit for about 30 minutes and wipe it off. If any stubborn spots remain, use a nonabrasive plastic scrubbie and another dab of paste to cut through the crud. Rinse the residue off with a moist sponge, and your oven will be as clean as a whistle. To make it even easier for the paste to do its stuff, wipe any loose grime out of the oven before you apply this cleaner.

Ammonia overnighter. Here's another easy oven cleaner to use while you're sleeping—pour 1 cup of ammonia into a glass bowl and set it in a closed oven overnight. The fumes will loosen the crud while you sleep. In the morning, pour the ammonia into a bucket of hot water and sponge away the grime. If you have some really nasty blackened spills on the bottom, lay a folded paper towel over them and saturate it with ammonia for extra cleaning power. Always wear rubber gloves whenever you use ammonia, and keep your kitchen well ventilated while you work.

Flow down. A baking soda spray will make the blackened gunk on oven walls give up its grip and slide down to the bottom. Put about 3 tablespoons of baking soda into a handheld sprayer bottle, fill the bottle with hot water, and shake it vigorously. Make sure the oven is cool, and spritz the walls with the mix, shaking it frequently as you go. When the grime collects on the bottom, wipe it away.

Spill catcher. To minimize your oven-cleaning chores, line a cookie sheet with foil and put it on the bottom rack underneath the dish you're baking to catch the spills. When you're done baking, just crumple up the dirty foil and toss it in the trash. If any spills happen to miss the cookie sheet and land on the oven, dip the crumpled foil into a paste made of baking soda and water and use the foil as a scrubbie to remove the goo.

The Great Clean-dini Speaks

Q. It seems like it's harder to clean my oven window than it is to clean the oven itself! What's the secret to removing that baked-on grease?

A. Use one of these quick and easy fixes to brighten up your outlook in a hurry:

★ Treat that window as you would a cruddy casserole dish—by soaking it in a mix of grease-cutting dishwashing liquid and water. How can you soak a window? Simple: Just saturate a cleaning cloth with the soapy water, plaster it to the window, and let it sit for about 15 minutes so the soap can penetrate the grease. Then scrub off the residue with a nonabrasive plastic scrubbie.

★ Shake a generous amount of Bar Keepers Friend® scouring powder on a wet sponge, and rub it all over the cool window. Wait about five minutes, then scrub the grime off with a nonabrasive plastic scrubbie.

★ Carefully scrape the hardened grease off with a paint scraper or a single-edge razor blade. And watch your fingers!

Grandma Putt's Magical Methods

You'll foil oven cleaning forever when you use this nifty trick from my Grandma Putt. The next time your electric oven is clean and cool, cover the bottom with overlapping sheets of heavy-duty aluminum foil, slipping the foil *under* the heating element, not over it. Then pesky spills will collect on the foil, and not on the oven. And when the crud builds up, just replace the foil.

Lemon scrub. When you combine the grease-cutting power of lemon juice and the abrasive action of salt, you have a great spot cleaner that'll scrub away spills in a flash—and make your kitchen smell good, too! Just mix 1 part fresh or bottled lemon juice with 1 part salt and apply it to the spills with a damp sponge. Let it sit for about 15 minutes so the juice can penetrate, then rub the spots with a nonabrasive plastic scrubbie. Wipe out the residue, and you're done!

Rack it up. Most kitchen sinks are too small to soak grimy oven racks, so put them in a bathtub instead. To prevent scratching the tub, line it with an old towel or two. Cover the racks with a few inches of warm water, add ½ cup of ammonia, and let them soak for about 30 minutes. The greasy grime will lift right off with a light scrubbing. Just make sure the room is well ventilated, and use long rubber gloves when you scrub to protect your skin from the ammonia.

Spray and wipe. As a last resort, if oven racks are really cruddy, spray them with WD-40® lubricant. Let 'em sit for about 15 minutes while the solvent works on the crud, and then wipe them down with a nonabrasive plastic scrubbie. Rinse the racks extra thoroughly before putting them back in the oven. WD-40 is smelly stuff, so do this job outside, or open a window or two for extra ventilation while you work.

Paintings

Hands off the antiques. If your artwork is old and valuable, don't try anything yourself beyond a simple dusting. Let the experts handle deep cleaning, or you could rub away the value of the painting along with the crud. That goes for prints, too, which can be just as costly as paintings and are even more susceptible to do-it-yourself damage.

Be gentle. Always use a very soft brush to dust paintings off. Flick away loose surface dust with a shaving brush, and use a baby's toothbrush or an artist's brush to remove dust from deeper textures.

Sure shot. In a hurry to dust a painting? Then use a can of compressed air to blow the dirt away. The air is forceful, though, so keep the nozzle several inches away from the surface and you won't loosen any paint. And don't try this trick if the paint is already beginning to flake or crack, or you may blow away the masterpiece in the process.

The Great Clean-dini Speaks

Q. The painting in my living room has gotten so grimy that I can hardly see the details anymore. Is there anything I can do to brighten it up?

A. There sure is—just start loafing! Remove the crust from a slice of fresh white bread, or grab a hunk out of the middle of an unsliced loaf of Italian or sturdy sourdough. Then ball up the dough and rub it gently over the surface of the dirty picture. Replace the bread "eraser" as soon as it gets dirty; you may need two or three loaves of bread to clean a large painting. Finish the cleaning by flicking the crumbs away with a soft brush.

Make it mild. If the surface of an acrylic or oil painting is sticky, mix a little dishwashing liquid in a bucket of warm water and give the artwork a gentle bath. Moisten a soft cotton or microfiber cloth with the soapy water and lightly blot the surface. Never rub because that can loosen the paint, allowing the water to soak into the canvas. And if the cloth drips, squeeze it out—moist, not wet, is the way to go.

Spitball. Saliva contains enzymes that break up grease, so when a painting gets grimy, moisten a cotton swab in your mouth and roll it over the painting's surface. Moisten a fresh swab when the current one gets dirty, and repeat until the painting is clean. This trick works best on small paintings because you can easily cover every inch and avoid blotches.

One potato, two potato... To clean a painting that's not a priceless treasure, cut a raw potato in half, and dab the artwork with the cut surface to pick up the grime. As the potato gets dirty, slice off the soiled end, and keep going until the painting is clean. Some folks swear by using a cut onion in the same way, so if you don't mind the smell, give it a try.

Hocus Pocus

DRY-CLEAN YOUR PAPER

Water, saliva, potato juice, and other cleaning methods will quickly ruin artwork that's painted or printed on paper. To safely clean prints, posters, or watercolors, you'll have to dry-clean them. Here's how to do it:

1. Start with a very soft shaving or artist's brush, and use it to gently wipe off the loose dirt.

2. Wipe the surface even more gently with a dry rubber sponge, which you can buy at paint-supply stores. This trick will work on oil or acrylic paintings, too, but be sure to use only the lightest touch, so you don't damage the artwork's delicate brushstrokes.

Smokers' stains. If you have—or had—smokers living at home, your paintings may be discolored by nicotine buildup. You can remove the grime by gently washing the surface with a sponge moistened with warm, soapy water and lemon juice. Use a few drops of grease-cutting dishwashing liquid, about 1/4 cup of fresh or bottled lemon juice, and 2 cups of water to make the cleaning solution. Keep a bucket of fresh water nearby so you can rinse out the sponge after every few strokes. Rinse off the soap with a clean, moist sponge and that dull, smoky film will disappear like magic.

Paint Stains

Pour on the alcohol. Don't throw paint-stained clothes in the ragbag when you can make those spots vanish in a hurry. Place the stained part on top of an old towel, pour rubbing alcohol on the spots, and the paint will dissolve like magic. Help it along by rubbing the fabric with an old toothbrush to get out deep-down stains, and then launder the item as usual. This trick works great on most clothes, but if you're not sure about the fabric, test it in a hidden spot first.

Sanitize the stain. To make a paint stain disappear, smear a glob of hand sanitizer gel onto the spot and rub the paint off with a nonabrasive plastic scrubbie or an old toothbrush. Use a butter knife to scrape off any excess paint as you work. When the goo is completely gone, launder the item as you usually do.

Spray 'n' scrub. To erase a messy paint smear almost instantly, spritz the area thoroughly with hair spray (the cheaper, the better), and scrape the spot with a flat-bladed knife. Use an old toothbrush to help lift the softened paint out of the fibers, especially on jeans and other coarse cloth. With a little elbow grease, that paint will vanish into thin air!

Powerful Potions

Washing Soda Scrub

Old-fashioned washing soda is the key to making paint stains disappear from granite, slate, sandstone, concrete, and other stone surfaces. It's related to baking soda, but it's more caustic, so be sure to wear long rubber gloves when you work with the stuff.

½ cup of washing soda

3 gal. of water

Mix the washing soda and water in a bucket, dip a soft-bristled brush into the mixture, and start scrubbing. Rinse thoroughly with fresh water, then let the spot air-dry. Washing soda works great on counters and vinyl floors, too, but it'll remove any wax along with the spot of paint. So you'll need to apply another coat of wax after the floor is dry.

Sneaker clean. Give this simple solution a try the next time you splatter paint on your sneakers. First, spray the spots with hair spray, and then scrub the stains away with a nonsoapy steel wool pad. Don't rub too hard—a light touch is all you need to make the paint disappear. This method also cleans paint off old leather work boots, but don't use it on high-fashion shoes because the steel wool will scratch the surface.

Slippery slope. Paint stains are easy to remove from nonabsorbent fabrics like nylon ski jackets. Just reach for a sanitizing hand wipe and swab the stains away. If the paint is stubborn, rub it with a nonabrasive plastic scrubbie and it should lift right off. Wipe it again with a fresh hand wipe, and the last traces will vanish. Then it's all downhill from there.

Bottoms up. Got stubborn paint stains on your clothes? Reach for a bottle of vodka. Pour a little on the stains, and rub it in with a nonabrasive plastic scrubbie or an old toothbrush. Then rinse the fabric with cold water.

Get the goo off Gore-Tex. To remove paint stains from Gore-Tex® without damaging the special finish, put the magic of Murphy® Oil Soap to work for you. Just pour a bit of the soap onto the fabric, scrub the paint off with an old toothbrush, and rinse it clean by wiping the area with a damp cloth.

Temper, temper! When your kids spill tempera paint on their clothes, scrape off the dried paint and then squirt some dishwashing liquid onto the stain. Blot the soap into the stain with a damp cloth, but don't rub because that may spread the paint. Leave the mess alone for 10 minutes, then launder the clothes as usual.

Grandma Putt's Magical Methods

Don't snarl when paint ends up in your hair—use my Grandma Putt's secret to make it vanish. Just pour some baby oil onto a cotton makeup remover pad, wrap the pad around your painted locks, and wipe the paint right off. Repeat the treatment if needed, and then shampoo your hair to remove the oily residue.

A little goofy. To remove a spot of paint from your light-colored carpet, start by scraping off as much of the dried paint as you can. Then spray or pour some Goof Off® onto a dry cloth, and blot the stain until it disappears. Be sure to test this trick on an inconspicuous part of your carpet first to make sure it won't lift the color or harm the fibers.

Crafty carpet trick. Acrylic craft paint is water soluble, so blot these stains away with a damp cloth while the paint is still wet. If the paint has already dried on your carpet, soak a clean cloth in a solution of $\frac{1}{4}$ cup of laundry detergent and 1 gallon of water, and lay the cloth on the stain. It may take an hour or two for the solution to work its magic, so check the stain every 30 minutes. When the paint becomes soluble again, blot it up with the cloth, and then blot again with a clean, moist cloth to rinse the soap out of your rug. If any residue remains, repeat the treatment.

Paneling

Save your back. Whether they're made from real wood or synthetic material, paneled walls don't need much cleaning to keep them looking good. Simply dust them from top to bottom about once a week—but not with an ordinary dust cloth. Use a long-handled mop with a dust-catching microfiber head instead so you can wipe down big sections lickety-split. You'll save a lot of time, and your back will be grateful, too.

Fingerprint kit. When grimy fingers soil the paneling around wall switches, wipe the smudges away with soapy water. Put a few drops of grease-cutting dishwashing liquid in a small bowl of warm water, dip in a cloth,

Powerful Potions

Paneling Cleaner 'n' Polish

Commercial oil soaps do a good job of heavy-duty cleaning, but you can make your own at home for just a fraction of the cost. Use this potion to clean wood or faux wood paneling whenever it gets a greasy, grimy buildup. It'll cut through the oily dirt in a flash and leave a fresh-scented shine.

¼ cup of lemon-scented dishwashing liquid

1 tbsp. of olive oil

1 qt. of warm water

Mix the dishwashing liquid, olive oil, and water in a bucket. Moisten a clean, dry cloth with the solution, and rub the paneling, starting at the bottom and working your way up. There's no need to rinse; just buff the paneling with a dry terry cloth towel to bring out the shine. Work in sections, and don't leave the solution on the wall for longer than a minute or two. Otherwise, it could penetrate the finish and leave a whitish haze. And buff the wood with the grain, not in circles, so your stroke marks blend in with the wood and don't stand out.

and squeeze out the extra water so that it's damp, not wet. Then rub the dirt away, rinse the spots with a clean, damp cloth, and buff the area dry with an old towel.

Knotty know-how. Knotty pine was all the rage back in the '50s—and it seems as if some of it hasn't been cleaned since then. Pine paneling darkens naturally as it ages, but you can take off the greasy crud that's accumulated on it over the years with a scoop of OxiClean® Versatile Stain Remover powder in a gallon of warm water. Murphy® Oil Soap or Pine-Sol® will also do the trick, although you may need to go over the wood more than once to remove the decades of dirt buildup.

Patios and Patio Furniture

Colored concrete cleanup. Stamped and colored concrete pavers are a favorite among do-it-yourselfers because they're easy to install and require no special skills. Keeping them clean is just as simple: Wet them down with a garden hose, squirt a little dishwashing liquid over the surface, and scrub away with a push broom. Rinse until the soap is gone, and let them air-dry before putting them back into service.

Stain paste. Removing stains from concrete pavers or a concrete slab is a snap if you slather on a thick paste made from powdered dishwasher detergent and hot water. Scrub it into the stains with a stiff brush and let it sit overnight. In the morning, rinse the paste off with a garden hose, and the concrete should look like new again.

Sweeping compound. To clean up loose dirt on the patio without raising a cloud of dust, use sweeping compound, which you'll find at most home-improvement and hardware stores. Sprinkle the compound lightly over the patio and use a push broom to sweep up the dust and debris. The fine-screened sand prevents the loose dirt from going airborne.

When life hands you lemons... If your grill or metal furniture has left rust stains on your concrete patio, wet the spots and cover them completely with powdered lemonade mix. Set a sheet of plastic wrap over each area, holding it in place with a rock or brick. Let it sit for about half an hour while the citric acid in the mix bleaches the stains away. Then scrub each stain with a stiff brush, and rinse off the lemonade with plenty of water from the garden hose. Just make sure the sugary solution gets as far away from the patio as possible, so ants don't take over your next cookout.

Cork scrub. To remove small rust spots from metal patio furniture, wet the end of a cork, sprinkle it with a little scouring powder, and rub that rust away. Then apply some baby oil to the bare spots to protect them from getting wet until you can dab on some touch-up paint.

The Great Clean-dini Speaks

Q. My concrete pavers look faded and dusty, with white powdery spots in some places. How can I bring back their original color?

A. As concrete weathers, the mineral salts in the mix come to the surface, just as they do on the outside of flowerpots. To make them disappear, scrub your pavers with a sturdy brush dipped in a solution of 1 part vinegar and 1 part water. Wait about 15 minutes so the acid in the vinegar can dissolve the mineral buildup, and then rinse the patio with a strong blast from the garden hose. Repeat the treatment if you can still see some whitish spots, and do it again about once a month to keep the natural buildup under control. To stop minerals from weathering out of your concrete and to make the color of the pavers really pop, apply a penetrating sealer that's available at most hardware stores.

Powerful Potions

Mold and Moss Remover

If your patio is plagued by slippery green moss, algae, or black mildew, this solution will get rid of it and make the surface inhospitable to further slimy situations, at least for a while.

- 1 gal. of oxygenated bleach
- 1 cup of trisodium phosphate (TSP) powder
- 1 gal. of hot water

First, dress in protective clothing, wear a pair of rubber gloves and goggles, and cover all surrounding vegetation, buildings, and materials with plastic so they don't get damaged by overspray. Then wet down the patio with a garden hose, and mix the bleach, TSP, and water in a bucket. Dip a scrub brush into the solution and begin scrubbing. Let the solution sit for about 15 minutes, then scrub the toughest stains one more time before thoroughly rinsing the patio down with the hose.

All-weather aluminum. Outdoor aluminum furniture has come a long way since the first folding chairs. It is now coated with special paint to hold up outdoors, while still being light enough to move whenever you want a cozier seating arrangement. But whether your aluminum is old or new, bare or coated, you should care for it the same way: by occasionally sponging it down with a mix of warm water and dishwashing liquid. Pay particular attention to the joints and crevices of the frame, and sponge the cushions or webbing with the same mix to freshen up the seats. Finish by rinsing everything off with a garden hose until all the soap bubbles are gone.

Car wax coating. Coated aluminum patio pieces will look their best if you protect the finish with car wax. Remove any cushions and apply the wax according to the directions on the label, then buff it off with a soft, clean cloth. Rain will bead up, and bird droppings will wipe off easily.

Hocus Pocus

BRIGHTEN YOUR WHITES

White plastic or resin patio furniture looks so fresh when it's new—and so dingy as it weathers. Try these tricks to brighten up your white patio furniture, planters, or trellises:

★ Wash the plastic with a mixture of 3 tablespoons of dishwasher detergent in 1 gallon of hot water. Let the solution sit for about 15 minutes, and then rinse it thoroughly. Be sure to wear long rubber gloves to protect your skin.

★ Scrub the pieces with a mixture of 3 tablespoons of powdered oxygenated bleach (like OxiClean® Versatile Stain Remover) in 1 gallon of warm water. Use a nonabrasive plastic scrubbie and plenty of elbow grease.

★ Restore the shine by wiping the surface with a cloth that's been sprayed with WD-40®. Buff off the solvent with a clean, dry cloth.

Sticky subject. If a nearby shade tree has showered your patio furniture with sap, dissolve the sticky mess with a mix of 1 part glycerin and 1 part warm water. Wipe the furniture with the mix, let it sit for a few minutes, then wipe the mess away with a clean, moist sponge. You'll find glycerin in the hand cream aisle of your local drugstore.

Blast from the past. To clean canvas beach chairs or chaise lounges, wet the fabric with a garden hose, rub a scrub brush across a bar of Fels-Naptha® soap, and give the canvas a good going-over. Rinse thoroughly, let the chairs air-dry, and you're done.

Cushion cleaner. If your outdoor cushions look dark and grungy, they've probably got mildew. Clean them up by applying a mixture of 1 teaspoon of borax, 1 teaspoon of dishwasher detergent, and 4 cups of warm water, soaking the seams and creases. Let the solution sit for 15 minutes, then rinse it off with a garden hose. Set the cushions on end to air-dry.

Pencil Marks

Simplest solution. The easiest way to remove pencil marks from both hard and soft surfaces is with an eraser. But the pink eraser on the end of the pencil can leave streaks, so use a clean art gum eraser to remove the marks instead. Its softer rubber is gentler on fabrics and walls, and it'll make the scribble marks disappear without a trace.

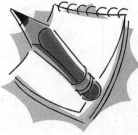

Crafters' friend. Using a pencil to outline the pattern on quilts or other craft projects can leave visible marks, especially if you use a soft, thick pencil. To erase all traces of your outlines on washable fabrics, try this trick: Mix ¼ cup of rubbing alcohol, ¾ cup of water, and a few drops of dishwashing liquid in a handheld sprayer bottle. Spritz the potion on the pencil marks, wait about five minutes, and rinse the marks away. Don't rub the fabric, and if you're not sure if your project is colorfast, try it on a leftover fabric scrap first.

Dirty desktop. Kids sure do love to "decorate" their furniture, but this terrific trick will eliminate even the worst scribbles from laminated wood furniture. Simply spray some WD-40® on a clean, dry cloth and wipe the artwork away. Follow up by wiping the furniture with a damp cloth to remove any traces of the solvent. Just don't use WD-40 near a flame or furnace, and be sure to open a window to let the fumes escape.

Grandma Putt's Magical Methods

When my Grandma Putt found pencil marks on her vinyl floor, painted woodwork, or laminate countertop (no doubt, courtesy of yours truly!), she put the gentle scrubbing power of good ol' baking soda to work. You can, too. Simply add a little water to the soda to make a paste, then lightly rub the pencil marks with it until they lift right off.

Pet Messes

Pet hair magnet. Cat and dog hair seems to stick to some fabrics like glue, and even a vacuum cleaner may not do a thorough job of cleaning it up. To get rid of the strays, wipe down your sofa with a damp washcloth. The rough texture of the terry cloth will pull the hairs out of the fabric and roll them up into a snarl that you can simply lift off. Rinse the washcloth frequently as you work, and wring it out so that it's merely damp, not wet, before wiping. To avoid hair problems in the future, drape a washable throw over the area your pet likes best.

Soak it up. To make it easier to neutralize pet odors in carpeting, remove as much urine as possible while it's still fresh. Start by setting a thick

Grandma Putt's Magical Methods

To neutralize odors and remove yellow or brownish urine stains on your carpet, mattress, or upholstery, give this potion a try. It's been working its magic since my Grandma Putt's day. Simply blot up the urine, then wet the stained area thoroughly with a mixture of 1 cup of white vinegar and 1 cup of water. Blot it with paper towels until it's damp, not wet, and then sprinkle about 1 cup of baking soda liberally over the stained area. Finally, mix ¼ cup of hydrogen peroxide with 1 teaspoon of dishwashing liquid, and pour the solution over the baking soda. (Always test the potion in an inconspicuous area first to make sure the peroxide doesn't bleach the color out of the fabric.) Work it in with a scrub brush until the baking soda is dissolved and the mixture penetrates the fabric or carpet fibers. Allow it to dry, and then vacuum up the residue. Cat urine spots can be really stubborn, so if you still see a stain, repeat the treatment.

Hocus Pocus

MAKE FLEAS FLEE

If you are displeased by fleas, try one of these tricks to get rid of 'em, and keep them away for good:

★ Sprinkle some powdered yeast on your pet's food, using about ½ teaspoon a day for a cat or small dog to about 2 tablespoons a day for a large dog.

★ Strong-smelling herbs help ward off fleas, so rub your dog with sprigs of fresh tansy, fennel, or pennyroyal; use peppermint, lavender, or rosemary sprigs on your cat.

★ Make a flea powder of equal parts eucalyptus powder, fennel powder, yellow dock powder, and pennyroyal powder (use rosemary powder instead of the pennyroyal for cats). Brush your pet's fur backward with one hand, and shake the powder on the skin at the roots of the hair. If fleas are already present, apply this powder daily for four days, and repeat as needed.

Fleas can quickly get out of control once your pet brings them inside, so nip pesky problems in the bud by vacuuming the floors and furniture frequently and thoroughly. Pay particular attention to the cracks along the baseboards, and don't forget to vacuum under the furniture, too. Dispose of the vacuum bag in an outdoor trash can ASAP, so the fleas don't escape. And to kill the fleas in your carpet, upholstery, or pet bed, sprinkle the surface and crevices with a mixture of equal parts baking soda and salt, let it sit overnight, and then vacuum up the powder—and the dead fleas—in the morning.

pad of paper towels on the area, then put a section of newspaper on top—and stand on it. You'll be amazed at how much urine the paper absorbs. Keep replacing the paper towels and newspaper until you can't soak up another drop, rinse the area thoroughly with fresh water, and follow the instructions in Grandma Putt's Magical Methods at left to keep the stain—and stink—from setting in.

Catty corner. After you blot up dear Kitty's accident in the corner of your carpet, make a mixture of 1/2 cup of white vinegar and 4 cups of warm water and pour it into a plastic handheld sprayer bottle. Spritz the stained area thoroughly, and then lay an old, folded cotton towel over it. Weigh down the towel with a heavy object to force the vinegar down into the fibers, and let it sit for about two hours. Remove the towel, raise the nap of your carpet with your fingers, let it air-dry, and it should be as good as new.

Scene of the crime. It's the scent of previous accidents that tempts pets to relieve themselves near that spot again and again. Our noses aren't nearly as sensitive as theirs are, so use these tricks—not your own sniffer—to make sure the trail is completely gone:

★ Never use ammonia to clean up accidents—it may remove the stain, but it'll encourage pets to reuse the area.

★ Scrub vinyl floors with a paste of baking soda and water to neutralize the acids in pet urine.

★ Use an odor-neutralizing cleaner before you attempt to steam clean your carpet. Steam can cause the proteins in urine to bond to the carpet fibers, and that's like setting up a sign that says "Bathroom Here!"

Hardwood helper. Urine can permanently stain wooden floors, so you need to act fast when your pet has an accident there. Wipe up the area with wet paper towels, then wash it with undiluted white vinegar. Work quickly so the wood doesn't absorb the liquid, and dry the floor with fresh paper towels. Repeat the vinegar wash, dry the spot again, and your floor will be fresh and clean.

A tisket, a tasket... If your cat decides to use a laundry basket filled with dirty clothes as a litter box, use an enzyme-containing detergent to dissolve the proteins and the stains, and add 1 pound of baking soda during the wash cycle to neutralize the smell. And while you're at it,

Powerful Potions

Anti-Skunk Shampoo

Skunk "perfume" contains an oil that makes it cling to pet fur—as well as to carpets, upholstery, and anything else your pet comes in contact with. So when your dog or cat has a close encounter of the skunky kind, keep him or her out of the house until the scent can be eliminated. You can try the old tomato juice bath remedy, but it requires a lot of juice, and even then, success isn't guaranteed. A chemist invented this potion, so give it a try:

- **1 qt. of hydrogen peroxide**
- **¼ cup of baking soda**
- **1 tsp. of grease-cutting dishwashing liquid**

Mix the peroxide, baking soda, and dishwashing liquid in a bucket, and be prepared for the foam—the peroxide will start fizzing up a storm. Put on a pair of rubber gloves (so the skunk oil doesn't rub off on your skin), wet your pet's coat with water, and pour on the potion, massaging it into the fur thoroughly. Use a washcloth to scrub your pet's face and the top of its head, and avoid the animal's eyes, nose, and mouth. After a thorough shampoo, rinse your pet with plain water, and take a sniff: If the skunk odor is still present, repeat the treatment. And if your skunked pet has brought the smell inside the house, set out bowls of vinegar to neutralize the scent.

freshen up your laundry basket, too, by washing it down with a paste made of baking soda and water.

Climbing the walls. When your cat sprays urine on the walls, start the cleanup by washing the spot several times with white vinegar. If the stain has penetrated the drywall, plaster, paneling, or brick, consider applying a clear, fast-drying sealer to keep the signature scent from perfuming your whole house. You'll find the sealer at most home-improvement or hardware stores; just follow the directions on the label.

Pewter

Easy does it. Pewter is mostly tin, so it needs a lot of TLC because it can be easily scratched or damaged. Never use steel wool or harsh abrasive cleansers, and don't set it on a hot stove or put it in the dishwasher. And when you do polish pewter, rub it in one direction and not in circles, so the strokes blend in with the metal.

Polish power. To bring out the glow of pewter pieces, dab a soft, dry cloth into one of these polishes and rub the tarnish away:

★ Mix 2 tablespoons of vegetable oil into ¼ cup of rottenstone powder to make a paste. Rottenstone (available at hardware stores) is made of weathered limestone and silica.

★ Stir some rubbing alcohol into ¼ cup of powdered whiting until you have a thick paste. Whiting is powdered white chalk, and it is available at hardware stores.

Wash off either paste with warm, soapy water, rinse, and buff with a clean, soft cloth.

Protect the patina. Old pewter often contains lead, which is what creates the grayish black patina that's treasured by folks in the know. Although you shouldn't serve food or drinks in old pewter pieces, you still need to clean them. To preserve the patina, wash with a little soap and water, and buff with a soft, dry cloth.

Grandma Putt's Magical Methods

Old-timers like my Grandma Putt had a terrific trick for polishing their pewter—they used cabbage leaves! Just peel off a few leaves from a head of regular cabbage and rub down the surface of your pewter pieces. The leaves will remove the grime and restore a gentle gleam without scratching the metal.

Phones

Clean calling. Keep your home phone clean by wiping it down with my Super Sanitizing Wipe on page viii. Spray the cleaner on a microfiber cloth, not directly onto the phone, and then wipe the grime from the handset and base. Use a cotton swab dipped in rubbing alcohol to clean the crud off the dial pad.

Germ control. Nasty bugs build up on the mouthpiece or handset every time you touch it. To keep germs away, wipe the phone with an antibacterial hand wipe whenever anyone in your house has a cold.

Weekly wipe. Clean your cell phone at least once a week by wiping it down with a baby wipe. It'll remove the oil from your fingerprints and do the same to any sticky lotions or food particles.

Leading the charge. A dirty connection can make it harder for your cell phone or cordless phone to recharge its battery. So dip a soft toothbrush into rubbing alcohol and gently brush the connection to remove any dirt.

Hocus Pocus

FIRST AID FOR SPILLS AND DUNKS

If your cell phone gets doused by a soft drink or other sticky liquid, act fast before the liquid penetrates the phone. Turn the phone off, take the battery out, and wipe it down with a soft cloth that's been dampened with rubbing alcohol to make the moisture evaporate quickly. If your cell phone gets immersed in water or ends up in the washing machine, dry it out by putting it in a bowl of uncooked rice overnight. If the rice is damp in the morning, repeat the treatment until it stops drawing moisture out of the phone.

Pillows

A dose of fresh air. To refresh feather or down pillows, try airing them out instead of washing them. Shake the pillows vigorously outside on a breezy day to loosen the dust and send it flying. Then hang them by their corners from a clothesline for a few hours, so the sunlight and fresh air can work their magic on the dust, germs, and odors. Finally, fluff the pillows up by tossing them in the dryer for about 20 minutes on low heat. Add a clean canvas tennis shoe or several clean tennis balls to the dryer to fluff up the feathers as they tumble around.

Double up. For machine washing, use the gentle cycle for washable pillows, and rinse them twice to make sure all the detergent is out of the stuffing. If your pillows are stuffed with foam or feathers, give them an extra spin cycle, too, to squeeze out as much moisture as possible before you pop them into the dryer. But don't try this trick on polyester-filled pillows because they may get lumpy from too much spinning.

Vinegar rinse. Don't add fabric softener when you wash or dry your polyester-filled pillows because it'll coat the fiberfill and make it less fluffy. Instead, add 1 tablespoon of white vinegar to the rinse cycle to cut the soap residue and leave the pillows smelling fresh and clean.

Bleach and latex don't mix. Soft, pliable latex pillows have a shocking reaction to bleach—the combination of chemicals can turn the water bright red. So never add bleach when you wash these types of pillows. And here's another trick that'll make latex or memory-foam pillows last longer: Wash them with their covers on or add zip-on pillow protectors, so the foam doesn't get chewed up.

Up with down. Protect the fine feathers inside of down pillows by washing them on the shortest, gentlest cycle your washing machine has to offer. Dissolve the detergent in the water first, before you add the pillows. Turn the machine off, then squeeze the air out of the feathers, and push the pillows into the water. When you take them out of the machine, the pillows are likely to have a noticeable odor— they'll smell like a wet hen. Don't worry: The scent will disappear when they're thoroughly dry. For more tips on dealing with down, see the entry starting on page 118.

Spot-clean throw pillows. To clean throw pillows without a full-fledged washing, dab them once a week with a damp washcloth. Depending on the fabric, treat spills with my Wet Spotter or Extra-Strength Dry Spotter potion (see pages 162 and 164). And if your dog leaves an odor on the pillows, sprinkle on some baking soda and let it sit overnight. Simply vacuum up the powder the next day.

Grandma Putt's Magical Methods

A pillow protector is a zip-on pillowcase that keeps perspiration, makeup, and other dirt from soiling precious pillows. Want to know an even better trick? Don't use one pillow protector—use two! My Grandma Putt always double-bagged her pillows, and as a result, she rarely ever needed to wash the pillow itself. Just zip the first protector over your pillow and add the second one, putting the zipper at the opposite end. Then pull on a pillowcase. When the pillow protectors get dirty, zip them off and pop them into the washing machine—it's a whole lot easier than washing the entire pillow!

Give 'em a squeeze. Throw pillows can get pulled out of shape in the washing machine. So when it's time to clean 'em up, give them a bath in your tub. Fill the tub with warm, soapy water, let the pillows soak for about 30 minutes, and then squeeze the soapy water through each pillow. Rinse them thoroughly under running water, massaging the filling to work out all of the soap. Press out the excess water and wrap the pillows in a thick bath towel to blot out even more moisture. Then put them in the dryer with a couple of clean tennis balls (to make them fluffy), and dry them on low heat.

Pine Sap

Cheers! Rubbing alcohol is pure magic when it comes to making pine sap vanish. It works great on both hard and soft surfaces—cars, windows, clothes, upholstery, wood, tile, and even carpet. Simply pour some alcohol on a washcloth and blot the sap. If the sap has already hardened, give the alcohol a few minutes to loosen the bond before you blot it away. Finish by washing the area with warm, soapy water. If you're using this trick on a big-ticket item like a car or winter coat, test it first in an inconspicuous spot.

Grandma Putt's Magical Methods

If you're not sure whether alcohol or my other sap-lifting tricks might damage fabric, try this trick from my Grandma Putt: Freeze the sap. Just lay the item in the freezer, making sure the sap is on top and not touching anything else. Wait a few hours, and then scrape the sap off with a dull knife or old credit card. It'll crumble to powder, so work over old newspaper, and get rid of the bits before they thaw and get sticky again. Use a soft brush or toothbrush on tougher fabric to remove any remaining frozen residue from the cloth. This trick works great on down vests and jackets, and it'll save you the trouble of having to wash the item afterward.

Baby your skin. Don't try to scrub gooey pine sap off your skin with soap and water because no matter how hard you rub, the stickiness won't budge. Use this trick instead—pour some baby oil on the sticky spot and wipe the sap away with a washcloth or paper towel. The sap will come right off, leaving your skin feeling soft as a baby's.

Greased lightning. Pine sap will slide right off a car or patio table if you rub butter, margarine, solid shortening, or vegetable oil on the spot. After the goo is gone, wash the area with warm, soapy water and rinse it thoroughly to complete the cleanup. This trick works on fabrics, too, but butter or other oily items will leave a stain behind. So after you get the pine sap off the fabric, pretreat the oily area by rubbing in some grease-cutting dishwashing liquid. Wait 15 minutes, then launder the item.

Handy sanitizer. To remove a smear of sap from floors, counters, or other hard surfaces, rub the spot with either a sanitizing hand wipe or a glob of gel hand cleaner. If the sap has hardened, use a nonabrasive plastic scrubbie to help the sanitizer do its stuff. You can use hand wipes or gel on fabric, too; just launder the item as usual after you wipe off the sap.

Sticky hair. Pine sap can really make a mess in hair, but it's a cinch to remove with this simple solution. Just work some mayonnaise or creamy peanut butter into the area and the stuff will slide right off. Shampoo your hair as usual, and the sap will be gone for good.

Pottery and Ceramics

Defect detective. Before you attempt to clean pottery or ceramics, examine each piece closely for any damage or previously repaired areas. If you notice any chips, cracks, or glue, don't immerse it in water or any other solution. And, of course, handle it with care when you dust it or sponge off the dirt, so fragile pieces don't break off in your hand.

Make mineral deposits disappear. To remove rust stains and calcium or lime deposits from glazed pottery or ceramic pieces, soak them in full-strength white vinegar. Rub the stains occasionally with a nonabrasive plastic scrubbie to help break them up. Light buildup should dissolve in about an hour, but heavy deposits may need to soak for a day or two. After the stains have disappeared, soak the pieces in distilled water for another couple of hours to remove the vinegar smell.

Simple wipe for ceramics. A damp cloth will wipe off most dirt from glazed decorative pottery or ceramic pieces. If you need a stronger solution for greasy spots, dampen a clean cloth with a mixture of 1 part white vinegar and 1 part water, and rub the grime away. Rinse thoroughly afterward, and dry the pieces with a lint-free cloth.

Paint specks. A sponge bath in soapy water will remove the grime from glazed pottery or ceramic pieces, but paint speckles are a different story. To make those specks vanish, you'll need to use an acetone-based nail polish remover. Simply dampen a cotton ball with the remover, and the paint will wipe right off. If you find a stubborn spot, just give the remover a minute or two to soak in before you attempt to wipe it away.

The Great Clean-dini Speaks

Q. My pottery vase has dark lines all over it, going every which way. What are they, and how do I make them disappear?

A. The lines are called "crazing," and it's a mark of age, which modern makers sometimes imitate deliberately. The glaze develops a network of fine cracks over time, and when dirt settles into those lines, it discolors the clay underneath. To lighten things up, soak your piece in a bucket filled with enough hydrogen peroxide to cover it. Let it soak at least overnight and for up to a week. If that doesn't do the trick, try a stronger 40% peroxide solution (available at beauty-supply shops). Wear protective clothing—including long rubber gloves—to prevent burns on your skin when you work with this stuff. And wear old clothes, too, because it'll bleach fabric in a hurry. Once the 40% solution has done its magic, wash the pottery in soapy water and rinse it thoroughly. Remember, this trick is only for glazed pottery, not for painted or unglazed pieces.

Unglazed craze. Your collection of Hummel® figurines, Christmas villages, Snowbabies™, bisque statues, or other unglazed pieces requires special care because these items aren't protected by a baked-on glaze. Never wash these precious collectibles, but dust them frequently with a soft, wide paintbrush. Or use the cool setting on a hair dryer to blow the dust away. And be sure to keep your treasures out of the kitchen, where the greasy residue from cooking can soil their surfaces.

What's for dinner? Most modern pottery and ceramic plates, cups, and other dinnerware can stand up to dishwashers because the decorations are underneath the glaze. Check the label on your pieces to make sure, though, before you stack them in the rack. If your dinnerware is hand-made, check with the artist—or play it safe and hand wash it. And never use harsh abrasives or steel wool pads on pottery or ceramics; if stuck-on food doesn't come off after a good soaking, rub the stubborn spots with a nonabrasive plastic scrubbie.

Silver threads among the gold. If your heirloom dinnerware is decorated with a band of gold or silver, wash the pieces by hand to keep that fancy trim in fine fettle. Even the trim on modern pieces can wear off with repeated cleaning in the dishwasher, so the extra time it takes to hand wash the dishes is well worth it.

Hocus Pocus

SILVERY SQUIGGLES

The matte glaze of "art pottery" like famous Roseville, Rookwood, and Van Briggle® can easily be marked by a stray pencil or a slight abrasion, leaving silvery marks on the item's surface. To remove the squiggles, rub them gently with an art gum eraser, brushing away the crumbs with a soft cloth. If you need stronger stuff, sprinkle a bit of Bar Keepers Friend® on a damp sponge and rub gently to remove the marks. Wipe off the residue with a damp cloth, carefully dry the piece, and put it back in its place of honor.

Quilts

Less is more. Have you ever wondered how those antique quilts managed to last a hundred years or more? One big reason: They weren't washed very often! Washing is hard on quilts because the weight of the wet fabric pulls on the stitches and fades the fabric. And an automatic washing machine can cause even more stress on the stitches. So to make a newly made quilt last long enough to be a family heirloom, wash it only about once a year. If the quilt is an antique, play it extra safe and wash it even less often—or not at all. When you need to wash an old quilt, follow the tips in "Prewash prep" and "Hand wash how-to" at right.

Blowin' in the wind. Whether a handmade quilt is old or new, the best way to clean it is to simply air it out on a clear, breezy day. Let the quilt blow in the breeze for a few hours to shake off the dust and leave it with a fresh scent. And in case you're wondering, dry cleaning is a no-no for old quilts—the chemicals might damage the fabric or thread.

The Great Clean-dini Speaks

Q. I have a stain on a brand-new quilt, and I'd hate to throw the whole thing in the wash. What's the best way to spot-clean a quilt?

A. This one's easy. Make a paste of Biz® Double Action Stain Fighter powder with a little water, apply it to the stain, and let it dry. Use the upholstery brush attachment of your vacuum to remove the residue. Repeat the treatment if necessary, and the stain will be history. This trick works great on new washable quilts, and it may even remove brown spots on old quilts. Just make sure your fabrics are colorfast first, so that only the spots run!

Dust with your vacuum. If you use a quilt as a wall hanging, dust it regularly with a hand vac or the upholstery brush attachment of your vacuum cleaner. Be sure to run the vac at low power so you don't loosen the stitches or embroidery. This trick works like magic on bed quilts, too. Vacuum them once a week to keep dirt from penetrating the fibers.

Prewash prep. If you must wash an old quilt, repair any missing stitches or rips first. Then test the quilt to make sure it's colorfast because many old fabrics aren't. Rub a damp white cloth on each different kind of fabric in the quilt, and if any color comes off, stop right there. Even after testing, quilt colors may run when they're saturated with water. Not scared off yet? Then follow the steps in my next tip.

Hand wash how-to. Before you dunk that quilt in water, gather up plenty of nice thirsty bath towels, and clear a space where you can lay the wet quilt flat after it's been washed. If the weather's nice, consider washing the quilt outside in a kiddie pool; it'll save your bathroom from all the drips and splashes. And keep in mind that washing is the last resort for cleaning a quilt. If it comes down to that, here's how to do it:

1. Fill the tub with cool water and a mild detergent like Ultra Ivory® dishwashing liquid or Orvus® quilt shampoo.

2. Let the quilt soak for a few minutes, and then gently swish it up and down to wash the dirt out of the fabric.

3. Drain the tub, refill with fresh, cool water, and rinse the soap out. Repeat until you don't see any more bubbles.

4. Support the quilt from underneath and gently squeeze the water out.

5. Lay out several thick bath towels and arrange the quilt on top of them so that it's lying flat. Top it with more bath towels and press the moisture out.

6. Dry the quilt outside on top of a sheet or towels. Make sure it's lying in the shade, so the sun doesn't fade the fabric.

Range Hoods

Ammonia power. When a range hood is extremely dirty, call on the grease-cutting power of ammonia to cut through the oily buildup. Simply add a squirt of dishwashing liquid and ¼ cup of ammonia to a bucket of hot water, dip in a sponge, and rub the grime away. Rinse with a damp cloth, and you'll really be cooking!

Dishwasher duty. The dishwasher can make short work of cleaning the metal range hood filter that covers the exhaust fan. Remove the filter, put it in the top rack of the dishwasher, and run it through the pots and pans cycle. The extra-hot water will scrub it clean, and you won't have to lift a finger. If the plastic or glass covering of the range hood's light is attached to the filter, leave it in place and it, too, will come out sparkling clean.

Cut grease like lightning. If you don't have a dishwasher, pick up a product called Greased Lightning® Multi-Purpose Cleaner & Degreaser in the cleaning products aisle. Remove the filter and place it in the sink, spray some degreaser on both sides of the wire mesh—and the dirt will dissolve right before your eyes. Wear long rubber gloves to protect your skin, and rinse the filter thoroughly once the grime is gone.

Make it melt. Here's another easy trick for getting rid of heavy dirt on a range hood's filter—melt it away. Line a baking pan with eight pages of newspaper, set the filter on top of it, and then put the whole shebang in an oven heated to "low" (250°F). The grease will melt off, flow down, and be absorbed by the newspaper. Check the progress after 30 minutes; if the filter's still greasy, give it another 30 minutes. When it's done, wash the filter in a sink full of hot, soapy water (or your dishwasher) to get rid of any lingering crud.

Powerful Potions

Range Hood Degreaser

Oily molecules that go airborne during cooking can build up fast on a range hood, hardening into a layer that takes a lot of elbow grease to remove. To keep the crud to a minimum, wipe the hood down every week or so with this simple spray. It'll cut the grease in no time flat, and save you from a tough cleanup job later on.

1 cup of white vinegar

½ cup of baking soda

2 cups of hot water

Mix the vinegar, baking soda, and water in a handheld sprayer bottle. Spritz the potion on the range hood (inside and out), and wipe the greasy film away. Rinse off the residue with a damp cloth, and the hood will be good to go. You can also use this degreaser on your stovetop and other large appliances.

It's in the bag! To loosen the gunky, stuck-on crud from a range hood filter, lay the screen in the bottom of a heavy-duty trash bag and pour 1 cup of ammonia over it. Tie the bag tightly, and let it sit outside (so it doesn't smell up your house) for 24 hours. Once the ammonia's worked its magic, rinse the filter off with a garden hose, and put it back in place.

Filthy fan? After you remove the range hood filter for cleaning, take a few minutes to spiff up the fan that's inside the unit. Unplug it if you can, and then dust the blades with a microfiber cleaning cloth. Once the loose dirt is gone, spray some of my Super Scrubber potion (see page 307) on a damp cloth, and wipe the blades clean. Check out the fan compartment; if it's really dusty, use the crevice tool of the vacuum cleaner to suck the dirt away. That way, your range hood will be fresh and clean, both inside and out.

Refrigerators and Freezers

Greasy spills. Make quick work of greasy meat drippings, salad dressing, or other oily spills by wiping them up with a cloth moistened with lemon water. To make lemon water, cut a lemon in half, drop it in a cup of water, and microwave it for about one minute to release the juice. The acid in the lemon juice will cut right through the oily residue and leave the fridge sparkling clean and lemony fresh.

Stuck-on spills. To loosen up food residue inside a fridge, heat 1/2 cup of white or cider vinegar in a microwave or on the stove top, pour it into a small heat-proof bowl, and set it in the fridge for about five minutes. The steaming vinegar will unstick those stuck-on spills, making it easy to wipe them away.

Grandma Putt's Magical Methods

I've always loved jelly on my toast, so my Grandma Putt kept my favorite variety on hand at her house. The only trouble was that those jars of strawberry jam sure left a lot of sticky drips in her fridge. She solved the problem by turning the plastic lids she'd saved from peanut butter, canned icing, or what have you into jelly jar coasters. They did a great job of keeping the gooey drips off the shelves, and when they got dirty, she'd wash them with the dishes.

A long shelf life. Be careful when you clean glass or plastic refrigerator shelves because replacements cost a pretty penny! To clean the shelves thoroughly, remove them and wipe both sides with my Inside/Out Fridge Cleaner potion at right. If they're loaded with hardened crud, let them soak for a few minutes in lukewarm, soapy water before you rub the residue off. And never wash a cold glass shelf with hot water: The sudden change in temperature could crack the glass. Let the shelves air-dry before you put them back.

Powerful Potions

Inside/Out Fridge Cleaner

Use this simple, but powerful, solution to clean both the interior and exterior of a fridge, including the gasket around the door. It'll remove dirt in a jiffy, kill nasty germs, wipe out lingering odors, and make mold disappear.

1 part white vinegar

1 part water

Mix the vinegar and water in a handheld sprayer bottle, spritz everything in sight, and wipe the grime away with a sponge or soft cloth. Don't forget to do the top of the refrigerator, too, even if you can't see the dust up there. And there's no need to rinse; the smell of the vinegar will disappear as the mixture dries.

Bin basics. It's easiest to remove crumbs and other food scraps from storage bins if you remove the drawers from the fridge first. Dump any loose debris in a wastebasket, and clean the bins with my Inside/Out Fridge Cleaner potion above. If spills have hardened on the bottom, soak the bins in warm, soapy water for a few minutes to loosen up the dried-on food. Then wash them inside and out with a soapy sponge and rinse thoroughly. Set them aside to air-dry before you slide them back.

Inside wipe. After you remove the shelves and bins, wipe down the inside of the refrigerator with a clean, damp cloth that's been sprinkled with a little baking soda. The soda provides a gentle abrasive for scrubbing off any stuck-on bits of food, plus it deodorizes while it cleans. Rinse off the residue with another clean, damp cloth and you'll be ready to reload.

Brighten up. To remove fruit juice, cola, ketchup, and other stains from inside a fridge, squeeze a dab of white non-gel toothpaste on the spots and rub it in with a damp cloth. Rinse well with a damp cloth when you're done, and the refrigerator will be smiling brightly!

Don't blow a gasket. When dirt collects in the grooved gasket around a refrigerator door, grab a toothbrush, dip it in my Inside/Outside Fridge Cleaner potion on page 263, and scrub that grime away. A toothbrush makes a great tool for cleaning around the hinges and in other tight places. After scrubbing, rinse the gasket with a clean, damp cloth.

Down and dirty. Dirty condenser coils will make a fridge work harder to keep cool, and that costs money. So you need to vacuum underneath the fridge and around the back every now and again to remove any loose dirt. Then every few months, do a more thorough job by removing the cover panel at the bottom and vacuuming out any debris.

Hocus Pocus

THE NOSE KNOWS

To keep the fridge smelling fresh and clean, instead of like last week's fried chicken leftovers, try these surefire tricks to neutralize the odors:

★ Baking soda is an old standby, and it really does work like magic. Just replace the box about once a month, and don't forget to keep the lid open.

★ Set half of a fresh-cut lemon on a saucer in the fridge with the cut end up, or do the same with a cotton ball that's saturated with fresh or bottled lemon juice. Remove it after a day or so.

★ Put several charcoal briquettes into an old dress sock, knot the end, and leave it on a shelf for a few days to absorb strong odors.

★ Dampen a cotton ball with a few drops of vanilla extract, set it on a saucer, and place it on a shelf until the cotton ball is dry.

★ Fill a shallow bowl or saucer with freshly ground coffee and place it on a shelf for a few days. Just don't spill it when you reach into the fridge.

Rugs (See also Carpets)

Ways to wash. Many throw rugs are machine washable, so check the label first to see if you've lucked out. If you did, wash them using the gentle cycle. To clean larger rugs, take them to a local Laundromat that's got extra-large machines. Set the dryer on low heat if the care label says it's safe to machine dry, or hang the rugs outdoors to air-dry in the shade.

Out, darned spot! Blot up spills on rugs immediately with a white cloth or paper towels. To remove stains, start with a gentle solution of dishwashing liquid and water, or try dabbing them with a mixture of 1 part white vinegar and 3 parts water. For tough stains, try the tricks in the Carpets entry on page 50, or look for the specific stain in this book. Use only a small amount of liquid when you spot-clean, so you don't shrink the rugs or leave visible splotches behind.

Q. I have a number of small, washable rugs that I clean about twice a year. Washing them just a few at a time solves the problem of my washing machine stopping halfway through because the load isn't balanced, but it seems like such a waste of time, energy, and water to have to do three or four loads. Any ideas on how I can wash them all at once, economically?

The Great Clean-dini Speaks

A. Have I got the solution—head to the car wash! Just lay the rugs flat in the car wash bay, or if the car wash has those large clips for hanging floor mats, hang the rugs off those. Then hose 'em down. When the water runs clear, roll up the wet rugs, cart them home (I put mine in large plastic trash bags in my trunk), and drape 'em over a railing outdoors until they're dry.

CLEAN AS SNOW

Believe it or not, fresh fallen snow is just the ticket for getting wool rugs clean. Take the rugs outside, shake off the loose dirt, and lay them right side up on the fluffy new snow. Then rub handfuls of the white stuff into the rugs. Let them sit for an hour or so, then shake out the snow—and the deep-down dirt. (You can flip the rug and do the underside, too, if you like.) Just make sure the temperature is below freezing, so the rugs don't get soaked by melting snow. When the rugs are clean, bring them back inside and lay them on several layers of newspaper until they're completely dry and as good as new!

Hocus Pocus

Pet hair problems? To remove dog or cat hair from throw rugs, put them in the dryer on the "air" setting for about 20 minutes. Add a dryer sheet to reduce static cling, and the pet hair will tumble right off the rugs— and into the lint trap.

Shampoo parlor. If you can't fit a throw rug into the washing machine, give it a bath outside. Vacuum the rug first, and then carry it outside and lay it flat on a clean surface. Mix up a bucket of baby shampoo and cold water, and sponge the rug sparingly with the solution. Wipe it until the sponge no longer picks up any dirt, and use a scrub brush to do the fringe. Rinse the rug with a clean, damp sponge and keep it lying flat until it air-dries. Then flip it over so the bottom dries completely, too.

Carpet fresh. Area rugs rarely need a full-fledged washing, but they can start to smell a bit musty and stale after a while. If a rug is too big to conveniently cart outside for airing out, use baking soda to brighten it up indoors. Just sprinkle baking soda lightly over the rug, let it sit overnight to neutralize the odor, and then vacuum the powder up the next morning. It'll leave the rug smelling fresh and clean, and you'll hardly have to lift a finger—much less a big, bulky rug.

Rust Stains

Squeeze play. There's no need to make a sour face when your favorite shirt gets spotted with rust stains. Simply rub the spots with a fresh-cut lemon, and then squeeze the juice directly onto the stains until the fabric is saturated. Lay the stained item outside in full sun for a couple of hours, and those rust spots will disappear. Launder the shirt as usual, but check the stains again before you put it in the dryer. If you can still see any rusty spots, repeat this trick to make them vanish completely.

What a rhubarb! Rhubarb juice is another great solution to use when your clothes or other washable items get stained with rust. Start by cutting five stalks of rhubarb into half-inch pieces, and then simmer them in 2 cups of water until they're soft. Strain off the rhubarb juice into a heat-proof bowl, and submerge the stained areas in the hot liquid until the stains disappear. Launder the items as usual, and the rust will be history.

Salt 'n' sour. Here's another trick from the kitchen to make rust stains disappear. First, saturate the spots with full-strength white vinegar. Next, sprinkle a generous amount of table salt onto the stains. Finally, rub it in using an old toothbrush, then let the fabric dry. You can speed up the stain-removal process by drying your garment outside in the sun. Launder the item as usual, and check the stains before you throw it into the dryer. If they're still visible, repeat the treatment. This salty solution works great on carpets and upholstery, too.

Best friend. Bar Keepers Friend® is a popular powdered cleanser for bathroom and kitchen use, but did you know you can also use it as a laundry treatment? To make rust stains vanish, rub them with a paste made of Bar Keepers Friend and water. Put a paper towel under the stained area, and let the item sit for a few hours. The rust stains should rinse right out.

Waterless winner. To remove rust stains from upholstery or clothes, try a dab of waterless hand cleaner like Goop®. Work it into the stains with an old toothbrush and wipe the residue off with a damp cloth. As always, test the cleaner first in an inconspicuous area to make sure it won't harm or fade the fabric.

Contemplate your naval jelly. This tried-and-true rust remover has been used for decades by military personnel on metal, floors, upholstery, and even clothes. Just rub a dab of naval jelly into the stain, and let it sit for about 10 minutes. Wash it away with soapy water, or launder the item as usual. Naval jelly is actually a form of phosphoric acid, so handle it with care, and make sure your skin and eyes are well protected.

Water woes. If your water has a lot of iron, or you happen to be doing laundry when your town is flushing the pipes, you may end up with a whole load of wash that's rust stained. Chlorine bleach will only set the stains, so solve the problem with this trick: Rewash your clothes in the machine using 1 cup of nonprecipitating water softener like Calgon® or Spring Rain® in the wash cycle. Don't use any bleach or detergent, and the rust stains should wash right down the drain.

Hocus Pocus

THINGS GO BETTER WITH COKE

The tangy taste of Coca-Cola® comes from the phosphoric acid in the recipe—the same acid that makes naval jelly such a good rust remover! To put this soft drink to work removing rust on metal, vinyl floors, chrome fixtures, and other hard surfaces, saturate a nonabrasive plastic scrubbie with cola, and scrub away. If the rust stain is on your clothing, pour the pop directly onto the fabric, and let it soak for about 10 minutes before laundering the item as usual. You can use other brands of cola, too—just make sure the ingredients include phosphoric acid.

Rusty cookware. Soak away rusty spots on steel, iron, or enamel cookware by filling a pan with a mixture of 1 part white vinegar or ¼ part lemon juice and 4 parts water. Let the pieces soak overnight, and if there's any rust remaining the next morning, scrub it off with a nonabrasive plastic scrubbie or steel wool pad. Rub the spots with a light coating of vegetable oil to head off further problems, and you'll be cooking like gangbusters.

Chrome cleaner. To make chrome faucets and fixtures shine and remove rust at the same time, try spraying WD-40® on them. Wait 10 minutes for the solvent to penetrate, then apply a little elbow grease with a nonabrasive plastic scrubbie. Make sure the rust stays away by buffing on a light coat of paste car wax to keep the chrome waterproof.

Foiled again. When your outdoor grill or patio furniture gets rusty, scrub the corrosion away with a ball of crumpled aluminum foil. Then keep rust at bay by rubbing on a coat of clear car wax so rain can't penetrate.

Lemonade stand. Citric acid makes a great antidote for outdoor rust stains, but scrubbing an entire patio down with a fresh lemon isn't very practical. As an alternative, try lemonade. Mix powdered lemonade with just enough water to make a thin paste, and scrub it into the stains with a stiff brush. Let it sit for about 30 minutes, and then scrub some more. Rinse the drink mix and rust stains off with a garden hose.

Grandma Putt's Magical Methods

My Grandma Putt used cream of tartar for baking—but she also used it as an all-purpose rust remover on her clothes, upholstery, and carpet. She made a paste by mixing it with a little water, and then she spread the paste on the stained areas. After 15 minutes, she washed the residue off, repeating the treatment if necessary. You'll need only a small amount of cream of tartar for most rust stains, so start with 1 table-spoon, and add more if it doesn't make enough paste to cover the stains.

Powerful Potions

Rust-Remover Soak

Believe it or not, molasses works just as well as any commercial rust cleaner. Use this unusual potion to make rusty tools, car parts, pots and pans, and other metal objects look like new again.

> **1 part molasses**
> **9 parts water**

Getting the molasses out of the bottle is the hardest part of this trick. To make the thick syrup pour more easily, zap it in the microwave in 15-second increments, checking it after each cycle. Once you've got the molasses moving, stir it into the water in a plastic bucket, add your rusty objects, and let them soak. Check the objects every day or so to see if the molasses has worked its magic. It may take three or four days before the rust gives up its grip, but it will eventually rinse right off. When the treatment is complete, rinse the objects thoroughly to remove any sticky residue.

Z is for Zud. To remove unsightly rust stains from a concrete sidewalk or patio pavers, wet the area with a garden hose, sprinkle a liberal amount of Zud® scouring powder on the stains, and scrub it in with a stiff brush. Zud contains oxalic acid, which will bleach stains away. Let it sit for about 30 minutes, and then scrub again before you rinse the area.

Rust-free paving. Old rust stains that have had time to penetrate concrete, brick, or other paved areas call for extra-strong measures, so pick up some oxalic acid crystals and whiting (powdered chalk) at a local hardware store. Dissolve the oxalic crystals in a bit of hot water, and add enough whiting to make a soft paste. Spread the paste onto the stains, let it dry, and then rinse thoroughly with a garden hose, using plenty of water. Protect your eyes and skin with goggles and gloves (and all surrounding vegetation with plastic) when you work with this cleaner.

Screens

Dust 'em off. Screen cleaning is usually a once-a-year job, unless you live on a dirt road. And speaking of dirt, that's the first step: Wipe the mesh and frames down with a microfiber cloth to remove any loose dust, dirt, and debris before you follow up with a good ol' bath.

Deep clean your screens. Screens collect a lot of grime, so you'll need a strong solution to make it disappear. Start by laying them flat, making sure there are no sharp objects underneath that could poke a hole in them. Wet each screen with a garden hose, dip a large sponge or soft brush into a bucket that contains 1 part ammonia and 3 parts hot water, and rub 'em down. Let the mix soak while you move on to the next screen or two. After the ammonia has had a few minutes to loosen the dirt, scrub it off with a sponge or brush. And don't get carried away with the elbow grease—you don't want to stretch or rip a screen.

Brush it out. Add a toothbrush to your screen-cleaning arsenal to tackle the crud in the corners, around the edges, and in the grooves of the frame. Wet those areas with the ammonia solution above, and then go to town.

Hocus Pocus

EASY AS 1, 2, 3
You might think it's easy to remember which screen came from which window, but take my word for it—it doesn't take much to get them mixed up. Here's how to make taking down and replacing screens a real breeze: Write a number (with a permanent marker) on each of the screens in an inconspicuous place, then write the same number on the corresponding window or door. And don't forget to mark which end is up, so you don't replace your screens upside down. Then when it's time to put the screens back up, the few minutes you spent marking them will pay off big-time.

Rinse and shake. After you've scrubbed the grunge off, rinse the screens thoroughly with a garden hose. Then stand them up with the edge on an old cloth, and give them a shake or two to remove any excess water. Lean the screens against a wall or railing—separately, not stacked—so they can air-dry thoroughly before you put them back in place.

Smooth sliding. While your screens are drying, clean out the grooves where they slide in the window or door frames. To reach into the narrow channels, wrap a strip of cloth around a screwdriver, dip it into the ammonia solution in "Deep clean your screens" on page 271, and run it back and forth in the grooves until they're clean. That way, your screens will slide nice and smooth, and they'll close tight, too!

Patch with polish. If one of your screens gets a hole in it that's big enough for bugs to get through, but not large enough to patch or replace, dab the hole with some clear nail polish. It's invisible and waterproof—and it'll keep those pesky mosquitoes outside, where they belong.

Sewing Machines

Cover it up. You'll have a lot less cleaning to do if you get in the habit of covering your sewing machine when it's not in use.

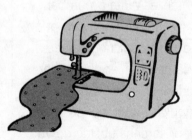

Not only will the machine stay cleaner, but you also won't have to worry about your next project picking up grime from a dirty case. This simple step will go a long way toward making sure your bobbin keeps bob-bob-bobbin' along!

Make it up. Have you misplaced the stiff lint brush that came with your sewing machine? Try using a clean makeup brush instead. A large makeup brush works well because the long, soft bristles can clean out all of the little nooks and crannies.

Q. The tension on my sewing machine isn't working right—my stitches are loose and uneven, and my thread keeps breaking. I haven't made any adjustments to the tension settings. What's the problem?

The Great Clean-dini Speaks

A. Oily dirt, no doubt. If you haven't cleaned the machine in a while, the fuzzy lint inside has probably turned into a greasy, grimy mess, thanks to the oil on the moving parts of the machine. Stray bits of thread can gum up the works, too. But there's no need to get all tense; just use a bit of sewing machine cleaning fluid to relax the situation. Here's how to do it:

1. Unplug the machine, remove the thread and bobbin, and lift the presser foot so the tension springs are loose.

2. To make sure the upper tension discs are working smoothly, soak a folded piece of fine muslin with cleaning fluid, and pull it back and forth between the discs. Repeat with a clean, dry cloth to remove the excess solvent and make sure all the grime is gone for good.

3. Moisten a cloth or small brush with cleaning fluid, and wipe away any dirt in the feed dog and in and around the bobbin case. Remove caked-on crud by picking it out carefully with a sturdy pin or needle.

4. Pull a thread back and forth under the tension of the bobbin to clean out any grime that's hiding in there. Rethread the machine, replace the bobbin, and you'll be back up to speed in no time at all.

Lose the lint. When a sewing machine starts acting balky, tearing thread or making uneven stitches, it probably needs a good cleaning. What's the biggest bugaboo when it comes to cleaning a sewing machine? The little bits of lint, of course. So you need to clean the fluff out frequently, before it causes a serious clog and/or damage. To do the job, first unplug the machine, then remove the needle, the spool of thread, and the bobbin. A small brush or a can of compressed air aimed in the right direction will get rid of that lint lickety-split.

Clear your throat. To get at lint that's deep down in a sewing machine, you'll need to remove the throat plate that covers the area around the bobbin case. To do so, slide the top plate toward you as far as it will go, and then unsnap or unscrew the throat plate. Use a lint brush or compressed air to whisk away the dusty debris in and around the bobbin case. Pick out any stubborn clumps or stray threads with a pair of tweezers, reattach the plates, and you'll be good to go!

Shades

Dust brush. An occasional dusting with a synthetic duster or microfiber cloth will keep most window shades clean. If the shade is made of fabric, you can use the upholstery brush attachment on your vacuum cleaner—it's a great dust buster. Dust the backs of the shades, and don't forget the tops and valances, too.

Sponge bath. Most window shades are washable, but that doesn't mean  you can throw them in a washing machine. To clean them, add a squirt or two of dishwashing liquid to a bucket of warm water, and sponge the shade gently with the mix. Rinse the sponge thoroughly, squeeze it out, and wipe the shades again to rinse the soap off. Then leave the shades down until they're completely dry.

Fingerprint kit. To make dirty fingerprints or other dirt marks disappear from vinyl window shades, spray a bit of my Super Sanitizing Wipe (see page viii) on a damp sponge, and wipe the prints away. And make sure you hit the bottom edge of the shade, too, where dirt tends to collect.

Fly specks. Tiny dark bug droppings can make a window shade look pretty ugly, so get rid of the specks with this quick trick. Dip a cotton swab into dishwashing liquid, dab the soap on the dark spots, and let it sit for about 30 minutes. Then wipe the area with a clean, damp cloth.

Try dry. If you're not sure how well a shade will take to wet cleaning, try dry cleaning instead. Here's how to do it:

1. Cover a work surface with a piece of plastic to make cleanup a cinch after you do the job. Then take the shade down and lay it flat on the surface.

2. Spot-clean stains by rubbing them with an art gum eraser, brushing off any residue.

3. Pour cornmeal into a shallow bowl, scoop some onto a corner of a dry, coarse terry cloth towel, and start rubbing the shade. Work with a gentle circular motion, making sure you do every inch until the whole shade is cleaned. The cornmeal will absorb the dirt as you work.

4. Vacuum the shade to remove any cornmeal residue, and rehang your nice clean shade.

HOCUS POCUS

CORD CLEANUP

If your window shades have light-colored pull cords, they can get pretty cruddy thanks to the natural oil in your skin—not to mention grubby fingers! So remember to clean the cords, too. Just dip a sponge or cloth into warm, soapy water, squeeze it out, and wipe the cord up and down while you hold it taut. Rinse with a damp cloth, and then let it air-dry.

Neat pleats. Pleated shades call for special handling, so that you don't damage the fold lines or crease the material in the process. For a pleated fabric shade, use the upholstery brush attachment of your vacuum, working carefully around the pleats. (Clean the bristles of the attachment before starting, so you don't add any dirt.) For paper or other pleated shades, use a "dry sponge" (available at paint stores) or a damp microfiber cloth to carefully wipe away dust, dirt, and other debris that are in and on the folds. And if the pleats start to look a little too relaxed, pull the shade up tight and let it stay in that position for several days until the folds look crisp again.

Shoes and Boots (See also Athletic Shoes)

Wipe 'em clean. To remove surface dirt from leather shoes and boots, use a damp sponge or premoistened hand wipe. A few quick swipes, and the dust and dirt will be gone in a flash!

Brush off mud. When shoes or boots get muddy, knock off as much of the stuff as possible, and then let the mud dry; it'll be easier to brush off once it does. Scrub the dried mud away with a stiff brush, and use an old toothbrush to get every last bit out of the seams and stitching. Wipe the footwear with a damp cloth, and it'll look as good as new.

Soften the smell. Here's a scent-sational tip: To deodorize smelly shoes and boots, slip a used fabric-softener sheet into each one. That way, instead of smelling like stinky feet, your footwear will have the fragrance of your favorite fabric-softener sheets. Is that "Meadow Mountain Flowers" I smell?

Summer splash. When ground-in dirt makes your flip-flops or plastic summer sandals look grungy, give them a bath—in the dishwasher! Simply clip the straps to the top rack with a clothespin, and run the shoes through the cycle. Just don't try this trick on sandals or flip-flops that have fabric or jeweled decorations; scrub that fancified footwear with a non-abrasive plastic scrubbie and dishwashing liquid or baking soda instead.

Q. How can I clean my daughter's UGG® boots? They seem to be real dirt magnets.

A. UGG sheepskin boots are a big investment, so it makes sense to use cleaning products that are made just for them; you'll find UGG cleaners, conditioners, and other products wherever the boots are sold. For the rest of the job, you'll need some baking soda and corn flour (a finer grind than cornmeal), which you can find at health-food stores, or in the Spanish food section of your local supermarket. Once you've got everything, follow these steps to clean your UGGs, inside and out:

The Great Clean-dini Speaks

1. Dampen a sponge in cold water and wipe the outside of the boots to remove any surface dirt.

2. Apply the leather cleaner, following the package directions.

3. Stuff the boots with newspaper or paper towels so they hold their shape, and let them air-dry. Don't set them near a heat source, and keep them out of direct sunlight.

4. Make a mixture of 2 teaspoons of baking soda and 2 teaspoons of corn flour, pour it inside the boots, and shake 'em up vigorously. Let the mix sit overnight to absorb odors, then shake the boots out the next day.

5. Finally, apply UGG® Sheepskin Water & Stain Repellent, and your boots will be ready to step out in style.

Zip it. If the zipper on your boots starts to get balky, run the business end of a pencil up and down it. The "lead" in the pencil is actually graphite, and it makes a great lubricant that'll help the sticky zipper run smoothly.

Stain blocker. To remove serious dirt from suede shoes or boots, buy a suede-cleaning block. It's sometimes called a suede eraser because it crumbles like an art gum eraser when you scrub off the deep-down dirt. Brush off any residue, then raise the nap on the shoes with a nailbrush or special suede brush. The block and brush are often sold together in a suede-cleaning kit at shoe stores. For more tips on cleaning suede, see the Leather and Suede entry on page 200.

Pantry polishes. To give leather shoes a nice shine, rub a small amount of olive oil or walnut oil into them with a soft, dry cloth. Use small circular motions to work the oil into the leather, and then buff with a soft, clean cloth to remove any excess oil and bring out the shine. The oil will soften and condition the leather, making it less likely to soak up water. Just be aware that this trick may darken lighter-colored leather, so test it first in an inconspicuous area before you go whole hog on the shoes.

Hocus Pocus

SALT STAINS

Do your leather boots or shoes have white stains on them because you walked in winter road salt? Here's an easy cleanup: Dip a soft, clean cloth in a mixture of 1 tablespoon of white vinegar and 1 cup of water and wipe the stains away. Polish the footwear afterward with a good leather conditioner, and then apply a stain protector to keep future salt stains from soaking in. Vinegar also does the trick of removing salt stains from suede boots or shoes. Just dampen a clean cloth with undiluted white vinegar and rub the white marks away. Rinse with a clean, damp cloth and brush the nap when the boots are dry to make it velvety soft.

Silver

Patina protection. When you burnish silver by hand for many years, it develops a deep, rich finish—the soft gleam that's called a patina. That's why the best way to care for silver service is to use it. When silver pieces sit on a shelf or lay tucked away in a chest, the finish will dull as it oxidizes. And when you do polish silver, keep in mind that the dark areas in the decorations are part of the patina—there's no need to make every last bit look shiny and bright.

Kitchen chemistry. This nifty trick uses a bit of chemistry to dissolve the tarnish on silver—without any scrubbing. Just put a sheet of aluminum foil in a heat-proof glass dish and lay the silver on top of it. Pour hot water into the dish until the silver is covered, add 1 teaspoon of salt, and then pour some baking soda in until it begins to foam. The tarnish will actually disappear right before your eyes! When the water cools, rinse the silver and dry it with a soft, clean cloth.

Baking soda rub. Simple and powerful—now that's the kind of magic I like! And what could be simpler than baking soda? Just make a paste of baking soda and water, dab some onto a soft cloth, and rub the tarnish off your silver. Rinse it thoroughly, and rub it dry with a soft, clean cloth. Keep in mind that baking soda is a very mild abrasive, so if you're worried at all about scratching the family heirlooms, use a commercial silver polish instead.

Grandma Putt's Magical Methods

Whenever my Grandma Putt boiled a pot of potatoes, she saved the water—not for soup, but to clean her silver. She simply soaked her silver earrings and other small pieces in the potato water for about 30 minutes and then dipped a soft cloth in the water to rub the tarnish away. It worked like a charm!

Hocus Pocus

ACID INDIGESTION

Foods that contain acid can discolor silver when they react with the metal, and salty foods can bring on the tarnish, too. That's why many silver serving pieces come with a glass liner. If your pieces aren't protected by a liner, don't use them to serve acidic foods like fruit juice, eggs, mayonnaise, or vinegar salad dressing, and keep them away from salty stuff, too, including olives. And always take off any silver jewelry before you go swimming because chlorine can damage it in a matter of minutes.

Keep rubber away. Rubber causes a chemical reaction that tarnishes silver and can even corrode it, so keep it away from this precious metal. Don't use rubber gloves when you wash or polish silver, and never put a rubber band around flatware. Even a rubber seal inside of a storage chest or a stray sealing ring from a canning jar may affect the finish.

Toothpaste scrub. To brighten up a small piece of silver, smear some white non-gel toothpaste over the surface, run it quickly under warm water, and rub it into a foam. Use an old, soft toothbrush to clean the grooves, or let them stay dark to add character to the piece. Rinse the toothpaste off under running water, dry the piece with a soft, clean cloth, and you'll be smiling at the results.

Follow the lines. Whenever polishing silver, use a straight back-and-forth motion and not a circular one. That way, the strokes will blend right into the surface. And be sure to use a light touch when you rub, letting the polish—not your elbow grease—do the job.

Ashes to ashes. The wood ashes from a fireplace are a gentle abrasive that works well for polishing silver. Just dab some powdery ashes on a wet cloth and rub the silver until it shines. Make sure you're using only fine-powdered ash, and not any that's got little bits of wood mixed in, which could scratch the silver.

Sisal and Jute

Don't water the grass. Sisal, jute, sea grass, and similar fibers are made from plants—and that means they're sensitive to water. They're tough and durable, but if they get soaking wet, the fibers are likely to shrink, causing them to wrinkle or pucker. Their color can also change, and too much humidity can cause mold and mildew to set in. So keep natural-fiber items indoors, and spot-clean them instead of drenching them with water.

Simple synthetics. Caring for man-made sisal couldn't be simpler, since you won't have to worry about stretching or shrinking the fibers. When vacuuming alone isn't enough to freshen the piece, use a damp mop to get it nice and clean. And since saturation isn't a problem with artificial fibers, you can be as tough as you like on stains; use my Two-Step Carpet Cleaner potion on page 51 to simply scrub them away.

Suck it up. Vacuum a sisal or jute rug frequently, using the strongest setting to pull the dirt out of the woven fibers. Ground-in dirt can damage and/or discolor the fibers if you spill something on the rug, so frequent vacuuming will make it last longer. Also do the underside, and suck up any dirt that has sifted down through the fibers to the floor.

Act fast. If fruit juice or another staining beverage lands on your sisal rug, first blot up as much of the liquid as you can, and then sponge the spot with a mixture of 1 part white vinegar and 1 part water. Blot the solution onto both sides of the rug if the stain has penetrated all the way through, and then blot it dry with a clean cloth. And remember—it's blotting that does the trick, not rubbing or scrubbing, which can stretch the fibers.

Tighten up. If a sisal rug is looking a little bumpy instead of lying nice and flat, give it a damp mopping to moisten the fibers, then let it air-dry. Sisal dries quickly, and the fibers will tighten up slightly—just enough to remove the bumps and bubbles.

MOLD REMEDIES

If mold or mildew shows up on a natural-fiber rug, it's a sure sign that the humidity is too high. So keep these rugs out of the bathroom, and don't use them outdoors if your summers are steamy. To remove mold or mildew, mix up 1 part chlorine bleach and 6 parts water in a handheld sprayer bottle and spritz the spots. Work the spray into the fibers with a soft brush, wait 5 to 10 minutes, and then rub the areas with a clean, dry cloth. Be sure to test the mixture first in an inconspicuous area to make sure it won't bleach the color; if it does, add more water to the solution and test it again.

On the spot. To remove stains caused by coffee drips, grease marks, or other problem liquids, start by vacuuming the sisal rug to make sure the loose dirt doesn't spread through the fibers when you clean it. Then whip up a bowl of soapsuds with a hand mixer, using grease-cutting dishwashing liquid and a little water. Dip a damp cloth into the suds, and sponge them onto the stains. Wait about 10 minutes, and blot the soap away with a clean, damp cloth. Dry the area with a hair dryer set on low, and the rug will look as good as new.

Watermark wet-down. Discolored blotches caused by spills are called watermarks, and sisal, sea grass, and jute rugs are notorious for them. Lots of dirt can hide in the woven fibers and underneath rugs made of these substances, and when any kind of liquid—including plain old water—meets the dirt, it'll dissolve and discolor the carpet. Once a watermark shows up, the only way to make it disappear is to wet the entire rug to make the spot blend in—and that's risky business with these moisture-sensitive fibers. To try it as a last resort, take the rug outside, spray it with a garden hose, and lay it over a railing or clothesline to air-dry. If bumps or other distortions appear as the fibers tighten, straighten the rug out by gently pulling the fibers flat.

Slate

The wet look. Unsealed slate turns dull and pales as it dries. So if you like the wet look, you need to apply a glossy acrylic slate sealant to the slab. Follow the directions on the label, and give it a couple of coats for better protection. Use a paint pad to apply the sealant; its rectangular shape will allow you to get into corners and along the edges without getting sealant on the baseboards or walls.

A simple wash. For routine cleaning of slate floors and countertops, use plain ol' water. Simply swab the slate with a wet sponge or cloth and let it air-dry. If the surface is extra dirty or greasy, use a solution made of 1 part white vinegar and 1 part water to cut through the crud. And avoid using detergents or other cleaning products because they can damage the slate and/or the sealant.

Q. My slate countertop has lots of scratches from slicing bread, dragging the toaster, and gosh knows what else. Is there any way to remove the marks without calling in the pros to refinish the whole surface?

The Great Clean-dini Speaks

A. You betcha! Just buy a bottle of food-grade mineral oil from your local pharmacy, and rub it in all over the countertop. To make sure the oil has soaked in deep enough to hide future scratches, perform this test: Run a knife lightly across the slate to make a scratch about an inch or two long. Then rub the scratch with your fingertip—the oil in the slate should make the mark disappear like magic. Reapply the oil once or twice a month, and your countertop will be a real smoothie.

Oil it up. To keep spills from penetrating an unsealed slate countertop, rub the surface with a bit of olive oil on a soft cloth. Olive oil won't turn rancid like corn or vegetable oil, and it'll give the slate a richer color and a gentle gleam.

White spot woes? If white spots appear on your slate countertop, they're most likely a buildup of minerals from water that's splashed onto the surface. To remove them, lay a cloth soaked in vinegar on the spots to dissolve the calcium and other minerals. Wait about 10 minutes, then rinse with fresh water. If that doesn't solve the problem, try a stronger mineral remover like CLR® or Lime-Away®.

Seal of approval. If you're still seeing spots after using the trick above, the minerals may have built up because water has penetrated the sealant. The remedy is to use acetone (available at hardware stores) to remove the old sealant, making sure you work with good ventilation. To reseal the surface, see "The wet look" on page 283.

Sliding Doors

Track it down. When a sliding door starts to stick, it's probably due to dirt in the track. So grab a trusty screwdriver, make yourself comfy, and start digging the gunk out. Use the flat blade like a spatula to shovel the crud out of the track, and then vacuum up the loose debris. Take your time, and work carefully so that you don't gouge the track or frame.

Slip-sliding away. After digging out and vacuuming up the worst of the debris, wrap a damp cloth around the screwdriver blade and run it through the track to get out every last bit of gunk. Spray the cloth with my Super Scrubber potion (see page 307) to remove any stubborn grime that remains. Let the track air-dry, and then apply a sliding door lubricant like Ultra Glide®. It'll dry fast, leaving your door ready to roll.

Bubble scrub. If you've neglected a sliding door track for quite some time, use Scrubbing Bubbles® bathroom cleaner to blast the dirt away. Spray the cleaner on the track, let it sit for a few minutes, and then rub it away with a damp cloth wrapped around a butter knife. You may need to use a damp cotton swab or a bent-to-fit pipe cleaner to reach into the really tight places.

Speedy squeegee. Clean the track and the frame of a sliding door before you clean the glass, using my Super Scrubber potion on page 307 to wipe down the metal or vinyl parts of the door. When it's time to hit the glass, switch to The World's Best Window Cleaner potion on page 354 and spray it on, working from the top down. Be sure to use a squeegee because it'll cut your window-cleaning time in half. And squeegeeing is so much fun that you might even be able to get the kids to do the job for you.

Weep no more. If you've got water leaking from the bottom of a sliding door frame into the house every time it rains, clean out the weep holes. Take a close look at the bottom of the door track and you'll see several small holes; that's where the water is supposed to drain outside after it rains. If water is running into the house or collecting in the channel, it means those weep holes are clogged. You'll need a thin, sturdy tool to poke out the crud—try a nail or an old drill bit. Once you've pushed the dirt out of the holes, pour some water into the track to make sure the weep holes aren't crying the clogged-up blues anymore!

Grandma Putt's Magical Methods

Here's a neat trick my Grandma Putt taught me. To unstick a balky sliding door, reach for the soap. Simply run a bar of white soap over the track, then open and close the door several times to work the slippery stuff into the moving parts. An old candle will also do the job—like soap, the wax reduces friction so your door slides freely.

Sporting Goods

Batter up! To clean a grimy baseball glove, lather it up with shaving cream that contains lanolin. Rub the cream in, and then buff it off with a soft, dry cloth. The cream will also moisturize and condition the leather, leaving it smooth and supple. Swab the cream out of the grommets with a pipe cleaner before it dries.

Grubby mitts? When baseball mitts or other leather sports gloves get really grubby, you can spiff them up with a citrus-based hand cleaner like Permatex® Fast Orange®. Rub it in with a soft cloth, folding the cloth as it gets dirty. Follow up by applying some petroleum jelly to the leather. It will help restore natural oils that'll keep the gloves pliable.

Grass-stained shoes. When baseball or other athletic shoes get streaked with grass stains, reach for the molasses. Spread a little bit onto the stains, and let the shoes sit overnight. Wipe the sticky stuff off with a damp cloth the next day, and the shoes will be good as new!

Grandma Putt's Magical Methods

When our childhood table tennis tourneys left a trail of dented balls, my Grandma Putt had a simple trick to make them good for another round. She dropped the dented Ping-Pong balls into a bowl of hot water for a few minutes. The heat caused the surface and the air inside to expand, and the dings popped right out. Yes, sirree, my Grandma P sure knew her way a-round!

Pedal to the metal. To keep a bicycle chain running smoothly, rub a candle stub on both the top and bottom of the chain and around the toothed edges of the front and rear gear sprockets. The wax will lessen friction and also create a barrier that keeps dirt from getting into the links and gunking up the chain.

HOCUS POCUS

SOCCER-KID STENCH

Protective gear for soccer and other sports gets mighty smelly because the foam and fabric hang on to odors. Lingering perspiration is the perfect breeding ground for bacteria, which makes them stink even more. Bacteria can cause health problems, too, so you need to keep the gear as clean and dry as possible. Try these tricks to ward off that nasty sports-gear stench:

★ When your children come home after practice, make sure the shin guards, shoes, and other equipment are set out to dry right away. Set the stuff where air can circulate freely, and aim a fan at them to help dry them more quickly.

★ Don't just let the uniform lie in a heap on the floor—pop it into the washing machine ASAP with a scoop of OxiClean® added to dissolve the sweat.

★ Spray Febreze® inside of gloves to help cut the odor, and sprinkle baking soda inside of shoes in between wearings.

★ Wearing stinky gloves can make a player's hands smell bad, too. So have your children scrub their hands with a fresh-cut lemon to get rid of the stench. (It works just as well for eliminating sports-gear smell as it does for eliminating odors from onions and fish.)

That's the goal. Keeping up with kids' soccer or hockey gear can be a real chore, so do as much as you can (as soon as you can) in your washing machine. Set the hockey helmet aside to clean by hand, but drop in shoulder pads, gloves, elbow pads, shin guards, and so on. Be sure to use a front-loading machine (without an agitator), and run the gear through on the gentle cycle. When it's done, let the equipment air-dry. As for that helmet, pour a bit of baby shampoo onto a sponge and wipe it down, inside and out. Rinse it well, and dry it with a bath towel.

A stiff handshake. It's easy to repair thin sports gloves that have gotten stiff and creaky after a round of golf or biking in the rain. Just put them back on after they've dried out, and rub them down with moisturizing hand cream. Apply the cream just as you would to your own skin, making sure to rub it into the backs, the palms, and in between the fingers.

Get a grip. To clean the leather grips on golf clubs, rub a bar of moisturizing bath soap onto a wet washcloth until you work up a lather, and then rub the suds into the leather. Rinse the cloth when it gets dirty, re-lather, and repeat the process until the grips are clean. Don't rinse the suds off because they help moisturize the leather. Simply buff the grips dry with a soft, clean cloth. If the grips are stained from sweat, rub in a waterless hand cleaner, and wipe the stains away before applying the moisturizing soap.

Ball brightener. Cleaning golf balls at home is quick and easy. Simply soak them in a solution of 1 cup of ammonia and 2 cups of warm water for a few minutes, rinse them with fresh water, and place them in an empty egg carton to dry.

Mat magic. If you've neglected your yoga mat for months, simply run it through the washing machine to clean it up. Use the gentle cycle with cold water for the wash and rinse. When the spin cycle is finished, remove the mat and roll it up in a big bath towel (like a jelly roll) to squeeze out all the extra moisture. Then hang it up or lay it flat to air-dry.

Tenting tonight. Today's tents rarely need a bath, but if yours gets muddy or dirty, set it up out in the yard and wet it down with a garden hose. Sponge off the dirt with warm water and a gentle soap that's made just for tents (available at most camping-supply stores). Rinse it thoroughly, and make sure it's completely dry before you put it away.

Don't be a sap. When pine pitch or other tree sap falls on your tent, bundle the tent up with the sticky part facing out, and set it in the freezer for a

Hocus Pocus

MILDEW MATTERS

If mold or mildew gets a grip on your tent, it can cause the urethane coating to peel right off as it works its way into the fabric underneath the protective layer. So if you notice a discolored area or dark, cross-shaped marks, follow these steps to stop the nasty fungi in their tracks:

1. Gently wash and thoroughly rinse the tent as described in "Tenting tonight" at left.

2. While the tent is still wet, rub any affected areas with a mixture of 1 cup of salt and 1 cup of bottled lemon juice in 1 gallon of hot water.

3. Let the tent completely dry by setting it out in the sun.

4. Peel off any bits of loose coating, and apply a commercial water repellent to seal the damaged areas.

If you frequently camp in damp conditions, consider applying a product like Tent Guard with Ultra Fresh™, which is specially designed to thwart the fungi.

few hours. When you take it out, you should be able to pick off the frozen sap with a fingernail. Or you can use a strip of duct tape (folded with the sticky side out) to lift the frozen gunk off. If the tent's too big for the freezer, try wiping the mess off with a cotton ball dipped in mineral oil.

Be a clean camper. Using a little common sense when camping will go a long way toward keeping your gear nice and clean. Always place a ground cloth under your tent, brush boots and clothes off before you turn in for the night, and sweep away any debris before you pull up the pegs. To avoid mold or mildew problems, make sure the tent and sleeping bag are completely dry before you stow them away, and never store them in a damp basement or garage during the off-season.

Powerful Potions

Yoga/Camping Mat Cleaner

To quickly freshen up a mat after a sweaty class or clean a grungy camping mat, use this aromatic, germ-killing spray. With just a few quick swipes, the mat will be free of grit and dirt and ready for your next adventure.

Distilled water

10 drops of tea tree essential oil

Fill a handheld sprayer bottle with distilled water, add the tea tree oil, and shake it vigorously. Spray the mat with the mixture after class, and wipe it dry with a paper towel. Tea tree oil (available at health-food stores) is noted for its antibacterial properties that'll keep your mat germ-free.

No sleeping on the job. When a sleeping bag needs cleaning, check the care label on the bag first; most bags are machine washable. Follow these guidelines, and the bag should come out smelling as fresh as a mountain meadow:

★ Wash it in a large, front-loading machine, so the bag has plenty of room to move. Visit a local Laundromat if you have a top-loading, agitator-type washer because this kind of machine can damage the bag's stitching or insulation.

★ Use a gentle soap (specially made for sleeping bags), and never use bleach or fabric softener.

★ Lift the bag from underneath when you remove it from the washer, so you don't stress the stitching. Dry it on low heat, checking frequently to make sure it hasn't twisted into a lump.

★ If the bag is stuffed with down, see the Down Clothes and Quilts entry on page 118 for more tips on how to clean it.

Stainless Steel

Microfiber miracle. These cleaning cloths are one of the best inventions since sliced bread, and they work like magic on stainless steel. For daily cleanup, simply dampen a microfiber cloth with plain old water—it'll remove dust and spots like a charm!

Cut the grease. If it's been a while since you wiped down your stainless kitchen appliances, use my Stainless Scrub on page 292 instead of a commercial cleaner. It works just as well at cutting through the greasy film, and it costs a whole lot less. Rinse the potion off with fresh water, and dry the surface to a sparkling shine.

Soap's the solution. To bust right through stubborn crud on stainless steel, dip a cloth into a solution of grease-cutting dishwashing liquid and water. Dishwashing liquid is gentle on stainless, but tough on dirt, so it does a terrific job on greasy stovetops and grimy refrigerators. Be sure to rinse the surface thoroughly after you wipe away the grime because soap residue can leave a rainbow hue on stainless steel.

Q. My stainless sink got blue streaks after I set a hot saucepan in it—and so did the pan. What can I do to get rid of the blues?

A. Those blue marks are heat stains because, as you've discovered, stainless steel discolors when it gets extra hot. The next time, don't set hot cookware in the sink until it cools down, and try not to let a stainless pan boil dry. To make heat stains disappear, rub them with club soda, olive oil, or Goo Gone® on a soft cloth until they're gone.

The Great Clean-dini Speaks

Powerful Potions

Stainless Scrub

Here's a homemade cleaner that's quick to whip up and safe for stainless steel sinks, cookware, and other surfaces. It does a great job of removing stains and discolorations, so the beauty of the stainless can shine through.

3 parts cream of tartar
1 part hydrogen peroxide
Rubbing alcohol

Mix the cream of tartar and hydrogen peroxide in a glass bowl and apply the cleaner with a soft, damp cloth. Let it dry, then wipe the residue off with a clean, damp cloth. Next, wipe the surface with rubbing alcohol, and then buff it dry with a soft, clean cloth. Use long, even strokes, working with the grain every step of the way.

Oil slick. To give clean stainless steel a super shine, rub the surface with a bit of oil. Olive oil or food-grade mineral oil works best because neither of these will turn rancid or create a film as other cooking oils might do. Rub the oil over the entire surface and remove any excess with a soft, dry cloth. The very thin layer of oil that's left behind will add a gleam and protect the surface from water spots and stains.

Feeling perky. To clean a stainless percolator, thermos, or other container, drop in two or three denture-cleaning tablets per quart of water, and let the container sit overnight. Rinse it thoroughly in the morning, and it'll be ready in time for the daily brew.

Don't get mugged. If your favorite stainless steel travel mug has gotten cruddy from coffee, tea, or cocoa, fizz those stains away with vinegar and baking soda. Put a couple of tablespoons of baking soda into the mug, add about ¼ cup of vinegar, and let them foam up like a volcano. Put the lid on, shake the mug so the bubbles reach all sides, then rinse the insides thoroughly with warm water.

Seeing spots. To make those darn white water spots in a stainless sink vanish in a jiffy, rub them with a soft cloth that's been moistened with a bit of cooking oil. Any kind of light-colored oil will do the trick—even a nonstick cooking spray. After the spots disappear, buff the surface with a soft, dry cloth to remove any extra oil.

Go with the grain. For a smoother finish, clean stainless steel in long strokes that go with the grain, not in circles. That goes for washing, drying, and especially polishing. When you rub stainless the right way, you'll end up with a brighter, smoother finish instead of unsightly circular tracks.

Avoid abrasives. Scratching the surface of stainless appliances, sinks, or cookware is a big no-no because it damages the protective layer that keeps the steel from rusting. To keep your finishes in fine fettle, avoid steel wool and other abrasive pads, as well as scratchy scouring powder. So how do you get stuck-on food off the bottom of stainless pots and pans? A good soak and a nonabrasive plastic scrubbie are all it takes. For more cleaning tips, see the Cookware entry on page 85.

HOCUS POCUS

GET IN THE SPIRIT

For a quick, streak-free shine, clean stainless steel with a spritz of vodka. Just pour a couple of inches of cheap, unflavored vodka into a handheld sprayer bottle, spritz the stainless, and wipe it down with a soft, clean cloth. It won't leave streaks or smears behind, and it dries like lightning—white lightning, that is! If there's any leftover vodka in the sprayer, store it in a cool, dark place for next time. And before you try this trick, make sure the item or surface is cool and no open flames are nearby.

Skin deep. Stainless steel is an alloy made of iron and chromium, with some of the chromium forming the hard "stainless" coating on the surface to prevent rust. But if any kind of acid remains in contact with the surface long enough, it can eat through that layer, letting moisture seep in and eventually causing rust. So always rinse off pickle juice, lemon salad dressing, and any other acidic foods instead of letting them set. And if you use vinegar for cleaning stainless, be sure to rinse the surface thoroughly afterward.

Easy stain removal. Stainless steel sinks can quickly accumulate gunk and grunge if you don't clean them every day. So here's a great trick for making even the grungiest sink look good again: Just spray it with a foam oven cleaner. Wait about 10 minutes for the foam to lift the crud, rinse the sink thoroughly, and enjoy the shine. Just be sure to open the windows first for ventilation, and wear rubber gloves while you work.

Stairs

Up the down staircase. On second thought, make that "down the up staircase" because cleaning from the top down is the way to go when you're sweeping wooden stairs. If you're vacuuming, you can work in whichever direction feels more comfortable. Some folks like to start at the bottom, moving the vac up as they go; others prefer starting at the top and moving on down. The choice is yours.

See spot run. When spots or stains show up on carpeted stairs, use carpet-cleaning soap to make them vanish. Dip a soft-bristled nylon brush into the concentrated cleaner, scrub the stains, and blot out the moisture with a clean, dry towel. Stand on the towel and move your feet around to get as much liquid into it as possible, and the damp spots will soon air-dry. You'll find other tricks for removing nasty stains in the Carpets entry on page 50.

Do the two-step. The most efficient way to clean fully carpeted stairs is to work your way down the staircase twice. Here's how to whip through this job in a flash:

1. Using the crevice tool of your vacuum cleaner, suck up the dirt along the edges and in the corners of each and every step.

2. When you've finished cleaning the cracks and crevices, replace the crevice tool with a regular vacuuming head, and clean the horizontal treads and vertical risers of each step. Pay special attention to the edges, where the carpet tends to get matted down from foot traffic.

See? The job goes much faster when you use the right tool—and when you don't have to constantly switch attachments.

Hocus Pocus

PET HAIR PICKUP

If your vacuum cleaner tends to leave pet hair behind on your carpeted stairs, here's how to put a little cleaning magic to work on Fido's fluff:

★ Pull on a heavy-duty rubber dishwashing glove, and dip your fingers into a bucket of water. Shake off the excess, and then sweep up the dog or cat hair with your wet rubber fingers. It'll roll right up, so you can simply lift it off and drop it into a plastic sack as you go. Rinse your gloved fingers every now and then because water is what turns the glove into a magic pet hair magnet.

★ Wet a cellulose sponge or rough washcloth, and wring out the extra water. Then stroke each step, lifting the pet hair off as it collects on the sponge.

★ Buy a dog-grooming "slicker brush" at a local pet-supply store, and run it over each step. Use a light touch, and peel the hair off as it collects on the fine wire bristles. This tool works best on carpets with low pile.

Grandma Putt's Magical Methods

My Grandma Putt usually reached for the oil soap when it was time to clean wood, except when it came to her stairs. In that case, she saved the soap for the banister only. She knew that any cleaning product that contains oil can make steps a little slippery—and even a little is too much when you need secure footing! So instead of using oil soap on her stairs, Grandma Putt used a simple mixture of ¼ cup of white vinegar in a bucket of warm water to do her damp mopping. There was no need to rinse, either, because the vinegar smell soon disappeared without a trace, leaving a nice clean nonslip surface behind.

Sweep often, mop less. Most of the dirt on wooden stairs is loose enough to remove with a broom, so do yourself a favor and sweep your stairs frequently. You won't have to wet mop as often, and you'll keep the dirt from being tracked throughout the house. Use a broom with angled bristles to reach into the corners and along the back edge of each stair, where dirt tends to settle.

Stop dirt in its tracks. No matter how you go about it, cleaning stairs is a chore. But it needn't be if you use this simple trick to keep your steps from getting grungy in the first place. Simply place a throw rug at the bottom of the staircase, and it'll catch a lot of the crud that would otherwise be tracked up the stairs. Use a rug with a rubber backing or nonslip pad to prevent it from sliding around when you come down the steps.

Sock the banister. Dusting a banister with a feather duster or cleaning cloth will remove most of the loose dirt, but it can send it flying in all directions, including onto neighboring posts. So use a microfiber duster or dust-magnet microfiber cloth to keep the dirt from migrating. And for a quick touch-up, slip a pair of old cotton socks over your hands and wipe each upright individually.

Stereos (See also CDs and CD Players)

Gnarly knobs. If a home or car stereo snaps, crackles, and pops when you turn it on, chances are the controls are gunked up with dirt. A quick spritz of a tuner/control cleaner and lube, like the kind RadioShack® makes, is all you need to get rid of the grunge. Pull or unscrew the knobs to remove them, aim the nozzle of the cleaner right where the shaft fits into the control, and give it a short, quick blast. Move the shaft back and forth to work the cleaner into the control, wipe off any excess, and replace the knobs. That stereo will soon be humming a different tune.

Hocus Pocus

MUSIC TO MY EARS

Personal music devices can get mighty grubby, so follow these steps to keep the tracks sounding loud and clear:

★ Keep MP3 players in their cases, and if the device has a screen, use a screen protector. That'll block most of the dirt, so you'll rarely need to clean it.

★ Use a soft, clean cloth to wipe the player and screen. Never use a paper towel, which can leave scratches.

★ To remove smudges and fingerprints, wipe the player with a soft, clean cloth sprayed with an ammonia-free glass cleaner. Never spray any type of cleaner directly on the device.

★ Wipe the earbuds and cords with the same cleaner and cloth.

★ Moisten a cotton swab with the cleaner to get into the tight places.

★ To minimize scratches, use a commercial MP3 cleaner like iDrops®. Put a few drops of the cleaner on a soft, clean cloth, and buff the surface lightly. You may have to repeat the treatment several times.

Cracking the code. When a car stereo displays the cryptic message "ER-0001," it's trying to tell you that it can't read the CD that's in the slot. Why? Probably because the stereo needs cleaning! For a quick and easy fix, slip in a laser-cleaning disc, which you can buy for a few bucks at most electronics stores. It'll take care of the dust and dirt that are causing your stereo to send out a digital cry for help.

Inside out. The best way to clean the inside of a stereo is with a can of compressed air. First, unplug the components at least 24 hours before you

The Great Clean-dini Speaks

Q. While cleaning out my mom's attic, I discovered a 30-year-old stereo, covered in dust. Any ideas on how to bring it back to its original luster?

A. You can make that old stereo look and sound good again with just a little TLC. Here's how to do it:

1. Wipe the case down with a clean, damp cloth to remove the layers of dust and grime.

2. Pull off or unscrew the knobs, and set them aside. Spiff up the plastic panel on the front by rubbing it with a cloth that's been moistened with white vinegar. If the aluminum has darkened over time, make a paste of cream of tartar and a little water, and rub it on briskly to bring back the shine.

3. Clean the grime off the knobs with an old toothbrush dipped in white vinegar. Take care of any dirt that might be hiding inside the controls with the "Gnarly knobs" trick on page 297.

4. Spray a clean, dry cloth with furniture polish and buff the wood on the case until it shines. Put the knobs back on, hook up the system, and enjoy your golden oldies!

plan to clean them—the electronics can hold a charge for a long time, and you don't want cleaning to be a shocking experience! Disassemble the stereo, and spray the compressed air at the dusty nooks and crannies and the circuit boards. Keep moving the can as you work because that blast of air is powerful enough to blow delicate circuitry out of whack.

Speaker of the house. Plain old dirt can interfere with a thumping bass or nice clear treble, so vacuum speakers to keep the dust down. Use the hose with no attachments to suck the dirt off the cover and out of the vents. If you can remove the cover, carefully vacuum the inside of the case, too, as well as the speaker cone itself. Just be sure to hold the hose close to, but not touching, the surface of the cone to avoid damaging it. When you use this little trick, you'll soon be hearing every note as clear as a bell.

Sticker Residue

The goo is gone. For an all-purpose solution to getting rid of that sticky residue from price tags, tape, or what have you, keep a bottle of citrus-based Goo Gone® or De-Solv-It® on hand. Either product works great on glass, plastic, painted wood, and lots of other hard surfaces. Just rub a little onto the pesky spot, wait a few minutes, and the stickiness will wipe right off.

Rub away. No Goo Gone® in the house? Try rubbing alcohol instead. Simply soak a cotton ball in it and rub the residue—the sticky stuff will come right off. Also known as isopropyl alcohol, this magic elixir works on metal, glass, mirrors, other hard surfaces, and even shoe leather.

Stick to it. When a sticker leaves its mark on any surface, grab a roll of handy duct tape and place a piece of it on top of the residue. Rub the tape with your fingernail and then swiftly tear it off—and presto! the sticky gunk underneath will be gone.

Hocus Pocus

VINEGAR TRICKS

White vinegar can be a big help when it comes to removing sticky stuff, whether it's the daisy appliqués in a bathtub or the labels on a new set of wineglasses. Here's how to use it:

★ To remove nonslip appliqués in a tub or shower, pour hot vinegar over the decorations, wait a few minutes, and carefully peel them off.

★ Remove a price tag or manufacturer's decal from glass, wood, or china by soaking it in white vinegar. Wait a few minutes, then rub the tag and glue off. Rinse under running water, or wipe the area clean with a damp cloth.

★ To loosen a stick-on hook from a painted wall, wet a sponge with vinegar and squeeze it slowly behind the hook to loosen the adhesive. After a few minutes, the hook should peel or fall right off.

Running hot and cold. To remove sticker residue from fabrics or hard objects, try heating it up—or freezing it off. Use a blow-dryer to soften the residue, then roll it up with your fingers. Or put the item in the freezer for a couple of hours, and carefully scrape off the remains with your fingernail or a dull knife. And next time you want to remove an entire sticker without leaving any residue behind, heat it with your dryer first and it'll peel right off. The goo will be gone with the wind.

Solvent solution. WD-40® loosens up just about any kind of hardware, from frozen bolts to rusty screws, and it works like magic on lifting sticky residue, too. Why, you can even use it on clothes! Simply spray it on the spot, wait a few minutes, and wipe it off. Remember to use this solvent outside or in a well-ventilated room because it has a strong odor. And since it's somewhat oily, you may need to follow up the treatment with soapy water to wash away any lingering traces of the solvent.

Slippery slide. To remove sticker goo from plastic objects, spray the spot with nonstick cooking spray, or saturate it with any kind of cooking oil. Wait a few minutes for the oil to soak in, then give it a swipe—the residue will slide right off. Finish the job by washing the item with soapy water to get rid of the oil. If the sticker residue has hardened, you may need to repeat the trick to remove every last bit of adhesive.

Down with decals. Removing a parking decal or other sticker from a car window isn't as simple as peeling off a price tag, especially after it's been baked on by the sun. You'll need a straight razor to scrape off the paper or plastic decal, and Goo Gone® to get rid of the residue. Scrape slowly and carefully with the razor blade, removing as much of the decal as you can. Then apply Goo Gone to the area, and wait about 30 minutes. Wipe the residue off, polish the window with your favorite cleaner, and you'll never know the decal was there.

The Great Clean-dini Speaks

Q. My children love to play with stickers, which means decorations end up all over my floors, the coffee table, and even the kids' clothes. Is there anything I can use to clean the sticky glue off all those surfaces?

A. Would you believe peanut butter? Yes, it's true— the very same stuff your kids ate for lunch can also clean up their messes. So the next time you need to get gluey goo off a floor or table, rub a dab of peanut butter onto the sticky spot, wait a few minutes for it to penetrate the residue, and wipe it off with a paper towel. You can even use peanut butter when a sticker leaves its mark on your kids' clothes. Peanut butter is oily, so after you wipe it off, rub a bit of grease-cutting dishwashing liquid onto the spot before you send the clothes through the wash—they'll come out as clean as a whistle!

Hocus Pocus

ERASE ALL TRACES

An ordinary pencil eraser is a great tool to turn to when you need to remove sticky residue from plastic computer cases, video games, and even laminate furniture. Simply rub the spot with the eraser until the stuff peels off, and wipe it clean with a damp cloth. An eraser works like magic on leather and suede, too. Brush off the eraser shreds with a damp washcloth, and your hide will look brand spankin' new!

Baby your books. To remove the stickers and residue from your kid's plastic school binder (so that it's good for another year), rub in some baby oil with a paper towel. Wait about 10 minutes, and the gooey stuff should wipe right off.

Smells clean to me! To remove the residue that duct tape leaves behind on a plastic surface, spray the spot with an aerosol deodorant. It'll quickly cut through the goo, which you can simply wipe away.

Toothpaste for TVs. Today's TVs often come with a manufacturer's sticker pasted on top, and those stickers are notorious for leaving a gooey mess behind. To remove the residue, rub a dab of white non-gel toothpaste on the spot and apply a little elbow grease. Toothpaste is a gentle abrasive, so it does a great job of removing stubborn glue.

Hello, my name is… Did you forget to remove your name-tag sticker before sending your shirt through the laundry? If so, then saturate the sticky area with rubbing alcohol, wait about five minutes, and rub the residue off with your fingernail. Test this trick on an inconspicuous spot first to make sure the alcohol doesn't affect the fabric.

Cleans on contact. Self-stick shelf paper can be such a challenge to peel off that you may be tempted to paper right over it. But before you give up on stripping the paper, soak the shreds with Avon Skin So Soft Original Bath Oil or Replenishing Body Lotion. Use a generous amount, and let it sit for at least half an hour. Then wipe off the last bits of paper and adhesive with a damp cloth, and wash the shelf with a soapy sponge to remove the oily residue. Rinse thoroughly, and let it air-dry before you reline the shelf with paper.

Grandma Putt's Magical Methods

My Grandma Putt was a big believer in recycling, and glass jars were one of her favorite things to reuse. But getting the labels off the jars...well, that was quite a chore. So instead of soaking and scrubbing, she used this clever trick: She'd saturate the label with cooking oil, wait 5 to 10 minutes for the oil to soak into the glue, and peel the label off. Then all it took was a little soap and water to remove the oil and leave the jar sparkling clean.

Stoves (See also Ovens; Range Hoods)

It pays to get fresh. Stovetop spills are easier to clean up when they're fresh, so wipe up spatters as soon as you see them. If a spill has already dried, lay a wet paper towel over it after the stove is cool, and wait about 10 minutes for the water to soften it up. Then simply wipe it clean.

Tough customers. To remove hardened globs of oatmeal, pancake batter, or other stubborn foods, first saturate the spots with water, and let them sit for about 10 minutes. Then use a nonabrasive plastic scrubbie to loosen the stuck-on food, and wipe the residue off with a damp sponge. Whatever you do, don't use steel wool pads or scouring powders on stovetops because they can easily scratch the surface.

Digital dustup. Use The World's Best Window Cleaner potion on page 354 to keep the digital display panels on your appliances bright and shiny. Spray a microfiber cloth with the potion, and run it lightly over the panels. And double-check the controls and displays after you've finished, just in case you've accidentally reset one of the buttons.

The Great Clean-dini Speaks

Q. I've tried everything to clean my drip pans and gas burner grates, but the crud just won't come off. Got any bright ideas for making it vanish?

A. Cooking spills can be a real chore because the heat bakes the stuff right onto the surface of the spill catcher. So if your drip pans, burner grates, or other stove parts need heavy-duty help, try one of these tricks to get them clean again:

★ Mix TSP (trisodium phosphate) powder with water (following the directions on the box), spread it over the surface, and scour the crud off with a nonabrasive plastic scrubbie. Wear rubber gloves and safety glasses to protect your skin and eyes.

★ Put the burner grates, drip pans, and metal burner rings in a large pot, pour in 1 cup of baking soda, and add enough water to cover the pieces. Bring the water to a boil, reduce the heat, and simmer for about an hour until the crud floats off.

★ If baked-on gunk remains after you try these tricks, try some fine-grit (220 grade) sandpaper to scrub it off.

★ When all else fails, consider buying a new set of drip pans and rings; they should cost only a few dollars each. Measure your pieces before you go shopping, and note how they're made so you buy the right kind.

Soak 'n' scrub. To loosen crusty crud on broiler pans, drip pans, or burner rings, soak them in a sink full of hot, soapy water (use grease-cutting dishwashing liquid) with 1/4 cup of ammonia added to it. Let them soak for at least two hours, or as long as overnight. The ammonia will loosen up the hardened grime, making it easy to finish the job with a nonabrasive plastic scrubbie.

Foil the drips. To save yourself a whole lot of cleanup work, use heavy-duty aluminum foil. Simply remove the drip pans and line each one with foil, trimming it to fit with a pair of scissors. Then the next time a pot boils over, all you have to do is replace the foil liner. For even more protection, use foil to line the drip tray under your cooktop, too.

It's elemental. Dirty burners can send smoke and smells throughout a kitchen, so wipe the cooking ring elements off while you're cleaning the stovetop. Here's how to keep them fresh and clean:

★ Make sure the burners are cool before you begin.

★ Wipe electric burners with a damp sponge or cloth (you can detach them and lift them out to get both sides), but never soak them or put them in a dishwasher.

★ If the gas burner grates need more than a damp wipe, lift them out and soak them in a sink full of hot water with a little grease-cutting dishwashing liquid added. Remove the crud with a nonabrasive plastic scrubbie.

Out with clogs. When you see yellow flames instead of blue ones around the rings that fire gas burners—or no flame at all in some spots—it means that the holes around the rings are clogged with grease or dirt. To fire things back up, unclog the holes by carefully poking each one with a pipe cleaner or piece of fine wire, like a straightened paper clip. Don't use a toothpick because it can easily break off in the hole, and then you've got real trouble.

Take control. To clean the control knobs on a stove, pull them off and scrub them in a sink full of hot, soapy water, using an old toothbrush. Be sure the control knobs are completely dry before you reattach them, or the results could be shocking! And if the knobs aren't removable, or if the stove has buttons on the control panel, wipe them down with a damp, soapy cloth, using a cotton swab to get into the tight spots.

Grandma Putt's Magical Methods

No one wants to smell last night's dinner the next day, so use Grandma Putt's tricks to minimize odors that arise while you're cooking:

★ To neutralize most strong kitchen odors, simmer ½ cup of white or cider vinegar and 2 cups of water in an uncovered saucepan for about 10 minutes, and then turn off the heat. Keep the pan on the stovetop for about an hour so the vinegar can work its magic. For a nice spicy scent, add a teaspoon of whole cloves to the mix.

★ Add 1 tablespoon of fresh or bottled lemon juice to the water whenever you cook cabbage, cauliflower, Brussels sprouts, or other cabbage-family foods.

★ If fishy smells linger after supper, simmer lemon slices in about 2 cups of water until the stink is gone.

★ Dab a few drops of lemon, lemongrass, orange, or grapefruit essential oil on a cotton ball, and set it in the kitchen. All of these oils neutralize odors, and leave a nice fresh, clean scent.

If cooking odors are a frequent, recurring problem, your range hood and/or exhaust fan may need a thorough cleaning. Check out the Range Hoods entry on page 260 for details.

Powerful Potions

Super Scrubber

Why keep a bunch of cleaning products on hand when you can use one potion to cover all parts of a porcelain stove—including the oven? This all-purpose spray loosens up crud and cuts through greasy spills like magic.

2 tsp. of white vinegar

1 tsp. of borax

½ tsp. of baking soda

1 squirt of grease-cutting dishwashing liquid

2 cups of water

Measure the vinegar, borax, baking soda, dishwashing liquid, and water into a handheld sprayer bottle and shake it well. Be sure the surface is cool before you use the cleaner, and then spray and wipe porcelain stovetops, drip pans, gas burner grates, ovens, and even the glass windows in oven doors. For dried-on spills, soak the spots with the potion, and wait about 15 minutes before wiping them up. Shake the bottle frequently as you work, and store it in a cool cabinet when you're finished. Just avoid using this cleaner on stainless steel or smooth cooktops because the borax might cause faint scratches.

Kitchen aid. For no-muss, no-fuss cleaning, let your dishwasher do the dirty work on greasy drip pans and gas burner grates. Instead of scrubbing the heck out of them, simply set the pieces in the top rack of the dishwasher and run them through the "pots and pans" cycle.

Easy bake. If drip pans are made of porcelain, take a look at the owner's manual: You just might be able to clean them in a self-cleaning oven. If so, simply set them upside down on the oven rack when you run the cycle, and the greasy crud will burn to soft gray ash. After the pans are cool, wipe the ash off with a damp cloth, let them air-dry, and put them back on the stovetop.

Go undercover. Many stoves have a spill-catching tray underneath the stovetop to catch anything that slips past the drip pans. It's way easier to wipe the tray frequently than it is to remove old spills, so get in the habit of lifting the lid once a week. A sudsy sponge should take care of most of the gunk in the tray. For really stubborn spots, mix a little baking soda with water and scrub away with a nonabrasive plastic scrubbie to get rid of the grime.

Hocus Pocus

SMOOTH MOVES

If your kitchen range has a smooth glass or ceramic cooktop, you'll need to treat it with kid gloves to keep it clean—and scratch-free. These smooth surfaces are all too easy to gouge or scrape, even with ordinary cleaning supplies. Plus, some food spills can etch the surface if you're not careful. Here's how to keep your cooktop as smooth as silk:

★ Use the nonabrasive stove cleaner recommended by the manufacturer, such as Cerama Bryte®, at least once a week. And remember: A little dab'll do ya—just a few drops will clean the whole cooktop.

★ Wipe it down after every use with a microfiber cleaning cloth to remove any fingerprints and water spots and leave the surface streak-free.

★ Use packaged window wipes for quick 'n' easy touchups.

★ Don't slide your pots, pans, or utensils across the surface, and never cut on it.

★ Wipe up sweet or sugary spills right away because if they heat up, the sugar can actually etch the surface with tiny pits.

★ Use a razor-blade scraper to remove any hardened spills. You can buy one made especially for smooth cooktops, which holds the blade at just the right angle—and keeps your fingertips out of harm's way!

Swimming Pools

Wash your tootsies! Kids jump in and out of the pool constantly, tracking in bits of grass and other debris every time they enter the water. To stop that dirt in its tracks, train your swimmers to rinse their feet off before they jump into the pool. Simply put a dishpan of water beside the pool for a quick rinse, and lay a rubber bathtub mat beside it so those wet tootsies have a clean place to stand. This one small step will go a long way toward keeping your pool water free of debris.

Save your back. Scrubbing a kiddie pool can really do a number on your back and knees. You can use a regular scrub brush to do the job, but why not make it easier on your aching back by using a long-handled pool brush? They're available anywhere swimming pool supplies are sold.

Q. Our grandchildren are frequent swimmers in our aboveground pool, and sometimes, one of them waits too long before taking a bathroom break and ends up urinating in the water. What's the best way to sanitize the pool before letting everyone back in?

The Great Clean-dini Speaks

A. Bathroom "accidents" can happen anytime and anywhere (especially in swimming pools), so even if your swimmers are out of diapers and into big-boy (or girl) pants, you'll want to clean the pool every couple of days. If an even worse accident happens and you see feces floating in the pool, drain the water immediately and scrub the pool vigorously with a mix of 1 part chlorine bleach and 9 parts water. Rinse it thoroughly, and before refilling, let it sit in the sun for a couple of hours to help kill any remaining bacteria.

Rake it off. Use a leaf rake to gather up wayward blades of grass, leaves, and other bits of debris that wind up floating in the pool water before they sink to the bottom. You can also use a regular swimming pool skimmer in your kiddie pool, if you have one handy.

Put a lid on it. An ounce of prevention is worth a pound of cure, so cover a pool when it's not in use to keep insects, leaves, and other debris from landing in the water. For a small kiddie pool, use a plastic tarp, setting a few heavy toys around the edges to hold it in place. For a larger pool, pick up an inexpensive cover at a local pool-supply store.

Made in the shade. Algae grow fast in sunlight, so if you want to slow down the green slime, set the kiddie pool up in the shade. You'll still need to change the water every two to three days, but less algae will mean less scrubbing when it comes time to clean the pool.

Clean with chlorine. Household chlorine bleach will kill bacteria and keep algae from growing in pool water. Use about $1/4$ teaspoon of bleach for every 10 gallons of water in the pool (that's about $2^1/2$ teaspoons of bleach for a 100-gallon pool). If you empty the pool every day or two, you won't need bleach at all.

Chemical kit. If you have a deep kiddie pool, you may want to consider using pool chemicals to keep the water clean between refills. Make sure you know how much water is in the pool. Look for products that are made for plastic pools, and don't go overboard: Follow the directions on the label and the recommended amounts to the letter. And to avoid skin and eye irritation, always wait a couple of hours after adding chemicals before you allow swimmers to enter the pool.

Recycle the water. If pool water is free of chemicals, don't let it go to waste! When it's time to drain the pool, bail some of the water out into a watering can before you pull the plug, and use it to give your hanging baskets, container plants, or garden a good drink.

SUNTAN LOTION STAINS

Slathering on suntan lotion can be messy business, so use these tips to prevent stains before the lotion soaks into your swimsuit or clothes, or gets tracked on to your carpet:

★ Simplify stain removal in the first place by buying a water-based lotion, rather than an oily one. Read the ingredients, and if mineral oil is listed, buy a different product.

★ Wash your hands thoroughly after you apply any lotion.

★ Spread a towel or two over your patio furniture and car seats to avoid staining the upholstery.

And if your tropical tan lotion does leave stains, use these tricks to make them disappear without going coco-nuts:

★ If you've got lotion on your clothes, wipe off as much as you can, then use an enzyme presoak before you launder the item. Or you can soak the fabric in a solution of 1 teaspoon of liquid laundry detergent, 1 tablespoon of white vinegar, and 1 quart of water, and launder it as usual.

★ For suntan lotion spills on hard surfaces, including plastic, tile, aluminum, and vinyl, dip a clean cloth into warm, sudsy water that's got a few drops of ammonia added to it. Rinse the area well and wipe it dry.

★ Lotion stains on walkways or patio pavers call for stronger measures, so use washing soda and water. Scrub the stains with a soft-bristled brush to work the soapy solution into the surface, and rinse it well with a garden hose.

★ Clean suntan lotion off carpet and upholstery by sprinkling the spots with baking soda or cornstarch to soak up the oil or liquid. Let the powder stand for half an hour, vacuum it up, and use my Extra-Strength Dry Spotter potion on page 164 if you can still see the stains. Always test the potion in an inconspicuous area first to make sure it doesn't damage the surface.

Table Linens

Enjoy your dinner. Spills and stains will happen, so don't whip the cloth off the table in the middle of dinner just to take care of it. Blot the spills up, then relax and enjoy your meal—you can take care of the problem later, after your guests are gone. Check the entries for Grease Stains on page 170, Wine Stains on page 356, and other stains by name. You'll find plenty of nifty tricks for solving any kind of tabletop disaster.

That hits the spot! Pretreat greasy food stains on dinner napkins or table linens with a dab of orange-based hand cleaner like GOJO®. It's made for mechanics, and you know what those grease-monkey paws look like. Lightly rub a little into the stains and toss the cloths in the wash along with the rest of your load.

Natural-fiber fix. If your tablecloth, napkins, or kitchen towels are made of linen or cotton, you're in luck because nearly all stains will disappear by soaking them in OxiClean®. Put 3 scoops of OxiClean Versatile Stain Remover powder in a sink, fill it about halfway with hot water, and soak the items overnight. If there's still a stubborn spot or two, rub some OxiClean directly into the spots before laundering the items as usual.

Grandma Putt's Magical Methods

To remove a really stubborn or mystery stain on an old white tablecloth, try my Grandma Putt's tried-and-true last-ditch effort: Put the cloth into an extra-large cooking pot, pour in 4 tablespoons of dishwasher detergent (liquid or powder), and add enough water to cover the fabric. Heat the mixture to a boil, and let it simmer on low for about 20 minutes, stirring occasionally. Lift the steaming tablecloth out with a pair of tongs, put it in a bucket, and then dump it in your washing machine. Wash it immediately on the usual cycle.

Q. I used my grandmother's old lace tablecloth for a dinner party, and my candles spilled over. I picked off some of the wax, but there's a lot more, down deep in the lace. Is there anything I can do to salvage this family heirloom?

The Great Clean-dini Speaks

A. There's no need to panic when candle wax drips onto your table linens, whether it's Grandma's lace or machine-washable cotton. Here's an easy trick that'll make it disappear in a hurry:

1. Set a box of frozen vegetables on the waxy spot for about 10 minutes, to harden it up. Then scrape off as much as you can with your fingernail or a dull knife. If the candle was white or made from natural beeswax, proceed to Step 3.

2. If the spill was colored wax, you'll need to treat the dye stain. Use my Extra-Strength Dry Spotter potion on page 164 or a commercial stain stick to remove the colored spot. You'll still have a grease stain, but don't worry—see Step 3.

3. Sandwich the stain between two layers of paper towels, and run a warm (not hot) iron over the top piece of paper. The heat will melt any remaining wax, and the oil and wax will get soaked up lickety-split by the paper towel.

4. To keep the stain from spreading, replace the top and bottom paper towels as soon as they get greasy, and keep ironing until no more oil soaks in.

5. Rub some grease-cutting dishwashing liquid into the spot, wait about 10 minutes so it can work on the stain, and then launder the item as usual.

Natural bleach. Household bleach may be too strong for old or delicate table linens, so use the gentle power of the sun to minimize spots, stains, and yellowing on white or light-colored items. Hang them over a clothesline, or dry them flat on the grass on top of an old sheet. Be sure to put them in an area where they'll get the full force of the sun for several hours. And don't try this trick on deeply colored cloth—Old Sol is likely to fade the color, as well as the stains.

Grease zapper. Grease stains are the most common type of mishap when it comes to table linens, and making them vanish is a cinch—as long as

Powerful Potions

Crochet Cleaner

Crocheted pieces take hours of work to create—and only a few seconds to get stained! If those stains refuse to yield to my other tricks, try this magical formula to make them disappear; it gets rid of just about any discoloration you can think of, even if you have no idea what caused the splotch in the first place. Plus, it'll leave your crocheted tablecloth, runner, or doilies crisp and bright.

1 cup of Vivid® Ultra Liquid Bleach
1 cup of Cascade® powdered dishwasher detergent
½ cup of white vinegar

Wearing rubber gloves to protect your skin, combine the ingredients in a large glass bowl, and push the stained crocheted piece into the mixture. Let it soak for about an hour, and rinse thoroughly. Dry the piece flat to prevent shrinkage, and stretch it gently to keep it in shape as it dries. If the piece is too big for the bowl, submerge only the stained part, and follow the soak with regular laundering in cold water using Vivid according to the package directions, along with your regular laundry detergent.

you pretreat the stains before you wash and dry the item. So inspect all linens for trouble spots before you toss them in the washing machine. Rub a squirt of grease-cutting dishwashing liquid into each spot, let the linens sit for about 10 minutes, and then launder them with an enzyme detergent to help dissolve the stains. Check the items again before you put them in the dryer because heat will set the stains. If you still see spots, repeat the treatment.

Anti-aging treatment. Lace tablecloths and white linens tend to yellow with age, but you can whiten them up by soaking the pieces in one of these simple recipes:

★ For smaller pieces, use a mixture of equal parts white vinegar and baking soda. Lay the items flat in a sink (with the stopper in), sprinkle them with 1 or 2 cups of baking soda, and add an equal amount of white vinegar. The combination will foam and hiss ferociously. Let the items soak in the solution for about half an hour, then rinse thoroughly. Repeat the treatment if necessary.

★ Soak the discolored linens in a solution of hydrogen peroxide. Peroxide that is sold for home use is a 3% solution, which may be enough to whiten a slightly yellowed cloth; if yours needs a stronger fix, buy 20% hydrogen peroxide at a beauty-supply store. Fill a sink with cool water and add 2 cups of 3% peroxide or 1/2 cup of the 20% variety. Soak the items for about an hour, rinse them in cool water, and dry them in the sun for an additional whitening boost.

Scorch stains. A crisply ironed tablecloth or tea towel sure looks great—unless it has a big brown scorch stain on it! And since cotton and linen require a very hot iron, it's all too easy to scorch linens when you let the iron rest just a tad too long in one place. To lighten the stain, brush any charring off, rub liquid laundry detergent into the spot, and launder the item as usual. If the stain is still visible, try nonchlorine bleach that's safe for all fabrics, or bleach the brown mark away by sponging it with bottled lemon juice and then laying the item in full sun for a few hours.

Decaf your cloth. When a splash of coffee or tea stains your table linen, run cold water through the cloth ASAP to rinse out the dark color. Then rub some dishwashing liquid into the spot before you launder the item, and use an oxygenating detergent to remove all traces of the stain.

Wrinkle reliever. You'll rarely need to heat up your iron if you use this trick to keep your polyester and poly-blend table linens wrinkle-free. Just  keep an eye on the dryer when you're laundering them, and remove them as soon as the cycle stops. Smooth out the still-warm linens, fold them neatly, and they'll be all ready to use next time. Oh, and if you do forget to take the linens out of the dryer right away? Why, just toss a very moist washcloth in and run them through another cycle for a few minutes. The moisture will relax those wrinkles in a jiffy.

Tiled Floors

There's the rub. Daily sweeping is a must for tiled floors. Why? Because the grit that gets tracked in on the bottom of shoes works like sandpaper on natural stone or ceramic tiles, causing fine scratches that dull the finish. A broom or dust mop will help, but to do a really thorough job of grit removal, use a vacuum. Switch it to the "hard floors" setting, so the beater bar doesn't hammer the tile. And use entry mats to trap the dirt—they'll go a long way toward stamping out the sandpaper.

Be a softie. A microfiber mop is best for cleaning tiled floors. It attracts dirt like a magnet, instead of pushing it into the grout lines or leaving it behind on the textured surface. To avoid scratching, stay away from scouring powders, steel wool, and other abrasive cleaners. Plain water does a great job on ceramic or stone tiles; for tougher dirt, add a squirt of dishwashing liquid or ½ cup of ammonia to your bucket. And rinse the floors thoroughly because soap residue will dull the shine.

You dirty dog! To clean extra-dirty grout, mix up a solution of Oxiclean® Versatile Stain Remover per the directions for heavy-duty cleaning. Go over grout lines with a sponge mop, rinse, and the grime should be gone.

Grubby grout. If white tile grout gets stained, try one of these tricks to lighten and brighten it up:

1. Spray a mix of 1 part hydrogen peroxide and 1 part water onto the spot, let it sit for 15 minutes, wipe it clean, and repeat if needed.

2. If the stain hasn't lightened, lay a folded paper towel over the area, and saturate it with peroxide. Cover it with plastic wrap so it doesn't dry out, and wait about an hour.

3. Still see a stain? Make a paste of baking soda and peroxide in a small bowl, wait for the bubbling to stop, and rub it on. Let it sit for an hour or two, spraying it with more peroxide whenever it starts to dry out. Wipe the residue off, and your grout should be white again.

So long to scum. If a tiled bathroom floor is spotted with soap scum or mineral deposits, scrape the splotches off with a plastic putty knife. Hold the knife at an angle, and push gently. You can also scrub scum-spotted tiles with a solution of 1 or 2 tablespoons of trisodium phosphate (TSP) in 1 gallon of hot water. Use a non-abrasive plastic scrubbie, and rinse the floor thoroughly.

Powerful Potions

Grout Scrub

Use this potion to spiff up grubby grout; it's safe to use on both the white and colored stuff.

  2 cups of baking soda

  1 cup of powdered borax

  1 cup of hot water

Mix the ingredients in a small bucket. Dip a nonabrasive plastic scrubbie or grout brush into the mixture, and rub it briskly along the lines. Rinse thoroughly with a cloth or mop dipped in plain water to remove the residue.

Grime scene. If the grout doesn't come clean when you wash the floor, scrub it with an old toothbrush that's been dipped in a paste made of baking soda and water. For deeper stains, fold a piece of sandpaper and rub it back and forth along the cracks. Just be careful to stay inside the lines to avoid sandpapering the tiles.

Seal of approval. Most tiled floors are sealed to prevent spills from soaking into the grout. But as the sealant wears off, stains can quickly penetrate the porous grout, and mildew may set in. Check the sealant by sprinkling a few drops of water on the grout. If the water beads up, you simply have surface dirt. But if the water soaks in, it's time to reseal the floor. For glazed tile, you'll need to reseal only the grout itself; for unglazed tile, you may need to treat the entire floor. Speak with a tile specialist for details on floor treatments.

Stick to it. Because peroxide and other cleaning products can bleach colored grout, always test them in an inconspicuous area before you work on a spot. And if your colored grout fails the test, buy a chalklike grout-cleaner stick at a tile store. It'll work wonders on those stained spots.

The Great Clean-dini Speaks

Q. My textured kitchen tiles were creamy white, but now they're dingy with dirt that just won't come off. Do you have a safe cleaner that's strong enough for my floor?

A. Here's a scrubber that really tackles the dirt on white or light-colored floors, even if the tile has a textured surface like yours. Simply cut a fresh lemon in half, dip the cut side into powdered borax, and scrub gently. The citric acid in the lemon will brighten up the tiles and grout, while the borax adds a gentle abrasive for extra scrubbing power. So pucker up, and you'll kiss that dingy floor good-bye!

Time to reflect. Terrazzo consists of marble chips and concrete that have been polished to a high gloss. To preserve the shine of a terrazzo floor, wash it with a mixture of 1 cup of liquid fabric softener and ½ gallon of water. For an even brighter finish, add 1 cup of white vinegar to the rinse water, then stand back and enjoy the reflection.

Pop your cork. Sweep or vacuum a cork tile floor every day to keep dirt from scratching the surface. For a more thorough cleaning, damp mop with a squirt of dishwashing liquid in a pail of water, and rinse with fresh water. And make sure the mop is only slightly damp, so you don't soak the cork.

Toasters and Toaster Ovens

Smudge solution. Because these appliances get a lot of hands-on use, fingerprints are bound to smear their surfaces—especially after a battle with butter and jam. To spiff things up, wipe them down with a cloth or paper towel that's been dampened with white vinegar. It'll cut the grease and leave a nice clean finish behind.

Shine stainless. Clean and polish stainless steel toasters and toaster ovens by buffing their exteriors with a soft cloth that's been dipped in rubbing alcohol. It'll remove fingerprint smudges and grease prints in a snap. Alcohol is flammable, so make sure the appliances are completely cool before trying this trick. And let the alcohol dry for at least an hour before you make your next batch of toast.

Improve your vision. To clean the window on a toaster oven, wipe it down with a solution of equal parts vinegar and water. If the window is spattered with hardened grease, rub it down with a dab of orange-based waterless hand cleaner (like GOJO®) on a soft cloth, or use a nonabrasive plastic scrubbie to apply a little elbow grease.

Hocus Pocus

MELTED-PLASTIC MAKEOVER

Toasters and toaster ovens can get mighty hot—hot enough to melt a plastic bread bag or other food wrapper that touches their surfaces. To remove melted plastic from these appliances, wait until they completely cool down, then rub the smear with a little nail polish remover. The melted plastic will wipe right off—like magic!

Salt shaker. To clean charred bread out of the nooks and crannies inside a toaster, just sprinkle 1 to 2 tablespoons of coarse kosher salt into the slots, cover the openings with strips of masking tape, and shake the toaster vigorously. The chunks of salt will dislodge the carbon buildup on the wires and other inside parts. Clean the salt out by shaking the toaster upside down and then wiping out the crumb tray.

Crumb catcher. Your toaster won't work as well when it gets "crummy," and in fact, it can even catch fire. So clean out the loose crumbs frequently. Simply unplug the toaster, open the crumb tray, and shake out all the loose bits. Wipe the tray clean with a paper towel, and brush off the inside parts with a soft pastry brush.

Easy-off oven cleaning. No, not the brand name—never use oven cleaner on a toaster oven. Instead, make it part of your routine to wipe the oven down after every use. Be sure it's unplugged and completely cool before you clean it. Then wipe the interior with a damp cloth. If the oven is greasy, use a cloth that's been dipped in hot water with a bit of dishwashing liquid added to it, and scrub off any stuck-on food with a nonabrasive plastic scrubbie. You can remove the racks to clean them in the sink, or simply wipe them off in place.

Toilets

One, two, three...go! Cleaning a toilet is a three-part job: the inside, the outside, and the seat. Here's a quick and easy method to power your way through all three parts without missing a beat:

1. Most toilet bowl cleaners need time to soak into the crud, so start by squirting, shaking, or pouring your favorite product into the water. Close the seat and let the cleaner do its stuff.

2. Meanwhile, clean the outside, working from the top down. Wipe down the lid, the tank (don't forget the handle), the outside of the bowl, and the surrounding floor with a disinfectant cleaner.

3. Clean the seat lid, both sides of the toilet seat, the hinges, and the top rim of the bowl.

4. Scrub the bowl, including the nasty part under the rim. Wipe up any drips, flush once, flush twice, and you're done.

Powerful Potions

Kitchen-Sink Solution

To make stubborn toilet bowl stains disappear, try a little kitchen cleaning magic. This potion works like a charm, and the best part is—you already have the ingredients at your kitchen sink.

Powdered dishwasher detergent

Water

Make a medium-thick paste of dishwasher detergent and water in a small bowl. Then head to the bathroom and lower the water in the toilet bowl (see "Lower the Water" on page 322 for the how-to). Apply the paste to the stained areas, close the lid, and wait about 15 minutes. Then swab the bowl clean.

Hocus Pocus

LOWER THE WATER

Before cleaning a toilet bowl, you need to lower the water level so you can work on those areas that need it the most. Here's how to get rid of the excess H_2O for easier access:

★ Pour about half a bucket of water all at once into the bowl.

★ Push the bowl brush quickly in and out of the exit hole a few times.

★ Shut off the water to the tank at the pipe, flush the toilet, and it won't be able to refill.

★ When you're done cleaning the toilet, be sure to turn the water back on.

Color-coded. If you regularly use yellow rubber gloves around the house, how about a purple, green, or blue pair for toilet duty? That way, they won't get mixed up with your other gloves and spread nasty germs to other parts of the house. Store them in the bathroom, and then use them only for toilet-cleaning duty.

Dispose of the germs. To prevent spreading germs or, worse yet, accidentally using a toilet sponge on your kitchen sink, always use paper towels to wipe down the toilet and the floor around it. When you're finished with the job, just throw the used paper towels in the trash.

Quick disinfectant. Brighten up a toilet bowl and kill germs at the same time by pouring $\frac{1}{2}$ cup of chlorine bleach into the water in the bowl. Close the lid, let the bleach sit for about 10 minutes, and then scrub the stains away. Don't mix bleach with any other cleaning products, and run the bathroom fan or open a window to exhaust the fumes during the treatment.

The real thing. To remove toilet bowl stains, pour a 2-liter bottle of Coke® or Pepsi® into the bowl, let it sit for about an hour, and then flush the toilet. Most stains will be gone, and you can polish off the rest with a little elbow grease.

In-tank hang-ups. Toilet bowl cleaners that hang or drop into the tank seem like a great idea, but the chlorine in them can be a real troublemaker. It degrades the rubber flapper, causing that annoying (and money-wasting) trickle of water into the tank. Toilet experts call it the "vacation syndrome" because the problem happens fast when the toilet isn't flushed regularly—like when you're away on vacation. Plus, these cleaners only clean the water, so you still need to scrub the rest of the toilet. With all these drawbacks, a trusty scrub brush makes a lot more sense.

Take two tablets. Here's a nifty trick to clean a toilet bowl from the water line down: Drop two Alka-Seltzer® tablets into the bowl, close the lid, let things soak for about 20 minutes, then brush the loosened crud away. You can also use two denture-cleaning tablets, letting the toilet soak overnight and swishing it clean the next morning. The fizzy action and mild acids do a great job of brightening things up.

Tangy tip. Citric acid also makes a great toilet bowl cleaner. Simply drop 2 teaspoons of Tang® or powdered lemonade mix into the toilet bowl before you go to bed. Let it work on the stains overnight, then the next morning, just brush and flush!

Grandma Putt's Magical Methods

When hard-water minerals build up in a toilet tank, the deposits keep the flapper valve from closing tight—and that leads to an annoying trickle. But my Grandma Putt never let her flapper valve cause a flap if jiggling the handle didn't make the toilet stop running. She'd shut off the water, flush the toilet to empty the tank, and scrub off the pesky buildup with Zud® scouring powder. Nowadays, you can also use Lime-Away® or CLR® to dissolve the minerals. Just remember to protect your skin and eyes while you work. When you're finished, turn the water back on and flush the toilet a few times to rinse out the residue.

Water deposits. To dissolve the hard-water mineral buildup in a toilet bowl, pour in a gallon of white vinegar and let it sit overnight. The acid in the vinegar will counteract the lime, loosening its grip on the once-tidy bowl. In the morning, scrub the mineral remains off with a nonabrasive plastic scrubbie. If your toilet is a real tough cookie, you may have to repeat the treatment.

Hard cases. If you're ready to give up on ever having a clean toilet simply  because of mineral stains or hard-water buildup, try a phosphoric acid cleaner like Snow Bol® or The Works® Disinfectant Toilet Bowl Cleaner. These thick liquids dissolve all kinds of stains and scum so fast you won't believe it. Be sure to protect your eyes and skin, and follow the directions to the letter. Then store the bottle safely away where kids or pets can't get anywhere near it.

Tools

You can handle it. Keep wooden tool handles in good shape by wiping them down every few months with a dab of boiled linseed oil. If a handle is pale and dry, sand it lightly to remove any rough spots or splinters, then apply the oil. Let it soak into the wood, then apply another coat. Wait about 10 minutes, wipe the excess off, and buff the wood dry with a soft, clean cloth. Now your tool handles will be smooth operators.

Dig it. To keep shovels, hoes, rakes, and other tools free from rust, make a sandpit. Start by filling a 5-gallon pail about two-thirds full of sand, and then mix in $\frac{1}{2}$ quart of motor oil (used is fine). Set it in a corner, and after working hard in your yard, plunge your tools up and down in the bucket a few times to quickly clean them up. The sand will scrub off

Grandma Putt's Magical Methods

Wooden tool handles have a tough life, what with working in mud and muck, on rainy days, and sometimes even being left outside in the elements. So my Grandma Putt came up with this magical mix to keep the wood in fine fettle, shielding it from cracking and splintering. Use it to wipe down all of your handles about once a month, or whenever you notice that the wood is starting to look a bit pale and dry.

Take a glass jar with a tight-fitting lid and mix 1 part white vinegar, 1 part boiled linseed oil, and 1 part turpentine in the jar. To use the mix, pour some of it on a dry microfiber cloth or old cotton sock, and rub it up and down the handle until the whole thing is covered. Wait about 10 minutes for it to soak in, and then repeat the treatment. Wait another 10 minutes, then wipe any excess off with a clean, dry cloth. Screw the lid on and store the leftover potion in a cool, dark place—it'll keep indefinitely.

dirt and rust, and the oil will give the metal a protective coating. You can leave the tools in the bucket, or wipe the sand off and hang them back up where they belong.

Get inhibited. One of the best ways to keep rust from getting its grip on metal tools is by spraying them with a rust inhibitor. The old-fashioned method is to wipe the metal down with a cloth that's been dabbed with mineral oil. Nowadays, you can do the job in half the time with rust-inhibitor sprays like Boeshield T-9® Corrosion Inhibitor and Lubricant. These sprays leave a very thin, waxy coating on the metal. Use T-9 to loosen existing rust so that it rubs off easily, then follow up with a light coat to keep rust away for good.

Steel yourself. To clean rusty hand tools, scrub the problem areas with steel wool. Wet the tools first, then rub the rust away with small circular motions. Rinse the residue off, dry the tools, and coat them with a little mineral oil or rust inhibitor to prevent the rust from creeping back in.

Rust remover. When rust sets in on hand tools, try this quick fix: Spray the metal with WD-40®, and rub it lightly with a nonabrasive plastic scrubbie. The rust will come right off, and you won't scratch the tools. Finish the job by wiping off the excess lubricant with a dry cloth, and store the tools in a clean, dry place.

TVs, VCRs, and DVD Players

Keep it simple. The best choice for cleaning the screens on these machines is the simplest: a soft, dry cloth. Use a microfiber or electrostatic dust cloth and wipe gently; don't rub or press hard because too much elbow grease can easily damage the coating. And never use paper towels or newspaper to wipe these screens because the cellulose fiber in the paper can scratch them.

Can you see me now? Use a dry cloth to dust a glass screen and a damp cloth to remove fingerprints and other smudges. If your TV is an older model that doesn't have special coatings on the glass, you can also use Windex® to clean it. Just spray the cleaner on the cloth, not on the screen, so that moisture doesn't seep into the cracks around the frame.

Flat screens. If a flat screen, rear-projection, or plasma TV needs more than a simple dusting, your best bet is to use a commercial cleaner that's specifically made for the particular type of screen (check the owner's manual for details). Turn the TV off, spray the cleaner on a soft, clean cloth, and use the gentlest pressure possible. You can find cleaning kits wherever TVs are sold.

Light touch for LCDs. To clean an LCD TV screen, use equal parts rubbing alcohol and water. Dip a soft cotton or microfiber cloth into the mix and squeeze it out so that it's barely damp. Wipe the entire screen, using a very light touch without any pressure at all. There's no need to rinse because the alcohol evaporates quickly. To clean around the edges of the screen, dip a cotton swab in the solution and run it lightly along each side.

Cabinet cleaning. Use a dry microfiber or electrostatic dust cloth to wipe down TV cabinets, whether they're made of plastic, wood-look vinyl, metal, or what have you. (Most cabinets are made of synthetic materials, even if they look like real wood.) The vents or grilles collect a lot of dust, so wipe away from the openings, toward the back of the speaker. And don't use furniture polish, even if the cabinet is made of real wood—it'll only attract more dust.

On with the show. VCRs and DVD players get very dusty because they give off static electricity that attracts loose particles like a magnet. So dust these components just as you did the TV—with a soft, dry cloth. Wipe away from the vent holes, making sure that dirt doesn't fall inside. And remember to clean around the cables, too. Use a small, soft paintbrush to get the dust off the cable connections, and be careful not to bend the connector pins.

Hocus Pocus

SHOOTING BLANKS

If a VCR starts acting up, showing nothing but a blue screen or lots of static, it probably needs cleaning. For a fast fix, insert a new blank tape and let it play for about 30 minutes to collect any bits of crud that are gumming up the works. Don't rewind the blank tape, or that dirt will fall back into the machine. If you're in a big hurry to watch a movie, check the VCR after you've run the blank tape for 5 to 10 minutes—that may be all the cleaning it needs to operate properly.

Department of the interior. Dust, hair, and other debris can easily work their way into the slots on a media player, where they can lodge on the optical lens that reads the discs or tapes—and that means skips or static will soon follow. Here's how to solve the problem:

★ Invest in an optical lens cleaner for DVD players. Then all you need to do is slip in the disc and let it run.

★ To clean a VCR player, start by blowing any dust out of the tape compartment with a can of compressed air. Hold the door open, aim the can inside, and give it a few short blasts. Be sure to keep the can moving while you blow out the dust.

★ Buy a head-cleaning videocassette and follow the directions on the package to clean the working parts of your VCR. The "wet" type, which uses a special cleaning fluid, works great at getting rid of gunk.

Grandma Putt's Magical Methods

Back in Grandma Putt's day, when all TVs had glass screens, cleaning off the smudges was a cinch—a spritz of window cleaner, and the job was done. But now there are a whole slew of screen types to deal with, and some of them are mighty finicky. So before you clean anything, do what my Grandma Putt would do anytime some new-fangled appliance entered her home: Read the owner's manual. That way, you won't mess up the big picture!

Wipe out. When DVDs get dirty and start acting funky at show-time, wipe them down with a clean microfiber cloth. Stroke outward from the center hole to the edge of each disc, not around in circles. If that's not enough to make the smudges disappear, try a damp cloth, or use a half-and-half mix of rubbing alcohol and water. Remember, don't use a paper towel, which can scratch discs and leave behind a trail of lint. DVDs can be cared for in the same way you care for CDs. See page 58 for more tips.

Upholstery
(See also Fabrics; Furniture; and specific stains by name)

Weekly dustup. Vacuum fabric-covered furniture about once a week to
keep it clean. Use the upholstery attachment to do the surfaces, and
the crevice tool to suck the crumbs up and dust along the seams and
in the corners. Be sure to flip the cushions and vacuum up the debris
that's sifted down between them. As for the pocket change that ends up
underneath the cushions—why, that's finders, keepers!

Read the label. Unless your sofa, couch, or other upholstered furniture is
old or antique, it should have a label on it that tells you how to care for
the fabric. Most often, it is sewn to a cushion, but
if it's not, you may need to get down on your hands
and knees to look underneath the piece. Modern
furniture labels use code letters for care; see
"Cracking the Code" on page 330 to find out what
they mean. Once you find the tag, be sure to follow
the manufacturer's cleaning advice to the letter.

A sudsy solution. If your upholstery can be safely cleaned using a water-
based solution, try this trick to either spot-clean or freshen up the entire
piece. Start by using a hand mixer to whip ¼ cup of dishwashing liquid
and 1 cup of warm water into a creamy foam. Scoop some of the foam
onto a cloth or soft brush, and lightly scrub the fabric. Lift the suds
off with a spatula as they get dirty. Wipe the fabric down with a clean,
barely damp cloth to remove any remaining soap, and you're done.

Test first. Because cleaning products can discolor, shrink, or otherwise
damage upholstery, always test the technique in an inconspicuous area
first before you start scrubbing a spot that'll be in full view. Chances
are, the trick you use will turn out to be safe—but pretesting is better
than trying to disguise a disaster with a throw pillow.

Nachos, anyone? When finger foods (like nachos) drop on your couch, they can leave a grease stain behind in no time flat. To make the oily stain vanish, blot the spot with a solution of 1 tablespoon of ammonia in ½ cup of water, but only if your upholstery is labeled W or SW (see "Cracking the Code" below for guidance). For more super solutions for snackin' spills, see the Grease Stains entry on page 170.

Fabric protectors. If your upholstery was finished with fabric protector, you won't have to fret too much about dirt and spills. But you'll still need to clean it. Fabric protectors make the upholstery less absorbent, but they're not an ironclad defense. Consult the fabric-care tag, and use the appropriate trick to clean the dirt and spills. And remember—a fabric protector wears off over time, so you need to reapply it according to the directions on the package.

Hocus Pocus

CRACKING THE CODE

The fabric-care label on modern upholstery uses a code letter—W, S, SW, or X—to tell you which cleaning methods are safe. Here's how to interpret the shorthand:

★ **W** is for water, but that doesn't mean you can saturate the fabric. It means that the soapsuds from water-based cleaners are safe to use—not the liquid itself, mind you, because soaking upholstery can easily leave water stains.

★ **S** is for solvent, and this letter means that you should use a water-free, solvent-based cleaner like AFTA®, and not soapsuds.

★ **SW** indicates that either water- or solvent-based cleaners are A-OK to use.

★ **X** says, hey, you, stop right there—neither water- nor solvent-based cleaners are safe for this fabric! So limit your cleaning to vacuuming or brushing, or you'll risk damaging the fabric.

Grandma Putt's Magical Methods

Slipcovers have never gone out of style. Grandma Putt and many housewives of her generation used slipcovers to easily hide hopelessly stained upholstery, protect new furniture from getting soiled, or give a room a fresh new look. And they still serve the same purpose today. They're easy to care for—simply vacuum them as you would regular upholstery. If the covers are washable, check the care labels to find out which cycle to use, load them loosely into the washing machine, and let them presoak to loosen the dirt. Take them out of the dryer while they're still slightly damp—they'll be easier to fit back into place on your furniture. Once you've wrestled the slipcovers back on, straighten the seams, crease the pleats, and reshape any ruffled edges. Let the covers air-dry overnight before you sit on them, or speed up the drying process by aiming an electric fan at them for a few hours.

Coconut cure. To clean leather upholstery, combine equal parts of coconut oil liquid soap and water, and whip the mixture into a frothy foam. Apply the foam to the piece, working on one area at a time—back, seat, then arms. Use a soft brush or cloth to gently rub it over the surface to remove the grime, then wipe the suds off with a barely damp sponge. Buff the piece with a soft, dry cloth to work the oily residue into the leather and leave it smooth and supple. You'll find a lovely bunch of coconut oil liquid soaps at organic foods markets and health-food stores.

White and bright. White upholstery is really elegant—until it starts getting dirty. To get rid of the grungy look, stroke white fabric furniture with a special latex sponge that has a texture like sandwich bread. You can buy it for a few bucks at most hardware stores. Don't moisten the sponge;

simply wipe it over the dingy upholstery to remove the surface grime. Its porous texture does a great job of loosening dirt and pet hair, too, so you can simply stroke the stuff away.

This'll floor you! If an upholstered piece of furniture is beyond the point of hand cleaning, try using a carpet-cleaning machine with an upholstery-shampooing attachment. You can rent one of these powerful machines at most supermarkets and convenience stores. Just fill the reservoir with an upholstery shampoo like RugDoctor® Upholstery Cleaner, and you'll be ready to suds, steam, and extract the grime with some really super suction.

Vacuum Cleaners

What's the limit? To keep your vacuum cleaner operating properly, replace the bag when it's about half full. Check it out before you begin vacuuming; by the time the vac stops picking up debris, the bag will be overloaded—and will have already missed a lot of dust and dirt. So keep extra bags on hand, and you won't be scrambling when your current one gets filled to capacity.

Going bagless. You won't have to worry about vacuum bags if you've got a bagless model, but don't think you're getting off scot-free. Bagless vacs have filters that need cleaning, and you'll still have to empty the dirt cup. It's a good idea to dump the cup into a plastic grocery bag, tapping it gently on the floor to make sure it's empty, every time you vacuum. Clean the filters as often as the owner's manual recommends, which is usually every few weeks. Empty and tap them into a bag, just as you did the cup. And work outside if you can, so you won't have to vacuum after you clean the vacuum!

LOST YOUR SUCTION?

If your vacuum cleaner stops sucking up dirt or leaves some dirt behind, there's probably a clog somewhere in the works. First, check the bag and filters to make sure they're not over-loaded. If they're relatively clean, then the clog is probably in the hose. Clear it out with these tips:

★ Carefully push a broomstick through the hose to remove any debris that's lodged inside, causing a major traffic jam. Hold the hose straight while you work, so you don't damage it.

★ Untwist a wire coat hanger and carefully pull out or loosen up any clumps in the hose. Work slowly and carefully to avoid poking a hole in the hose.

★ Bend the end of a coat hanger into a small hook, put it inside the vacuum cleaner opening where the hose connects, and use it to fish out any debris.

Beat the brush. The beater bar is the spinning brush underneath a vacuum cleaner that loosens dirt so it can be sucked up. Take a look at it every now and then, and pull off any hair, threads, and other debris that get wrapped around it. You'll need to remove the brush to do a thorough job. Examine how the brush is installed before you remove it, so you can replace it afterward. Clean off the metal axle, too, and unscrew the caps on the ends and dust those areas to complete the job.

Filter check. Modern vacuum cleaners have a filter to catch fine particles of dust that would otherwise go airborne. Check the owner's manual to find out how to clean or replace your filter. If it's made of foam or plastic, you can usually rinse it clean, letting it air-dry completely before you put it back in place. If the filter is made of paper, carry it outside and shake off as much crud as you can, or replace it according to the manual's recommendations.

Heap o' savings. Paper HEPA filters cost a pretty penny—and they get clogged up fast with all the dust and dirt they catch. To avoid having to clean or replace these filters often, use a paper towel to catch the bigger particles before they get to the high-priced HEPA filter. Here's how:

1. Use a two-ply paper towel (Bounty® two-ply paper towels work best). Separate the layers of one towel by carefully peeling them apart.

2. Wrap one separated sheet around the HEPA filter, saving the other for next time. Secure it with tape.

3. Replace the now-covered filter, and vacuum as usual.

Listen for trouble. If the tone of your vacuum cleaner suddenly changes, switch it off immediately because you've sucked something up that's preventing it from working right. Unplug the machine and find whatever it is that's gumming up the works. If your vacuum has come to a sudden stop, as it will if you accidentally suck up the fringe on a rug, check the belt, too; it may have ripped, melted, or gotten pulled out of place. Keep an ear on your vac—and it'll keep you out of trouble!

Paper clip catcher. Paper clips, staples, and other metal debris can jam a vacuum cleaner and even poke a hole in the hose. To keep them out of the way, add a magnetic bar to the front edge of your vacuum. It'll attract metal objects before they get sucked up and muck up the works. You'll find these bars at office-supply stores and vacuum cleaner shops.

Grandma Putt's Magical Methods

Pet hair, loose string, and straggly fibers can work themselves into a real snarl around a vacuum cleaner's beater brush. It's difficult to work a scissors blade under the stretched stuff, so my Grandma Putt used a better tool: the seam ripper from her sewing kit. After she'd sliced through the tangled mess in a few spots, she used a kitchen fork to remove the mess. Once the brush was tangle-free, it went back to giving her rugs a good beating.

Vases

Sink your teeth in. Here's an easy way to clean a vase without using any elbow grease: Just fill it with hot water, drop in a couple of denture-cleaning tablets, and let it soak overnight. This treatment will even work on mineral deposits, although you may have to repeat it. If the neck of the vase is too narrow for a denture tablet, simply break the tab in half, and bombs away!

Fizz power. To remove dried-on leaves, muck, or other debris inside a vase and make it look like new, try this trick. Pour 1 cup of baking soda into it and then slowly add 1 to 2 cups of white vinegar, depending on the size of the vase. This concoction will hiss and foam like crazy, which will loosen the gunk. Add a little more vinegar when the baking soda simmers down, and let it foam again. Scrub the vase with a bottlebrush and rinse it thoroughly under running water.

Tight quarters. If you can't fit a bottlebrush or cloth into the tight neck of a vase, use some salt to do the scrubbing. Pour about ¼ cup of coarse kosher salt into the vase, add about 1 cup of water, and cover the opening with your hand. Then shake the vase vigorously and swirl it around to let the salt scrub down the walls. When you're done, rinse the vase thoroughly to make sure all traces of salt are gone.

HOCUS POCUS

BAG THE BUNCH

To keep a vase from getting stained with mineral deposits or green scum in the first place, put a clear plastic bag inside it, and fill the bag with water. Just don't poke a hole in the bag when you add your bouquet. After the flowers have all faded, remove the bag, and stow the vase back on the shelf until next time. With this trick, you'll never have to scrub off a mineral ring buildup again!

Overnight soak. To remove stains from the inside of a vase, fill it with white vinegar or ammonia and let it soak overnight. Empty the vase, rinse it out, and scrub it with soap and water to finish the job. If you decide to use ammonia, set the vase outside to soak, so you don't have fumes in your house.

Vinegar shake. To get rid of caked-on scum or mineral deposits in your favorite vase, pour in 1/4 cup of white vinegar and add 2 tablespoons of uncooked rice. Put your hand tightly over the top, and then shake, rattle, and roll. The vinegar will dissolve the crud, while the energetic action of the rice will scrape off the scum.

This'll crack you up! To clean a vase with a narrow opening, try using eggshells as an abrasive. Simply crumble the clean, dry shells from two or three eggs into the vase, and add a drop or two of dishwashing liquid and about 1/4 cup of warm water. Cover the top with your hand, and shake and swirl the vase in circles to scrub the inside.

Vinyl

Let's dish. Dishwashing liquid is the best all-purpose cleaner for anything made of vinyl. It cuts through dirt and grease in a flash, and it won't harm the material. So whenever a kiddie pool, patio furniture, storage container, kitchen floor, or other vinyl surface needs a good scrubbing, squirt some dishwashing liquid in warm water and sponge the grunge away.

Down with dingy. If a vinyl floor looks dirty no matter how hard you scrub it, you could be dealing with discolored floor wax or polish, or dirt that's worked its way under the glossy finish. To strip off the old wax, pour ammonia straight from the bottle onto the floor, and spread it over

Powerful Potions

Once-a-Week Wash for Vinyl Floors

Vinyl floors have a built-in shine, so there's no need to use wax or polish, unless they've gotten dull from years of abuse. Before you apply a commercial product, though, try this powerful potion—it's a super-easy solution for keeping sheet vinyl and linoleum looking spiffy, and it costs just pennies to make. Plain water is enough to remove light dirt from the floor, and the vinegar will cut any grease and give the floor a gentle shine. Best of all, there's no need to rinse!

1 cup of white vinegar
1 gal. of water plus 1 bucket of rinse water

Mix the vinegar and 1 gallon of water in a bucket, dip in a sponge mop, and have at it. Keep another bucket of clean water nearby to rinse the mop whenever needed. And don't worry about the vinegar smell—it'll disappear as soon as the floor dries.

the surface with a damp sponge mop. The mop will soon start picking up dirt as the ammonia dissolves the wax, so rinse it out frequently and keep mopping until the floor and mop are clean. Then rinse the floor with plain water, let it dry, and reapply wax if you like. And to keep that finish looking its best, use my Once-a-Week Wash for Vinyl Floors potion above instead of cleaners that contain ammonia, which will cut through the wax. Also avoid powders like Spic and Span®, which may permanently mar the finish.

Scrub off scuffs. To remove scuff marks from a vinyl floor, try a little dishwashing liquid on a damp sponge. If you need more cleaning power for a troublesome area, use a nonabrasive plastic scrubbie instead of a sponge. You can also rub the spots with a pencil eraser, a dab of baking soda, or some white non-gel toothpaste to make the marks vanish.

Now, that's awesome! If you simply can't get the dirt off a vinyl floor with regular damp mopping, try LA's Totally AWESOME® liquid cleaner. You'll find it at dollar and discount stores; just look for the big word *Awesome* on the label. The "original" type works great on cutting through old floor wax and general grunge. Use about 1 part AWESOME to 10 parts water for everyday dirt, and a stronger solution for tougher cleaning; mix it according to the directions on the label.

Grandma Putt's Magical Methods

If you're a true audiophile and own a priceless collection of vinyl records, you probably have your own favorite tricks for cleaning them. But when my Grandma Putt wanted to wipe off kids' fingerprints, or clean up LPs she found at garage sales, she used plain old soap and water. It worked great, and it didn't harm the vinyl. Here's how to do it:

1. Find a basin big enough to hold an LP. Put in a few inches of warm water and a squirt of dishwashing liquid.

2. Holding a record by the edges, submerge it in the water, then remove it and wipe both sides with a soft cloth that's thoroughly wet with the soapy solution. Wipe around the disc following the grooves because that's where the crud collects.

3. If some or all of your records are really filthy, use a wet, soapy toothbrush to clean the surfaces after you've dunked each one.

4. Rinse each cleaned record under warm water, and wipe it dry with a microfiber cloth, again working with the grooves, not against them.

Have a seat. Abrasive cleaners can scratch vinyl upholstery, and household cleaners may make it brittle, so always use gentle dishwashing liquid instead. Dampen a soft cloth in a bucket of warm water with a squirt of dishwashing liquid added to it, and rub the upholstery to remove the surface dirt. Rinse the upholstery with a clean, damp cloth and let it air-dry. For stubborn stains, visit an auto-supply store and buy a vinyl cleaner that's specially made for auto upholstery.

This side up. A once-a-year cleaning will keep vinyl siding looking like new. The secret? Work on a cloudy day to prevent streaks, and start at the bottom and clean upward. All it takes is a few good squirts of dishwashing liquid in a bucket of hot water, applied with a long-handled car wash brush to soap up the siding. (You can also pour the soapy water into a hose-end sprayer to wash down a large area in a hurry.) Then rinse the siding with a garden hose. Vinyl siding is usually installed without a waterproof barrier behind it, so spray the water at the siding the same way rain falls—from the top down. And use a spray, not a blast, to keep water from getting in behind the vinyl.

Don't fence me in. Vinyl fences and garden trellises require much less maintenance than those that need painting, and they're easy to clean, too. Use a soapy solution of water and dishwashing liquid along with a soft-bristled brush or cloth to rub the dirt away. Rinse 'em clean with a garden hose, and remember to work on a cloudy day, so the detergent doesn't leave streaks on your nice clean fence or trellis.

Outdoor living. Because vinyl sheds water, it's a popular material for outdoor furniture. When your patio pieces start looking grungy, check out the Patios and Patio Furniture entry on page 241 to clean them, or try a product called Quick n Brite®. It's a biodegradable, environmentally safe paste (or liquid) that cleans the toughest dirt from just about anything—including airplanes! And it works quickly to brighten up vinyl fences and siding, too.

Vomit Stains

Act fast. When there's an "unpleasant surprise" on a rug, furniture, or bed, take care of it right away before the liquid has a chance to soak in. It's much easier to clean up a problem that hasn't gone too deep; if it soaks in, you'll have a much bigger job on your hands. So scoop it up, blot as much moisture as you can, and then use one of the tricks in this section to take care of the stain. Remember: You'll get the best results when you act quickly on a fresh vomit stain.

Super scooper. The first step in dealing with an upsetting accident is to remove as much of the stuff as you can. Paper towels help, but here's a great trick to scoop up the mess: Cut a stiff paper or plastic plate in half to form a flat edge, and scoot it under the puddle. It'll pick up most of the stuff, and then you can finish gathering up the remaining evidence with paper towels.

Grandma Putt's Magical Methods

To help soak up any lingering moisture and neutralize the sickly smell from vomit, Grandma Putt would sprinkle a layer of baking soda over the area after she'd blotted up as much moisture as possible. She'd let it sit for about an hour, then she'd vacuum up the residue. You can try this trick, or use 1 part borax powder and 2 parts cornstarch in place of the baking soda. Like baking soda, this mix will absorb moisture and eliminate odors.

Sponge the stain. All vomit stains are different, but once you've got the stuff scooped up, sponge the area with water, using a blotting motion. Don't saturate the stain, and rinse your sponge frequently. That'll help dilute and remove the stomach acid, so that stain removal will be easier. Plain water works great on walls and floors, and it may completely remove the stain on fabrics, too.

Kitchen aid. Dishwashing liquid makes a great treatment for vomit spots because it lifts out the grease and most food stains. Use it as a laundry pretreatment on washables. Or moisten a sponge with a mixture of dishwashing liquid and a little water and dab stains away on upholstery, carpet, or other nonwashables. Rinse the soap out of the area by blotting it with a clean, moist cloth.

Pretreat your washables. If a stained item is machine washable, rub some dishwashing liquid into the spot, wait about 10 minutes, and then launder the piece in cold water with an oxygenating detergent. The dish soap will lift most of the stain off, and the detergent will scrub the rest away. Just check the article before you throw it in the dryer; if you can still see a stain, repeat the treatment.

Sensitive subject. Some sensitive fabrics react badly to ammonia and other cleaners, so try this trick for anything that's made of washable acetate, triacetate, rayon, silk, or wool. After you scoop up and blot the mess, moisten a folded paper towel with my Wet Spotter potion on page 162 and lay it over the stain. Let the towel sit for about 30 minutes, spraying it every now and then with the potion to keep it wet. Then rinse the spot with cool water, and launder as usual. If the item is marked "dry-clean only," don't use this trick; take it to the dry cleaner instead.

Two-step stain removal. Dishwashing liquid and ammonia are great allies when it comes to getting vomit stains out of carpet, upholstery, or clothes. Mix a little dishwashing liquid with water and sponge the stains—that may be all it takes to make them disappear. If you need additional power, blot the stains with a cloth that's been moistened with ammonia. Rinse by blotting with a clean, wet cloth or sponge, and the stains should be gone. Dishwashing liquid is safe for any washable fabric, but don't use ammonia on wool carpet or silk, rayon, or other delicate fabrics. And always test a hidden area first to make sure the ammonia won't affect the dye or damage the fabric.

Powerful Potions

Vomit-Stain Remover

Use this solution to quickly remove most "recycled food" stains on carpet, furniture, mattresses, and clothes. It's safe for almost any fabric, but test it first in an inconspicuous area to make sure it doesn't affect the dye or otherwise damage the material you're working on.

> ½ cup of rubbing alcohol
> ½ cup of white vinegar
> ½ cup of water

Mix the ingredients in a handheld sprayer bottle. Lightly spritz the stained area, wait a few minutes, and blot the stain. Repeat the steps until all traces are gone. The alcohol in the mixture not only helps remove the stain, but also makes the solution dry quickly.

Leather and suede solution. To remove vomit stains from leather or suede upholstery or clothes, whip up a bowl of creamy foam, using a few squirts of dishwashing liquid and about ¼ cup of water. Lift off as much of the residue as you can, apply the foam with a sponge, and gently rub it in. Wipe away the foam with a clean, damp cloth. After it dries, apply a leather conditioner, or brush the suede to raise the nap.

Use your head. Accidents can happen in the strangest ways, so if vomit somehow ends up in your hair, the smell may linger even after you wash the stuff out. To get rid of the stench, try washing your hair with Head & Shoulders® shampoo, which works great for neutralizing nasty odors. Let it sit on your head for about 10 minutes after you lather up. If you still catch a whiff of that stomach-turning aroma, plaster your hair and scalp with a paste made of baking soda and water, pull on a shower cap, and let it sit for a few hours. After you shampoo as usual, the smell should be gone.

Q. My dog threw up on the carpet, and now I can't get the smell to go away. I've tried baking soda and Febreze®, and both of them worked for a while, but the odor soon came back. What's the trick for getting rid of that awful smell?

The Great Clean-dini Speaks

A. Before you put your pet in the doghouse, try Nature's Miracle® Stain & Odor Remover or OdoBan® Odor Eliminator, following the directions on the bottle. You may need to repeat the treatment a couple of times to get rid of the smell completely. Odoban is used in nursing homes, so you know it's powerful stuff.

If these products don't make the smell disappear, the problem may be deeper than you suspected. The liquid in the vomit may have soaked through the carpet into the backing, the pad, or even the floor beneath it. That's when it's time to try these tricks:

★ To remove moisture that's soaked into a carpet, rent a water extractor from a local hardware store. Follow the directions on the extractor, and run it over the area to pull out any moisture that has penetrated below the surface.

★ Lift the rug to check for wet spots in the backing or the pad. Keep going through the layers until you see where the stain has stopped; the liquid in vomit can cause a permanent stain if it penetrates a wooden floor. Treat the deep-down stains the same way you treated the carpet.

★ If the smell is coming from deep within wall-to-wall carpeting, you may want to consider a patch job as a last-ditch effort. Slice out a square of the stained area and replace the carpeting and the pad with matching squares.

Welcome to the club! When your pet has an accident that dries before you notice it, scrape up what you can with a spoon, and then bring out the bubbly—the bubbly club soda, that is! Pour club soda right on the spot, count to 30, wipe away the residue with paper towels, and blot up the moisture. Repeat until the stain is gone.

Mattress makeover. It's not difficult to remove a surface vomit stain from a mattress, but if the vomit has soaked in, the filling may have absorbed the liquid and resulting odor. Here's how to get rid of the stinky problem:

1. Saturate the spot with hydrogen peroxide and let it sit for at least five minutes or so.

2. Blot the area with paper towels or a clean cloth until the spot is dry. If you can still detect an odor, repeat the treatment.

3. Sprinkle baking soda generously over the towel-dried area and rub it in. Let the spot dry completely, then vacuum the powder up, and you'll have sweet dreams again!

Walls

Bust the dust. Dust doesn't build up on walls as quickly as it does on tables and other horizontal surfaces, so you'll only need to dust them once every few months. Use a long-handled duster or the upholstery brush attachment on a vacuum cleaner to do the job, and work from the top down. In between full-scale dustings, sweep away any cobwebs that settle in the corners where the walls meet the floor and ceiling.

Fingerprint kit. To remove smudges and dirty fingerprints from painted or papered walls, rub the spot gently with an art gum eraser. You can also use a dry rubber sponge, which is available at paint-supply stores. It'll erase the grunge from your walls lickety-split.

The bucket brigade. Wall washing goes a lot faster when you use two buckets: one for the cleaning solution and the other to rinse the sponge. Work from the bottom up, and rinse each section before going on to the next. Change the water frequently, so you aren't wiping dirt back onto the walls as you go. And check for streaks when you finish; if you see any, give them another going-over to blend them in.

HOCUS POCUS

KEEP A SCRAPBOOK

When you put up new wallpaper or a border in a room, save some scraps to use for testing cleaning products and techniques. That way, you can experiment to your heart's content—without risking damage to the real thing.

Don't be a drip. Hold a wet sponge in your hand, raise your arm to wash a wall, and what happens? That's right—water runs down your arm. To prevent the drips from running away, slip a terry cloth ponytail holder over your wrist before beginning. It'll neatly catch the drips before they can slide down your sleeve.

Stocking up. Textured wall finishes are popular because they hide the seams and imperfections in the drywall. But the rough surface can shred a sponge in no time flat, leaving bits and pieces clinging to the wall until you pick them off, one by one. So instead of using a sponge to clean textured walls, try a balled-up handful of old nylon panty hose or stockings. They'll scrub the nooks and crannies without falling apart.

White or rye? If your wallpaper isn't washable, use a couple slices of fresh bread to rub the dirt away. Simply wad the bread into a fist-size ball, and have at it. Replace the bread when it gets dirty, and be sure to use a brand that doesn't have seeds, nuts, or other ingredients that might scratch the paper or make a mess. Soft white sandwich bread works best, although some folks swear by unseeded rye.

Fantastic foam. Vinyl won't absorb water, but moisture can seep into the seams when you're washing a vinyl-covered wall, causing the wall covering to lift, peel, or pucker. To prevent problems, use soapy foam instead of soapy water to clean it. Just whip ¼ cup of dishwashing liquid and 1 cup of warm water with a hand mixer until the mixture is the consistency of whipped cream. Dip a sponge or cloth into the foam and rub the dirt off the wall. Wipe the foam off with a barely damp cloth or sponge, and the seams will stay nice and tight.

The Great Clean-dini Speaks

Q. I quit smoking more than a year ago, but I still can't get the nicotine stains off my walls. My cleaning products barely make a dent, no matter how hard I scrub. Is there any hope, or do I need to call in the painters?

A. I have just the cleaning magic you need; there's plenty of hope (and help) in these surefire solutions:

★ Wash the walls down with Mr. Clean® Multi-Surfaces Liquid Cleaner at full strength. Wear rubber gloves, and use a rough terry cloth towel to remove the crud.

★ Mix 1 part LA's Totally AWESOME® Concentrated Cleaner with 5 parts water, and the gunk will practically fall off the walls.

★ Use my "Handling heavy-duty dirt" trick at right to make the last traces of your old habit disappear.

Always wear protective clothing and ventilate the room whenever you work with these powerful products. Wash the walls from the bottom up, wipe the drips so they don't leave tracks, and rinse the walls thoroughly after the stains are gone. And last, but definitely not least, test the solution in an inconspicuous area first before tackling a whole wall to make sure it doesn't affect the paint.

Powerful Potions

Wall-Washing Wonder

When it's time to wash down an entire wall, mix up a bucket of this potion. It'll make the greasy film, dirty fingerprints, and general grubbiness vanish into thin air.

  1 cup of ammonia
  ½ cup of white vinegar
  ¼ cup of baking soda
  1 gal. of warm water

Mix the ingredients in a scrub bucket, dip in a sponge, and wash the wall from the bottom up. Work in overlapping sections, so you don't miss any spots. Rinse with fresh water, and the wall will have a new lease on life. Don't forget to wear rubber gloves to protect your skin from the ammonia, and open a window or two for ventilation while you're working.

Candle wax cleanup. To remove candle wax that's splashed or dripped on a painted or papered wall, heat it with a hair dryer turned on the highest setting, and blot the melted wax up with a paper towel. Keep heating and blotting until no more wax or oil soaks into the paper. If the candle left a stain behind, dampen a Mr. Clean® Magic Eraser®, and run it over the spot until it's gone. This trick works great on crayon marks, too!

Handling heavy-duty dirt. If painted walls have been neglected for years, or if they're stained with nicotine or soot, trisodium phosphate (TSP) will get rid of the dirt and discoloration though you may have to repeat the treatment. Test TSP in an inconspicuous area first to make sure it doesn't damage the paint. Then mix 1 to 2 tablespoons of TSP powder in a gallon of warm water, wash the walls from the bottom up, and rinse them thoroughly. Wear protective clothing, and cover all rugs, floors, and furniture to shield them from drips and splashes.

Washers and Dryers

Pocket check. Tissues, pens, coins, and other overlooked items can ruin a whole load of laundry, and they can clog the dryer vent if they get that far. To prevent problems, keep a basket by your washer and double-check all pockets before you toss the clothes in. After all, the more junk you can catch ahead of time, the better off you'll be!

Tidy up. Use a damp microfiber cloth to clean the outside surfaces, knobs, and control panels on your washer and dryer. Wipe out the inside of the machines, too, especially after you wash a load of muddy clothes or fuzzy fabrics.

 **Grandma Putt's Magical Methods**

With a busy household to look after, my Grandma Putt sometimes forgot to take a load of towels out of her washing machine. When she opened the lid the next morning—phew, they sure stank! So if you notice a musty, nose-wrinkling aroma after washing bath towels, keep them in the washer and try my Grandma Putt's trick: Run them through an extra rinse—with vinegar. After the tub is filled with fresh water, pour in 1 cup of white vinegar, run the rinse cycle, and the bad smell will disappear by the time they're done.

So long, scum. Hard water, soapy detergent, and liquid fabric softeners can leave quite a scummy stew in a washing machine's hoses and other parts, causing a mighty bad smell. To clean the scum out of places you can't see or reach by hand, give your machine a vinegar treatment about once a month. Pour in 2 cups of white vinegar and run it through the cycle with hot water. After the cycle stops, run a rag around the top of the tub, the underside of the lid, and any other areas you can reach; the vinegar that was in the steam will make it a lot easier to clean those parts, too.

Dispense with the mess. Pouring laundry liquids and powders into washing machine receptacles can make a gooey or powdery mess. If you wipe the cups and spouts out frequently, the residue won't cause a stink or get smeared on clean clothes when you take them out. Scrub fabric-softener cups in hot, soapy water, and use cotton swabs to clean the tight spots in the bleach dispenser and other receptacles.

Hocus Pocus

TIME FOR A TOUCH-UP

When the enamel coating inside a washing machine or dryer drum gets chipped, nasty rust spots may form on the bare metal—which will leave streaks and stains on your clothes. So buy a touch-up kit at a local hardware store now to fix the dings as soon as you notice them. Dab some touch-up paint on any chips around the machine doors, too, because rust can get started when you transfer wet clothes.

You stinker! If the fabric-softener receptacle on a washing machine is part of the center agitator, it just might be the source of the bad odor you're smelling. Sloshing water can easily cause soap and softener (not to mention plain old dirt) to get stuck beneath the receptacle. To fix the problem, take the fabric-softener holder out, scrub the slimy black gunk off, give it a rinse, and pop it back into place.

The sweet smell of clean. If your washer smells musty, then mold or mildew has probably gotten a grip inside the machine. Before you reach for a screwdriver, try this: Run the machine through its longest cycle with hot water and chlorine bleach. Check the owner's manual, and use the maximum amount of bleach that is safe to use in a single cycle.

Powdered preferred. Liquid laundry products leave a residue in washing machines, and that's where bacteria and mold can set in. Here's a simple trick that'll prevent sour or musty smells: Switch to powdered detergent, and don't use liquid fabric softeners.

HE help. High-efficiency (HE) washers use less water and seal more tightly than older machines—but they're notorious for raising a stink. Why? Because mold and mildew build up fast when there's not much air circulation. And since HE washers clean efficiently with cold water, dirt and detergent residue often don't dissolve completely. The resulting residue stays in the machine, instead of running down the drain. To turn the tide, use all five of these tricks:

★ Check the owner's manual to make sure it's okay to use bleach on your machine, then do the following: Mix 1 cup of bleach with 2 cups of warm water. Using a sponge or soft cloth, wipe inside the door seal with the bleach solution. Leave the door open and let the seal air-dry.

★ Leave the door slightly open after removing every wash load. This will allow the seal to dry out, and odors should disappear.

★ Use the hot water cycle every few loads of laundry to dissolve any scum that might be building up.

★ Be a little stingy with detergent: Use about three-quarters of the recommended amount, being sure to measure it out.

★ Every month or so, wipe around the inside of the door seal with a paper towel to remove any slime that may have accumulated.

A fresh idea. To prevent a musty stench in a high-efficiency (HE) washer, you may want to try affresh™ oxygenating tablets. Just drop one in and run the cycle with hot water to scour off the bacteria and dirt buildup. According to Whirlpool®, which makes the tablets, the product releases tiny fizzing bubbles that loosen the scum around the seals, tub, and hoses, so the next load of laundry should come out smelling fresh and clean.

Q. There's an awful smell in my front-loading washing machine. I've cleaned every bit I could reach, and I've run vinegar and bleach through it, but nothing seems to get rid of the smell. My washer's only a few years old, but I'm ready to trash it, unless you have a cure for the stink.

The Great Clean-dini Speaks

A. Front-loaders can be real stinkers, all right, and it's commonly because of the trap. Have you ever wondered why you don't find stray coins in the machine? That's because any overlooked candy wrappers, pocket change, and even the occasional sock go down into a trap where the water leaves the machine. The debris that collects in there soon gets gunked up with soapy slime—and that's the perfect breeding ground for really bad smells.

You'd think manufacturers would make it easy to get to the trap, but you'll have to do a bit of work to clean it out. Here's how:

1. Unplug the machine. Look for a front panel under the door, unscrew it, and set it aside. (If your machine doesn't have a removable panel, check the owner's manual for further instructions.)

2. Set a few old bath towels nearby because you'll need them to catch the water that pours out when you open up the trap.

3. Find the plastic trap, and turn it counterclockwise to open it. As the water spills out, soak it up with the towels.

4. Wipe out all of the debris and crud in the trap.

5. Turn the trap clockwise to close it, replace the front panel, plug in the machine, and it'll be good to go!

Hocus Pocus

DEALING WITH AN INK DISASTER

No matter how careful you are about checking pockets, sooner or later a troublemaking item is probably going to sneak through and make a real mess of things inside your dryer. When an ink pen leaves gooey smears and dried stains, use one of these tricks to erase the mess:

★ Rub the stains with a cloth that's saturated with nonacetone nail polish remover, and rinse them well with a clean, moist sponge.

★ Run the dryer a few minutes to warm it up a little, and then rub solid vegetable shortening onto the stains. Wait a few minutes for the oil to penetrate the stains, and wipe them away with a paper towel.

★ Squeeze a dab of shampoo onto a damp cloth, and apply it to the stains with plenty of elbow grease. After the ink is gone, wipe the suds away with a moist sponge.

★ Spritz the stains with hair spray, and wipe them clean with a damp cloth.

★ Spray WD-40® on the spots, let it sit for a few minutes, and wipe the stains and solvent away with a damp sponge.

★ Get rid of the gunk by rubbing the spots with Goo Gone®, then wiping the residue up with a damp cloth.

Be sure the laundry room is well ventilated when you try these tricks, and don't keep your head in the dryer because the fumes can give you a real headache. And if one technique doesn't do the job, wait an hour or so before you try another one. If the problem is melted crayon and not ink, you'll find some surefire solutions for getting rid of that gooey mess in the Crayon Marks entry on page 100.

Lint detective. With all the lint that clothes shed in the dryer, it seems like they should be threadbare after a few washings. But those bits of fibers just keep on coming. That's why it's important to empty the lint trap every time you use the dryer—and during the cycle, too, if you're drying fluffy fibers like a new pair of sweats. When the lint screen is blocked by fuzz, the dryer has to work harder to put out the hot air. And that means higher energy bills, a shorter life span, and possibly even a fire if the dryer overheats. So clean the screen!

What's down there? Lint cleanup doesn't stop at the screen—those flying fuzzies collect around and under it, too. After you remove the screen, shine a flashlight down into the slot, and see if there's a whole bunch of stuff just waiting to be vacuumed out. Don't forget to remove the lint that gathers around the rubber seal and the door, too. To finish up, about twice a year, slide your dryer away from the wall and vacuum the floor underneath it, where dust and lint hide out.

Windows

Made in the shade. Heat will make any window-cleaning solution dry too fast, leaving streaks in the process. To avoid this problem, don't clean windows when the sun is streaming through them. Try to do this job on a cloudy day, or work on windows that are out of the sun. And if, for some reason, you simply must clean a sunny window, do it in the morning, when the glass is still cool.

Go lint-free. Rubbing windows with a wad of paper towels will leave bits of lint all over the place, so use a soft, lint-free cloth instead. Old cloth diapers are a great choice because they're highly absorbent and super soft. Or you can use a microfiber cloth or chamois. And skip the fabric softener when you wash window-cleaning cloths: It reduces their absorbency and may leave streaks on the windows.

Powerful Potions

The World's Best Window Cleaner

This potion works just as well as anything you can buy at the store, and it costs a whole lot less. The reason? The store-bought stuff is mostly water. So mix it up yourself and start spritzing!

½ cup of rubbing alcohol

2 tbsp. of ammonia

¼ tsp. of grease-cutting dishwashing liquid

Water

Pour the alcohol, ammonia, and dishwashing liquid into a handheld sprayer bottle, add enough water to fill the container to the top, and shake the mixture well. If you're doing a lot of windows, double the first three ingredients and use enough water to fill a 3-gallon bucket to two-thirds of its capacity. Apply the cleaner to the windows with a sponge, starting at the top, and wipe it off with a cloth or squeegee; there's no need to rinse. And nothing goes to waste because any leftover potion will keep indefinitely in a cool cabinet.

The latest news. Wiping wet windows with a wad of newspaper will give them a great shine, but here's something to consider before you crumple that paper: The ink may smear, leaving black marks on the window frame and your hands. Fortunately, many newspapers are now printed with ink that doesn't run when it gets wet, but it's still a good idea to wear rubber gloves and be careful around the frames, just in case.

The simplest cleaner. A little dishwashing liquid in a bucket of water works great to clean most windows, especially if you use a squeegee. Add only a small amount (about ⅓ teaspoon per 3 gallons of water), so you don't get lots of suds or leave streaks behind when you wipe the cleaner off. You won't even need to rinse the glass unless it's absolutely filthy—just rub it dry with a soft, lint-free cloth and you're done.

Shining clean. White vinegar is an old standby for cleaning windows because it not only cuts the crud, but also adds plenty of shine. Use about ½ cup of vinegar per gallon of water, and your windows will turn out sparkling clean.

Power wash. Exterior windows get a lot grubbier than their inside cousins, so start with a good stiff spray from a garden hose before you begin scrubbing. This will wash off surface dirt, knock down cobwebs, and help loosen the grime before you apply the elbow grease. If the windows are really filthy, rub the worst of the dirt off with a nonabrasive plastic scrubbie. Then follow up with a sponge or cloth dipped in your favorite window cleaner, and squeegee them to perfection.

Squeegee clean. Using a squeegee properly is fast, fun, and easy. Here's how the pros make it look so simple:

1. Lay a folded cloth on the sill to catch any drips. Wet a sponge with the cleaner, and apply it to the window in a big, backward S, starting at the upper left corner and ending at the lower right corner. Reverse it if you're left-handed.

2. Use a dry cloth to wipe a 1-inch-wide strip along the top of the glass. That's where you'll start each squeegee stroke.

3. Clean the window from top to bottom using vertical strokes. Wipe the blade with a towel at the end of each stroke to prevent drips.

4. Do one last sweep across the bottom of the glass if needed, and dry the sill with the towel. There—now, wasn't that nice?

Extend your reach. Here's another great reason to invest in a good-quality squeegee: Most of them are made to screw onto an extension pole, letting you reach the tops of tall windows without a ladder. If you have high windows, an extension handle is well worth the investment. But before you buy one, check the broom closet—you may already have a broom or mop handle that can be unscrewed and used with the squeegee.

Grandma Putt's Magical Methods

Figuring out which side of the glass a streak is on can be awfully frustrating. You peer, you smear, you walk outside and back in again. To tell the difference at a glance, my Grandma Putt came up with a great trick: She used vertical strokes on the inside of her windows, and horizontal strokes on the outside. Then if that doggone streak was horizontal, why, she knew it was on the outside looking in!

Go like a pro. A good squeegee makes short work of window cleaning, so ignore the cheap plastic kinds at discount stores. Spend a little more money and invest in a professional squeegee for about $10—it's well worth the price. Because the soft rubber blade has no imperfections, it'll do a streak-free job, and you can even replace the rubber strip when it wears out. A 12- or 14-inch blade is a good size for most home windows. You'll find professional-quality squeegees at all janitorial-supply companies and most hardware stores.

Wine Stains

White or red? White wine is easy to remove because there's no color to stain the fabric. Just flush the area with water and rub in a little dishwashing liquid before you toss the item into the washing machine. Red wines, on the other hand, can make a real mess because the color will quickly seep in. Check out the following solutions to make red wine stains vanish.

High water. My Grandma Putt treated fruit juice stains on her tablecloth by holding the cloth over the sink while she poured boiling water through it. Wine is just fancy fruit juice, so put the teakettle on and pour hot water on (and through) the stains while they're still fresh. Get a helper to hold the cloth over the sink while you carefully pour.

Powerful Potions

Red Wine Remover

This mixture is hands down the absolute best way to make red wine stains disappear, whether they're on carpet, clothes, or furniture. It works like magic on fresh stains, old stains, and even stains that have been through the washer and dryer. The only drawback is that you'll need to mix up a fresh batch whenever you need it because leftovers won't keep well.

1 tsp. of dishwashing liquid
1 cup of hydrogen peroxide

Stir the dishwashing liquid into the peroxide in a small glass bowl. (If you're using the popular blue dishwashing liquid, don't be surprised if it becomes clear as you stir.) Soak a clean cloth or sponge in the mixture, squeeze out enough liquid so that the applicator is wet (but not sopping), and then blot the wine stains until they fade away. The peroxide in the mixture has a mild bleaching action, and although it shouldn't be strong enough to lift the color out of fabric, test it in an inconspicuous area first, just to make sure.

Salt solution. When a glass of wine gets tipsy on a tablecloth, immediately cover the stains with salt. Pour a generous amount onto the spots, covering them completely. The salt will soak up the wine and counteract the stains while you finish the meal. After your dinner guests have departed, shake off the salt, rub some dishwashing liquid on the spots, and launder the cloth in cold water.

White after red. Pouring or blotting white wine on a red wine stain is an old remedy that works best when the spill is fresh. You can also pour club soda on the stain; the fizzy bubbles will lift out the red wine in a hurry. Wait a few minutes, and then blot up the excess moisture with paper towels. If you can still see the stain, repeat the treatment, or try one of the other tricks in this section to get rid of the stain for good.

Carpet cleaners. When you've got to clean up red wine stains on carpet, start by blotting them with a wet cloth, then spray the spots with a stain remover like Shout® or Spot Shot®. Blot them again with a moist cloth, and the stains will disappear fast. Avoid rubbing when you clean carpet stains, so you don't spread the problem or damage the fibers. You'll find more carpet-cleaning tricks in the Carpets entry on page 50 and the Rugs entry on page 265.

Give it a shot. All-purpose stain remover Quick n Brite® comes in a concentrated liquid that you mix with water, and it's so effective on red wine stains that a single spritz makes the stains vanish. Plus, it's environmentally safe. Just test it first in an out-of-the-way area, especially if you have dark carpet, to make sure it won't affect the color of anything except the pesky stains.

Zippers

Don't get agitated. To keep clothing zippers in good condition, always close them before you throw the items in the washing machine. Why? Because all that sloshing and agitating can bend or break the teeth if they're exposed. Closing zippers protects other garments, too, because an open zipper can catch loose threads or cause a pull in a favorite blouse—and that'll really make you agitated! And always close the zipper when you hang up jackets and other clothes to help the garments retain their shape.

Oral surgery. If a zipper starts to get balky, check all the teeth for one that may be bent and need attention, or for debris that might have gotten stuck. Use a straight pin to pick out any fuzz or gently push the teeth back into place. Then run the zipper up and down a few times to make sure it's working smoothly again.

Wax the tracks. Metal zippers are notorious for losing their easy gliding ability. If straightening the teeth doesn't fix the problem, try greasing the tracks. Open the zipper and hold it taut, and run a natural-colored beeswax candle, a white votive, or a bar of paraffin along the teeth. You can also use a bar of white soap or a piece of waxed paper. Open and close the zipper a few times to work in the lubricant, and you'll be back to zipping right along in no time at all!

Hocus Pocus

DON'T FORCE THE ISSUE

When a bit of fabric or a thread gets caught in a plastic zipper, don't try to force it any further. Just fold the zipper right at the problem spot, and pinch the coiled teeth until they open enough to gently pull the offender out. Then pull the zipper all the way down, and open and close it a few times to knit the teeth back together again.

Get the lead out. If a zipper won't zip up or down smoothly, close it and run the business end of a pencil along the teeth. Pencil "lead" is really graphite, and the tiny bits that flake off as you do this trick work wonders as a lubricant. Open and close the zipper a few more times, and repeat the treatment if it's still acting stubborn. Whatever you do, don't try this trick on a light-colored zipper, unless you like "drawing" attention to your work.

Fast first aid. If you're out on the town and a zipper gets stuck, don't get embarrassed—get balmy! Pull some clear lip balm out of your purse and run it up and down along the teeth to provide lubrication. It should get things rolling again. If you happen to lose a zipper pull, insert a paper clip through the hole and use it until you can get a more permanent fix. And when the teeth of a zipper open up at the bottom, zip up the slider, and attach a safety pin horizontally across the teeth just above the break to prevent it from opening up further.

Index

A

Acetate fabrics, 169, 341
Acetone, 225, 284. *See also*
Nail polish remover
Acids
cautions, 84, 109, 125, 270
silver and, 280
stainless steel and, 294
Acne cream, 181
Acrylic fabrics, 128, 132, 176
Adhesive residue, 163,
299–303
Affresh™ oxygenating tablets,
350
AFTA® Cleaning Solvent,
164
Aftershave, 227
Air cleaners, 1
Air filters, 1–3
Alcohol (rubbing)
for cleaning
carpets, 51
CDs, 58
cell phones, 251
chrome, 67
computers and print-
ers, 80, 82
crystal chandeliers,
158
leather, 175
toasters and toaster
ovens, 319
TVs, VCRs, and DVD
players, 327
in Powerful Potions
Daily Shower Spray, 21
Granite Countertop
Cleaner, 99
Lens Cleaner, 155

Super Sanitizing
Wipe, viii
Vomit-Stain Remover,
342
World's Best Window
Cleaner, The 354
for stain removal
coffee, 76
grass stains, 168
grease stains, 174
hair dye, 214
ink stains, 180, 182,
202
lipstick, 210–211
mustard, 224
nail polish, 227
paint, 237
pencil marks, 245
pine sap, 254
tar, 8
for sticker residue, 299,
302
on wood furniture, 148
Alcohol (vodka), 238, 293
Algae, 25–27, 41, 142–143,
153–154, 310
Alka-Seltzer®, 43, 86, 190,
208, 323
Allergens, in bedding, 22, 23
All-Purpose Cleaner, 18
Aloe vera, 171
Aluminum awnings, 12–13
Aluminum foil
for cleaning
barbecue grills, 16, 269
chrome, 66
patio furniture, 269
silver, 189, 279
for protecting stoves, 233,
234, 305

in Silver Shine potion, 140
Aluminum items, 226, 243
Aluminum siding, 3–5
Ammonia
for cleaning
barbecue grills, 14
brick, 40
chrome, 67
cookware, 88, 89
curtains and drapes,
104–105
fireplaces, 136
glassware, 158, 159
gold, 165, 166,
188–189
irons, 186
ovens and oven racks,
232, 234
range hoods, 260, 261
screens, 271
stoves, 305
tiled floors, 316
vases, 336
vinyl, 336
contraindications, 81, 85,
223, 337
in Powerful Potions
DIY Ammonia
Cleaner, 4
Easy Oven Cleaner,
232
Everyday Counter
Cleaner, 95
High-Powered Handle
Cleaner, 45
Prewash Spot Cleaner,
127
Soot Scrub, 138
Wall-Washing Won-
der, 347

driveways, 7
fiberglass, 134, 135
gold, 166
houseplants, 178
lamp shades, 197
marble, 215
paintings, 236, 237
paneling, 240–241
patio furniture, 243
rugs, 265
shades, 274, 275
shoes, 11, 277
stainless steel, 291
suede, 213
sunglasses, 156
table linens, 313, 315
tiled floors, 316
upholstery, 329
vinyl, 336–339, 346
windows, 354
as lubricant, 46–47
in Powerful Potions
Old Salt, 226
Paneling Cleaner 'n'
Polish, 240
Prewash Spot Cleaner,
127
Red Wine Remover,
357
Two-Step Carpet
Cleaner, 51
Wet Spotter, 162
World's Best Window
Cleaner, The, 354
for stain removal
coffee, 76, 282, 316
egg, 124
grease stains, 170, 172,
174, 282, 315
ink stains, 182
ketchup, 192
makeup, 210, 211, 212,
214
mustard, 224

paint, 239
pine sap, 255
tar, 8
vomit, 341, 342
wine stains, 357
Distilled water, for cleaning,
40, 58, 184, 255. *See also*
Hard-water deposits
DIY Ammonia Cleaner, 4
Dog odor, 145, 253. *See also*
Pet hair; Pet messes
Dolls, 183
Doorknobs, 116–117
Door knockers, 116–117
Doormats, 50, 316
Doors, 116–117, 284–285
Down clothes and quilts,
118–120
Drains, 121–122
Drapes, 103–105
Drink coasters, 6
Drink mixes
for cleaning, 39, 114, 115,
323
for rust stains, 242, 269
Driveways, 7–9, 173. *See also*
Concrete
Dry cleaning, 131
Dry-cleaning solvent, 164
Dryel®, 131
Dryer sheets
for cleaning, 47, 66, 89,
100
for deodorizing, 11, 34,
276
for static control, 132
Dry sponge (latex sponge),
31, 276, 331–332, 344
Duct tape
for cleaning, 289, 299
residue from, 302
Dusting methods
blinds, 30–31
books, 34–35

ceilings, 60–61
china and porcelain, 63
doors, 116
furniture, 146
houseplants, 177
paintings, 235, 236
pianos, 220
shades, 274
TVs, VCRs, and DVD
players, 326
unglazed ceramics, 257
walls, 240, 344
Dust masks, 3, 55. *See also*
Safety precautions
Dust mites, 22, 23
Duvet covers, 118
DVDs and DVD players,
326–328
Dye stains, 133

E

Easy Oven Cleaner, 232
Eggs, 76, 179, 204
Eggshells, 208, 336
Egg stains, 122–124, 133
Emery boards, 225
Enamel, 87, 124–126
Enamel Broiler Pan Cleaner,
125
Enzyme detergent, 122, 123,
133, 167, 248–249, 315
Epoxy, 162
Erasers. *See also* Mr. Clean®
Magic Eraser®
for cleaning
ivory jewelry, 190
lamp shades, 198
leather gloves, 160
pottery and ceramics,
257
shades, 275
suede, 205, 225
vinyl, 337

M

Magic Sheet®, 88

Makeup brushes, 177, 210, 272

Makeup stains, 175, 210–214

Marble, 99, 215–216, 226–227

Marble Poultice, 216

Marbles, for coffeemakers, 75

Margarine, 254

Marker stains. *See* Ink and marker stains

Mattresses, 22

Mayonnaise, 149, 179, 205, 219, 255

Meat tenderizer, 73, 228

MERV, 1, 2

Metal and hardware cleaners. *See also* Hardware; *specific metals*
  Copper Cleaner, 92
  High-Powered Handle Cleaner, 45
  No-Scrub Brass and Bronze Cleaner, 38
  Silver Shine, 140
  Stainless Scrub, 292

Microwave ovens
  cautions, 217
  cleaning, 217–218
  as cleaning tool, 112
  Soot and Smell Dissolver for, 218

Mildew. *See* Mold and mildew

Milk
  for cleaning, 37, 140, 169
  in Houseplant Wipe, 178
  for stain removal, 76, 180–181

Milk stains, 133

Mineral oil
  for cleaning, 67, 136, 148, 205, 292
  for crayon mark removal, 101
  as lubricant, 46
  for pine sap removal, 289
  as protectant, 37, 43, 66, 107
  for rust prevention, 325
  for slate scratches, 283
  for stain removal, 211

Mineral spirits, 102, 145, 146, 148

Minimum Efficiency Reporting Value (MERV), 1, 2

Mint, 131

Mirror-cleaning potion, 4

Modacrylic fabrics, 128, 132

Molasses
  for grass stains, 168, 286
  in Rust-Remover Soak, 270

Mold and mildew
  awnings, 12
  basement walls, 85
  bathrooms, 19, 20
  decks, 109
  leather, 200–201
  luggage, 176
  needlework, 230
  odor from, 68, 176, 348, 350
  sisal and jute, 282
  tents, 289
  washers, 349, 350

Mold and Moss Remover, 243

Montmorillonite clay, 153

Moss, removing, 41, 142–143, 243

Mothballs, 131

Moths, 130–131

Motor oil, for cleaning tools, 324–325

MP3 players, 297

Mr. Clean® liquid cleaner, 346

Mr. Clean® Magic Eraser®, for cleaning
  athletic shoes, 10
  burn marks, 42
  cabinets, 44
  cookie sheets, 90
  crayon marks, 100, 102
  doors, 117
  fiberglass, 134, 135
  lamp shades, 198
  suede, 205
  walls, 347

Mud, 51, 52, 276

Multipurpose cleaners. *See also commercial brands*
  All-Purpose Cleaner, 18
  DIY Ammonia Cleaner, 4
  Super Sanitizing Wipe, viii
  Super Scrubber, 307

Multitool knives, 194

Muriatic acid, 84

Murphy® Oil Soap, 44, 239, 241

Musical instruments, 219–221

Mustard stains, 222–224

Musty odors. *See* Mold and mildew

N

Nail polish
  for repairing screens, 272
  stains from, 225–227

Nail polish remover
  for cleaning, 186, 218, 256, 320

Vinyl walls, 346
Viscose rayon fabrics, 127
Vivid® Ultra Liquid Bleach, 314
Vodka, 238, 293
Vomit-Stain Remover, 342
Vomit stains, 340–344

W

Wall-cleaning potions
 Paneling Cleaner 'n' Polish, 240
 Wall-Washing Wonder, 347
Wallpaper, 103, 170, 173, 345
Walls
 basement, 85
 crayon marks on, 100, 101
 general cleaning methods, 344–347
 nail polish on, 227
 paneled, 240–241
Walnut oil, 148, 202–203, 278
Washers and dryers, 102, 316, 348–353
Washing soda
 for cleaning, 173
 in Powerful Potions
  Silver Shine, 140
  Washing Soda Scrub, 238
 for stain removal, 123, 311
Washing Soda Scrub, 238
Water leaks, in sliding doors, 285
Water marks
 leather, 201
 sisal and jute, 282
 stainless steel, 293
 wood, 149
Waterpik®, 188

Water softeners, for cleaning, 268
Wax paper, 25, 49, 184, 359
WD-40®
 cautions, 63, 183
 for cleaning, 234, 244, 326
 as lubricant, 25, 209
 for stain removal
  crayon marks, 100
  grease stains, 172
  ink stains, 183, 352
  pencil marks, 245
  rust stains, 269
  tar, 8
 for sticker residue, 300
Wedding gowns, 71
Wesley's Bleche-White®, 10
Wet Spotter, 162
Whiting, 185, 216, 250, 270
Windex®, 326
Window cleaners
 DIY Ammonia Cleaner, 4
 World's Best Window Cleaner, The, 354
Windows, 353–356
Window shades, 274–276
Wineglasses, 158, 159
Wine stains
 carpets, 53–54
 clothes, 69–70
 fabrics, 129
 general treatment methods, 356–358
 marble, 215
 Red Wine Remover, 357
Wood ashes
 for cleaning, 14, 39, 149, 280
 cleaning up, 137
Wooden cutting boards, 106–108

Wooden tool handles, 324, 325
Wood furniture, 42–43, 146–149
Woodwork, 102, 245
Wool-embroidered pieces, 229
Wool fabrics
 stains on
  grass stains, 168, 169
  grease stains, 172, 173
  makeup, 211
  nail polish, 225, 226
  scorch, 185
  vomit, 341
 washing, 132–133
Woolite®, 119, 174, 193, 197, 229
Wool rugs, 266
Worcestershire sauce, 38, 136
Works® Disinfectant Toilet Bowl Cleaner, The, 324
Works® Tub & Shower Cleaner, The, 115
World's Best Window Cleaner, The, 354

Y

Yeast, for flea repellent, 247
Yellow dock, 247
Yoga/Camping Mat Cleaner, 290
Yoga mats, 288, 290
Yogurt, 37

Z

Zippers, 278, 358–359
Zout® Triple Enzyme Clean stain remover, 101
Zud®, 270, 323